UNION MAN

UNION MAN

By David J. McDonald

E. P. DUTTON & CO., INC. | NEW YORK | 1969

190

B
MacD

to my beloved Rosemary

LIST OF ILLUSTRATIONS

following page 128

UNION MAN

Prologue

They turned on the floodlights when we stepped out of the conference room. Sweat trickled down inside my collar. I'd faced these lights and the television cameras many times before, but never like this, never with a heartache. Always before, I had faced them in triumph, to announce an agreement that would mean a better life for the steelworkers I represented. This time, I faced them to say that someone else would be taking over my job before I was ready to give it up—and that the mantle would pass to him peaceably and without recriminations.

I'm not really sure when I came to that decision. I suppose it was made in my heart shortly after I was wakened and told the incredible news that late returns from Canada had given my opponent an apparently unbeatable lead. But my brain probably hadn't accepted it until just a few minutes earlier, in a meeting of the Executive Board of the United Steelworkers of America. I think most of the board members expected me to contest the election. God knows, there were grounds enough, and there were plenty of people urging me to do it. It would have taken only a letter to the Department of Labor in Washington to impound the ballots and throw the election into a recount that might drag on for months. But I was the only one who could make that decision, and it had to be made in anger, out of an absolute determination to see the fight through, no matter what the destruction along the way. I simply hadn't the heart for it. I wasn't fighting mad. I was heartsick.

So I rose in the Executive Board meeting and looked around that table at men I thought had been my friends—some of them for decades—and I said: "I'm not going to contest this election. I'm not going to invoke my rights to demand a review of the voting. There's been too much turmoil already. The purposes of this union are served by unity, not dissension, and I've always been dedicated to those purposes. I love this union, and I'm not going to be a party to breaking it apart."

I sat down, unable to trust myself to say more. And the members of the Executive Board—including some who had campaigned just a few days earlier for my opponent—stood and applauded. When the applause stopped, I rose from the table and said: "The press is waiting outside. I'm going out and tell them what I've just said here." I looked directly at my opponent and asked, "Would you like to come along?"

He did, and we stood rubbing shoulders before the reporters and the television lights. I was suddenly conscious of his nearness, and I looked at him in a detached sort of way as if I'd never really seen him before. I. W. Abel is a humorless man of medium stature and diffident manner. He looks at the world solemnly from behind a pair of heavy eyeglasses. I had chosen him—as a compromise candidate because he was both inoffensive and unknown—as my secretary-treasurer when I had been elected president of the United Steelworkers of America thirteen years earlier. He had served quietly, and without any particular distinction all those years. Looking at him now, I realized he had been busy in other directions, too, even though he had denied any such activity almost up to the minute he declared himself in opposition to me.

As I studied him beneath those powerful lights, I knew that the faith in human nature that had sustained me so many times before had been badly shaken, and I was grieved at that. But I shrugged and tried to put it behind me by repeating to the reporters the statement I'd made to the Executive Board a few minutes earlier, and—quite unexpectedly—the reporters applauded, too. Then I turned to Abel and looked directly into his eyes and said, "I ask you, Abe, will there be any recriminations or any reprisals?" And he answered a flat "No"—the only word he spoke during that brief conference, a word that was to be as prophetically untrue as all the denials of his opposition to me had been.

Suddenly, it was all over—forty-two years of intimate, exciting, rewarding—and sometimes heartbreaking—association with the labor-union movement in the United States of America. The reporters said, "Thank you, gentlemen," and it sounded like an epitaph as the hot lights went out. There was a run for telephones and an undercurrent of small talk while the TV technicians packed their equipment. Then the room was lifeless. The news was made.

As I left that empty room, I was proud, and the pride softened the heartache a little.

My wife and my friends were waiting for me, and we talked far into the night. This was a group that had always looked first to the future, but this night we looked to the past, because soon everything would be past, and as we talked, it all came alive to me again—the long route I had traveled to the leadership of the greatest labor union in the world.

1

I suppose there were three things in my childhood that shaped my attitudes and my destiny as president of the United Steelworkers of America.

Most important, I had a deep love and respect for unionism—deeper, even, than Andrew Carnegie's passionate hatred of it. Then, I knew no hard-core poverty or destructive emotional upheavals within my family. There were plenty of tough times, but they were never intolerable. And, finally, I never *really* hated anything or anybody. I grew up with congenial people in surroundings I didn't think of as poor until others told me they were many years later. My outlook was generally one of optimism and hope, and I never regarded myself as a social reformer, although there were plenty of things that needed reforming in the industrial society into which I was born in Pittsburgh, Pennsylvania, on November 22, 1902.

On that day, *The New York Times* carried a front page story headlined: SETTLEMENT OF COAL STRIKE MAY BE NEAR. Beneath this head, the readers of *The Times* were told:

> The mine workers have agreed with the mine owners to attempt to adjust the differences between them outside the Anthracite Coal Commission. The proposition was made on a compromise basis and negotiations will be entered on at once with a reasonable hope of settlement.
>
> The rough prospectus which is to form the basis of negotiations is a 10 percent increase in wages, a 9-hour work day and trade agreements between the miners and the companies by whom they are employed.

My father saved that paper for me and showed it to me years later. Today, I have it framed and hanging on my wall. The 1902 coal agreement was a milestone in trade unionism in the United

States. It eliminated the open-end work week and introduced negotiation and compromise with labor as an *equal* partner.

But that clipping has also been a constant reminder to me that
rights dearly won are seldom permanent. They can always be
taken away from the apathetic, the fainthearted or the weak. The
coal operators later took away the nine-hour day and a good many
other things—including the dignity and humanity of the coal
miners. Eventually, I helped win them back. But in 1902, that was
still many years in the future.

My social catechism was learned around our kitchen table.
That's where my family and our visitors congregated, supposedly
to play cards, but actually to talk. The talk was mostly about the
efforts of the workingman to better himself and the determination
of the leaders of industry to break these efforts, by force, if necessary.

What else would the talk be about around my kitchen table?
When I was born, my father—a gregariouss, soft-spoken Irishman
of medium stature and great physical and moral strength—was
walking a picket line, trying to save a dying union. My mother's
father, Patrick Kelly, was financial secretary of the Sons of Vulcan,
the first union of ironworkers in the United States. Her two
brothers carried scars from beatings by company cops on picket
lines.

This talk of violence and dishonor done the workingman got
under my skin and into my blood, but somehow it didn't poison
my mind. I remember once bringing home a library book that
glorified the efforts of a group of scabs who had broken a railroad
strike in the Lehigh Valley. I used to sit around the table, reading
while the adults talked, and this night I became aware of a sudden
silence. I realized slowly and self-consciously that everyone was
looking at my book; then my father told me gravely that what the
book said was not true and I should take it back to the library the
next day.

We lived in an undersized block, just long enough for three
brick houses set neatly in a row. The street was cobblestoned and
the air laden with smoke and soot, but I accepted this as a simple

fact of life and have no recollection of being bothered by it. From our tiny, fenced-in backyard or the windows of our second-floor bedrooms, we could feel the waves of heat and look into the inferno of the steel rolling mill where my father worked.

I know that Pittsburgh fifty years ago was an ugly, dirty city, but my youthful memories of it are mostly warm and affectionate. My mother was a great beauty and a strong woman who saw to it that the family problems of poverty, of unemployment, of hostility to the dream of trade unionism she and my father shared did not erode the childhood pleasures of my stepsister, Mame, my young brother, Joe, my sister, Margaret, and me. Dad taught Joe and me to play baseball and football—to play them well—and he always talked to us about the importance of a formal education he never had. There was grass and there were trees nearby and dozens of kids—who, like us, felt no sense of deprivation. And in the evenings, there were those exciting, heated sessions around our kitchen table.

They were never confined to men. My mother was usually on hand, and often there were other women, too. The talk was salty and to the point. These were men and women of action. They had to be to survive.

They would drink my father's beer and wipe the foam from their lips with a sleeve and talk of heroes—always union men fighting overwhelming odds—and villains who all came out sounding like Andrew Carnegie. He was the arch villain of them all. The people around our kitchen table loathed him, and I remember as a boy trying to visualize the degree of evil he represented and finally giving it up as hopeless.

There was adventure, too, and history. Maybe the history was one-dimensional—the world as seen through the eyes of the workingman—but it was more fascinating than most of the books I was always carrying home from the library. My kitchen history course started with the Molly Maguires, a militant group of Irish immigrants who tried to force Pennsylvania anthracite coal operators in the 1870's to provide a living wage and rudimentary safety conditions for the miners, who were dying by the hundreds in mine accidents. The operators fought back with guns and strikebreakers and finally through captive courts that sentenced nineteen Molly Maguires to hang on mostly trumped-up murder charges. Although these martyred miners were heroes to my parents' generation, they were also recognized as violent men, and by 1910—after four decades of violence to try and establish the rights of labor unions to exist and bargain collectively—some workingmen were wondering if there might not be a better way.

The past gave them little cause for hope. America's evolution from a nation of small entrepreneurs and craft workers to huge industries, tied together by trusts and cartels, had seen no parallel organization of the labor that made the system work. I remember reading once that, just before the Civil War, the *Charleston Mercury* said in an editorial that "slavery is the natural and normal condition of the laboring man." A lot of wealthy Americans— north and south—in the nineteenth century believed that, and whenever workingmen tried to organize to gain a greater share of the wealth they were producing, they were beaten back by state and Federal troops, usually on the grounds that they were trying to overthrow the cherished American concept of a free society.

While the heroes of that society—J. P. Morgan and John D. Rockefeller and Andrew Carnegie and James Mellon and Jay Gould—were buying their way out of military service and building huge fortunes from Civil War profits, Irish immigrants were fighting the war. Small wonder that when it ended and these men went back to work in the mines and factories, they wanted to be treated as human beings.

It wasn't to come easy. My Grandfather Kelly arrived from Ireland in time to soldier in the Civil War. Then he helped organize the Sons of Vulcan at the steel plant in Sharon, Pennsylvania, where he found work after the war. Because the union was outlawed, the members had to meet secretly. My grandfather hid the meager dues he collected beneath a loose stone in his cellar against the day when they might be used to support a union movement with at least a whisper of hope of success.

My own father arrived in the United States in 1886—at the age of sixteen—after working for four years in the iron mills of Wales and crossing the Atlantic in the steerage hold of the *Mauretania*. Dad worked his way to Springfield, Illinois, where his Uncle David got him a job in an iron mill. Together, they organized a lodge of the Amalgamated Association of Iron, Steel and Tin Workers.

I can still remember my dad, eyes hardening, jaw working, describing what happened when the union asked for recognition. The company refused and ordered the men to disband the union or get out of the mill. The union called a strike, instead, and the company brought in an army of Pinkerton detectives and newly arrived East European immigrants from Chicago to scatter the picket lines and reopen the plant. The strikers built barricades in front of the mill gates to beat back the invaders. Both groups were armed and ready for open warfare.

That's exactly what they got. My dad—a frightened lad of seventeen in a new country he thought offered hope and equal opportunity for all people—found himself sharing a barricade with a huge Britisher known to the other workers only as "John Bull." When the Pinkertons charged, firing pistols at point-blank range, John Bull drew himself up, put a rifle to his shoulder and fired into the attackers. So did some of the other strikers. But their firepower was small, and their stomach for killing even smaller, and they were overwhelmed by the strikebreakers.

The scabs poured into the mill, leaving a battleground of broken heads and bodies behind them. Dad ran for his life, hooking a freight train to St. Louis, where he was unable to find work, then riding boxcars in the dead of winter back to Pittsburgh in search of a job. One of his traveling companions died of exposure in the frigid boxcar, and the others had to leave him there— frozen stiff—rather than risk arrest and beating by the railroad cops who patrolled the yards. In Pittsburgh, Dad learned that John Bull had been sent to prison for life for the shooting of a Pinkerton. But at least the Springfield experience accomplished one important thing for Dad: he'd learned skills in operating a rolling mill that made it much easier for him to find work in the tough years ahead.

Through these troubled times, the Ancient Order of Hibernians

—a society of which I'm still proud to be a member—served as a gathering place for Irish-Americans to talk over their problems, help one another and hope for better treatment of the Irish workingman in his new country. In the last decade of the nineteenth century, things *seemed* to improve. The Amalgamated union grew steadily in strength and numbers—until it was suddenly and violently ambushed by its toughest, most intractable opponent: Andrew Carnegie. At Homestead, Pennsylvania, in July, 1892, trade unionism in the steel industry was virtually destroyed.

Big business was beginning to run scared. The first really effective national labor organization—called the Knights of Labor—had grown to a membership of more than 700,000 by 1890. Business was calling it a secret, anti-Christian society aimed at taking over the country, then using these lies as an excuse for hiring private armies to break up its member unions. The nucleus of these armies came from the Pinkerton Agency, which the managing editor of the *New York Sun,* John Swinton, called "a private armed force, kept for the service of such corporations or capitalists as may hire it for the suppression of strikes stirred by the turning of monopoly screws." Swinton's was one of the few Establishment voices raised on behalf of the workers. Another was James Cardinal Gibbons of Baltimore, who said publicly that the Knights of Labor were a legitimate society of workingmen and carried this message to Pope Leo XIII in Rome, inspiring the Pope's famous encyclical on the rights of labor. In our house, Cardinal Gibbons was a saint.

But to Andy Carnegie he was a meddler and troublemaker, giving aid and comfort to the Amalgamated Association of Iron, Steel and Tin Workers, by 1890 the largest and strongest union in America with almost 100,000 dues-paying members. When the union began to challenge his absolute dynasty, Carnegie hired a notorious union hater named Henry C. Frick, put him in charge of the Homestead plant and told him to destroy the union there. The result was a bloodletting that enfeebled the will of steelworkers to organize for almost forty years. In that sense, at least, Carnegie was successful; but the price of that success came high.

Frick triggered the Homestead violence by telling workers there he was cutting wages from 10 to 40 percent. When the union officers demanded a hearing, Frick shut down the plant and locked out the workers. He expected to reopen with strikebreakers and scabs, but he didn't anticipate the degree or dedication of the resistance to his actions. Almost overnight, six thousand workers and their families began picketing the plant, sealing it off from the outside. So Frick sent to New York, hired 300 heavily armed Pinkerton agents and put them aboard two armor-plated scows several miles below Homestead. Then he had the scows towed through the river entrance of the Homestead steel plant.

The Pinkertons marched down the gangplank, eight abreast, rifles at the ready. For an instant the strikers faltered. Then an Irishman named William Foy—an authentic labor hero—stepped forward and challenged the Pinkertons. He was shot dead on the spot, and instantly the plant gates became a battlefield. When the Pinkertons retreated to their ship and the gunfire subsided, there were seven pickets and three Pinkertons dead and fifty others grievously wounded. The Pinkertons were besieged and finally surrendered. The strikers won that battle, but they lost the war. Carnegie, with limitless resources, kept his plant closed for 143 days, finally starving the workers into submission. When they came back, it was on his terms, but the legacy of hatred he passed along to the steel industry poisoned relationships between the companies and their workers for many years.

In her biography of Elbert H. Gary, the first president of United States Steel, Ida M. Tarbell says: "The terrible Homestead strike left a suspicion and bitterness in the minds of men and management which made natural free cooperation out of the question. There was a will to war on both sides. Management had been the victor, and as a body it was resolved that unionism never again should strike roots in its plants."

My Uncle Jack—my mother's brother—had had a leg broken by a club-swinging Pinkerton. Uncle Jack had enjoyed the satisfaction of smashing the strikebreaker before dragging himself—his leg trailing helplessly behind—up a long hill to my grandmother's home where he lay out the rest of the battle. I had only a dim memory of my mother's other brother, Jim—a giant of a man who helped organize the bridge builder's union, then was knocked from a scaffolding to his death in the Monongahela River by a runaway crane dangling a steel girder. These were tough, dedicated people, filled with the tradition of unionism and a dream of democracy that would penalize no man for being Irish, for being a Catholic, for being poor, or for striving to obtain for himself and his family a fair share of the proceeds from the work of his own hands.

The harshness of their struggle for survival was brought home to me when my dad was badly hurt in a mill accident. He'd gone back to work at Jones & Laughlin Mill No. 9 in Pittsburgh when an effort to make a new life, away from the steel mills, had failed.

During the Panic of 1907—when there was no work to be had —Dad decided to invest the family savings in a hotel and saloon a few miles away. We had to move, and after our household goods had gone in a horse-drawn wagon, I remember traveling to our new home on the streetcar, with my mother carrying Joe, who was just a baby then. The hotel was a mistake. It was in a German neighborhood, and we sure as hell weren't German. Segregation along nationality lines was almost total in those days, so few of our neighbors traded at our saloon.

My parents stuck it out for five years, but things never really got much better. We still weren't German, and our Irish friends in the old neighborhood had their own saloons. The two things I remember best about that period were starting school and the violin. I had a pretty serious bout with meningitis, and while I was recovering, I asked for a violin because I'd seen the barber across the street playing one and it intrigued me. I got a package deal: a violin and the barber for a teacher. The therapy turned out to be a lot more valuable than the music it produced.

School became something of a problem, too. Naturally my mother sent me to a Catholic school, which was fine with me except that I couldn't understand anything the nuns were saying. When I finally reported this at home, my mother found out all the teaching was being done in German. So I was hauled to a public school populated mainly by Protestants. My inclination was that I would rather not go to school than go where Protestant teachers would be, and my mother had to convince me daily with a paddle that I was wrong. I took a lot of convincing.

I never really started to make it in school until we moved back to the old neighborhood, and I went into St. Stephen's in the fourth grade. My dad finally lost the hotel and saloon and went back to the mills. Things were picking up in the steel industry, and Dad had skills that made it easy for him to get work when there was work to be had. Then, when I was in the fifth grade, I learned about the desperate need for some sort of workmen's compensation—the hard way.

I was called out of a class by one of our neighbors who had come to the school office. She told me I was to go home and wait for my mother, that my dad had been in an accident and my mother was with him but she would be home soon. I remembered from those kitchen table talk sessions some of the things that could happen to men in steel mills, and I guess I imagined them all on the way home. Thank God my mother got there soon after I did. She was calm and composed—my mother was calm in every crisis I can remember—and as soon as I saw her, I knew things weren't as bad as I had been imagining.

But they were bad enough. My dad was a guide setter in a steel rolling mill. His job was to steer white-hot steel billets into a machine that rolled them into structural steel. Dad saw one of the guides on the machine slip and knew that a breakdown in the whole line would follow very quickly. So he signaled the table operator to stop the machine while he adjusted the guide. While Dad was behind the rolls to make the adjustment, the operator—who apparently missed Dad's signal—started another batch of billets through. Dad was trapped behind the machine, and a searing strip of steel hit him in the thigh, literally cooking his leg. He fell back and grabbed the sides of the trough through which the steel was pouring, holding himself away from it. Had he fallen into the trough, he would have been instantly mangled. He told me later all he could think of was "Mary and the kids" as he somehow found the strength to hold himself above the trough in the stench of his own burning flesh while 150 feet of rolled steel passed beneath his legs. Then the machine was stopped and Dad collapsed in the empty trough.

He was in the hospital for six months, and during that time, I did a lot of thinking. For the first time, I realized that most steel plants didn't have even rudimentary safety guards to protect the workers. The accident to my dad couldn't happen today, and it shouldn't have happened then. A few dollars' worth of safety devices would have prevented it, and I made a resolution to do what I could to force the owners, if necessary, to provide that protection.

Then there was the matter of simple survival. When Dad's paycheck stopped coming, we had no money. For six months my mother was faced with the problem of feeding a young, hungry and growing family without a regular income. Once again, the injustice hit me. My dad had been hurt in line of duty, sacrificed to a saving of a few dollars in safety equipment. Yet, the minute he was of no further use to the company, his income stopped and his family was thrown on its own resources to survive a crisis which was in no way their doing. From that moment, workmen's compensation was not a catch phrase to me. It was the difference between hunger and survival, between hope and desperation.

We survived without emotional scars because of the unwavering strength of my mother. She rented rooms and Joe and I worked at odd jobs when we could. And once in a while the good Lord stepped in to help. One noon we were sitting at the kitchen table, staring glumly at the cornmeal mush that had become our major item of diet, while mother opened the mail that had just arrived. Suddenly she began to laugh and cry at the same time as she waved a check for $20 that fell from an envelope, a dividend from an investment Dad had made years earlier and long forgotten. Another day, Joe found a dollar in a pool of muddy water while scuffing his way home from school. He ran the rest of the way, bursting into the house with his treasure. These were moments of almost hysterical joy in our household. They meant some boiling meat to augment the mush and at least a momentary relaxation of the struggle for survival.

My mother kept her head high, and it never occurred to us to do otherwise. She let us know that we weren't "shanty Irish" and she never let us forget the importance of school. I was doing well—so well that I skipped the sixth grade entirely and was graduated from grammar school at the top of my class. And when Dad got back to work—walking with a limp on the right leg he wouldn't let them amputate in the hospital—the world looked pretty good to us. We had a suit of clothes apiece and a phonograph to play while we kids did the dishes in the evening and some green fields close by for football and baseball. It was easy to forget for long spells the drabness and the soot and the insecurity—and the resolutions.

There were two ways out of the mills—through politics and by acquiring some sort of skill that was marketable in a white-collar job. My parents pointed me down the second route—which meant walking four miles to Holy Cross High School where I could take a commercial course and learn typing, shorthand and bookkeeping along with the standard subjects. Mother was up at 4:30 every morning to pack Dad's lunch pail and send him off to work with a big breakfast under his belt. She saw me off at 7 A.M., carrying my lunch wrapped in a roll of newspaper. I saved several miles of walking each day when Dad got me a pass to use the Jones & Laughlin hot metal bridge across the Monongahela River. There were many winter mornings I would cross that bridge in a darkness thickened by smoke and perforated by the fires from the mill that would light occasional patches of the muddy waters below me. It always made me think that I was getting a preview glimpse into hell, and I would hurry a little faster to put it behind me.

The commercial course took two years. Before I completed it, I lied about my age—I was still fifteen—and got a job running messages and typing orders in the office of the polishing mill at Jones & Laughlin. I worked eleven hours a day—from 7 A.M. to 6

P.M.—for the magnificent sum of twenty-two cents an hour. But during the few months I spent in that job, I got a close look at every type of operation to be found in a steel plant. I was a young, cheeky kid, big enough to take care of myself but gifted with enough blarney to avoid most fights. I was never afraid of fighting, but I never really enjoyed it either. I usually got rid of my hostilities playing football.

Jones & Laughlin was known among steelworkers in those days as the "butcher shop." The title was well earned. Accidents were frequent and safeguards were virtually nonexistent. The men in the mill warned me about the danger points—the hot steel, the furnaces and soaking pits, the locomotives and the overhead cranes—and I saw enough firsthand evidence carried out of the mill almost every day to convince me that these dangers were very real.

While I was working, I went to school evenings and on Sunday, and I was graduated with my commercial class in June of 1918. With that behind me, I started looking around for a better job. We were involved in World War I, then, and a lot of men were being drafted. So a big kid of sixteen with a good school record and a tendency to brashness could have his choice of jobs. I almost doubled my wages when I landed in the toolroom of the National Tube Company's Continental Works, where my father had worked when he first came to Pittsburgh. The hours were the same—sixty-six a week—but now I was taking home $23.76 per week. And I was learning about people.

I'd heard my dad's friends talk about "Hunkies." I knew vaguely that they meant East Europeans without education and with very little grasp of English. In my new job, I met my first Hunky, a sweeper named "Wash" who had been crippled in a mill accident and given the meanest job in the factory by a beneficent boss when he recovered sufficiently to work. He liked me, and when the superintendent was gone, Wash would open his desk, take out a handful of parts catalogs, wave them at me and say, "You smart. You know how read. You read dese books and you be a big man, too." Wash knew he couldn't aspire to such managerial wonders as reading a catalog, but he thought I could. And some-how, this thought gave him pleasure.

There was Walt Larkin, big, hard-muscled, the machinist son of a Pittsburgh cop. Walt taught me to run a lathe and to box. We'd spar around during our lunch hour, and once he hit me over the heart and I dissolved like a punctured balloon. He was distraught and didn't want to box with me again, but I insisted, and I became pretty good with my hands.

There was Chappie Connare, a real honest-to-God Englishman with an accent, who was such a fine machinist that he was kept on the job in spite of the fact that he was the only dues-paying, card-carrying union member permitted around the premises. There was Con Duncan, an old man—he must have been almost sixty— who was chief mechanic and therefore automatically the fount of all wisdom and philosophy. He dispensed advice with a sort of benign patience, some of it useful. I remember him telling me once, "Just because a couple of your friends have a falling out is no reason why you should side with one or the other." Probably no more relevant counsel was ever offered a future union leader. And there was Fritz Reil, a tall, disjointed redhead who once cut off a chunk of his ring finger on an unprotected lathe, had it bound up and returned to his machine.

I filed my first grievance for Fritz, although, God knows, the whole concept of grievances would have chilled the people who ran the steel companies in those days. Anyway, I raised hell with the superintendent about the lack of safety guards after Fritz's ac-cident, and a few days later the sheet metal workers were making covers for the lathes. I don't know if I had anything to do with it or not, but it made me feel good to think that I did. And it gave me some stature around the plant.

These were the people who shaped my views in those early days. As I hustled tools around the plant, meeting all sorts of peo-ple in all kinds of jobs, I began to understand that there are a lot of different viewpoints that bear consideration, and the terrain each person can see is strictly limited by the height he commands and the direction in which he's looking. I found very little inclination on the part of either the workingmen or the few management people I met to venture a look in the other guy's direction.

The big difference, of course, was that management had all the power and labor—at that time—had none at all. So management generally had its way completely, and as long as the owners didn't give a damn about the people who worked for them, the prospects for plant safety or accident benefits or social security or protection against unreasonable demands were pretty dim. Not all owners or managers were like this, of course, but on one thing—I quickly discovered—they were united: they definitely didn't want workingmen organized into any sort of cohesive unit that could bring concentrated pressure to bear on the employers. They not only didn't want it, they were prepared to kill, if necessary, to resist it. And here is where the lines were drawn. Because they *did* kill and thereby fed a fire of anger and resentment that hasn't been damped down in the breasts of some working people three generations later.

While I was learning these lessons, I was also impressed by the fact that education would open doors otherwise closed to me. But I couldn't stop working; my family needed the money. So at sixteen, I enrolled at Carnegie Tech three nights a week to finish out my four years of high school.

During my forays around the mill, I also found out why union organizers weren't getting anywhere. Steelworkers were simply scared to death of losing their jobs—and they had no doubt at all that this is exactly what would happen if they openly supported unionism. I kept insisting we should share in some of the fat profits of Carnegie and his friends, and the only way we were going to accomplish this was by organizing. I got away with this kind of talk, I guess, because I wasn't afraid of being fired and I was young enough so that the foremen tended to be more amused than irritated.

Another thing that helped was my reputation as an "eye doctor." First aid was primitive, at best, administered in our mill by a former gate watchman who was too senile to do anything else. I took eighteen splinters out of a riveter's eye one day when the first-aid specialist couldn't even see them; after that, workers with eye problems came to me for help until the plant management was finally shamed into hiring a nurse.

Not all of my co-workers were friendly, though. A lot of them were suspicious of me because I was going to night school, and they would call me "Education" and belly up to me and say, "Who the hell do you think you are, anyway?" Most of the fights I couldn't avoid started with guys who resented my interest in an education and got on me about it.

I suppose the main driving force in my life at this point was Father James LaValle, the assistant pastor of St. Rosalia Catholic Parish in Greenfield, where we moved after we lost our hotel. Greenfield was a mill town full of tough Irish kids, and Father Jimmy decided to make sure that all this energy got released in a positive direction. He put pool tables and a bowling alley in an old house on the parish grounds and then started a sandlot football team that soon was beating the best semipro outfits around Pittsburgh. I played left tackle on several of those St. Rosalia teams, but the project of Father Jimmy that *really* got to me was his dramatic club. I'd always resisted that sort of thing as sissy, but playing for Father Jimmy was something else again, whether it was on a football field or the stage. I enjoyed acting, and I was good at it. Years later, those plays I did for Father Jimmy prodded me into a drama major in college and almost into another career.

But in 1920, there were other educational decisions to be made. Armed with a high-school diploma and two years of experience playing football for Father Jimmy's irregulars, I was offered an athletic scholarship at Kiski Prep School, where the Eastern colleges farmed out their football prospects. It was tough to turn down, but for the first time in my life, my family was living well, with my paycheck augmenting my dad's. That seemed to me more important, at the moment, than anything else. Besides, I was young. There was still plenty of time for more schooling. So I stayed on at Continental, polished my commercial skills and kept looking around for places to use them. And before I was twenty, a man with whom I was to spend the next thirty years moved over my horizon and came iinto view. His name was Philip Murray.

2

Just before I met Phil Murray, I got involved in my first labor dispute. The AFL was making a feeble pass at organizing the steelworkers, so the United States Steel Corporation, which owned the plant where I was working, decided to throw us a bone by letting us vote on whether or not we would like to work an eight-hour day. The whole thing was a joke because there was no pay increase in the package, so in effect the workers were being asked to cut their own income by shortening their working day. To nobody's surprise, the eight-hour day was turned down, but I campaigned hard for it—both because I didn't enjoy getting up at 4:30 to go to work and because I wanted to register defiance in some vague way.

My campaigning irritated both the plant management and my new boss, a thin, crabbed man named Harry Strobel, who hadn't liked me when he was assistant superintendent and liked me even less after he was promoted. We got off to a bad start when the Monongahela flooded, backed up into the sewers and left a foul mess in one end of our plant. Strobel told me to go clean it up, and I told him that wasn't my job. We had some words that ended up with him calling me a "smartass kid" and threatening to fire me. About the same time, my dad went out on one of those pitifully ineffective strikes that achieved little more than to let the employers know that a few workers still had guts enough to seek a redress of grievances on a picket line.

AFL fieldmen were trying to organize enough steelworkers to force recognition on the steel companies, but they weren't making much headway. I went to several meetings with my dad and listened to the organizers and then decided—even though the little plant where I worked wasn't involved—that I should stay away from work as a private protest of my own. When the strikers lost their battle and returned without a union, I reported back, too, but Strobel got on me, and I knew I'd better start looking around. So the next week I applied for a job with the Pennsylvania Railroad. The interviewer liked both me and my credentials. He told me to report for work the following Monday, then as I was leaving the office, he called me back. He was reading my employment form, and without looking at me, he said, a little too casually: "Is Holy Cross a Roman Catholic high school?" I told him it was, and he said, "I'd forgotten that the job I had in mind for you on Monday has already been filled. You'll hear from me when we find something else." He hasn't called yet.

I figured that waiting for the Pennsylvania Railroad to decide that Catholics are employable human beings might take too long, so I found a job as a typist in the office of the Wheeling Steel Corporation. The salary wasn't much—$80 a month—but the hours were spectacular, nine to five in an office in downtown Pittsburgh, where the soot was lodged on white collars instead of blue and the air had a chance of blowing clean when the wind came from the right direction.

The day I went to the mill to pick up my tools and personal effects was a small triumph.

Strobel spotted me, came hurrying over and said, "I have a goddam good notion to fire you."

And I said with what I thought was magnificent dignity: "You're too late, Harry. I quit."

It was an exit line I've never forgotten.

Everything about my new job was fine except the money, which was always gone long before payday. I groused about that in the evening bull sessions around McMillan's Drug Store in Greenfield, and one night a local football hero named Mark Stanton asked me if I was just talking or really interested in another job. I told him I was looking, and he said: "I turned down a good one today because I'm going to St. Vincent's to become a priest."

Then he explained that Philip Murray, who was a vice-president of the United Mine Workers of America, was looking for a male secretary. I'd never heard of Phil Murray, but his boss—

John L. Lewis—was a bigger-than-life hero to most working people because he had just won some important concessions for his miners from the coal operators after a long and bloody strike in 1919. So I was intrigued, and I asked Mark how I could get to Phil Murray to apply for the job.

The way to meet anybody of stature in Pennsylvania in the 1920's was to know the right politicians. The power centers in those days were the political wards, and the men with muscle were the politicians who ran them. The State of Pennsylvania for the first thirty years of the twentieth century belonged to the Republican Party. It was as much a one-party state as the Democrats in the Deep South, and anybody with political aspirations in Pennsylvania had to be a Republican, period. There was no Democratic Party in Pennsylvania to speak of until Franklin D. Roosevelt ran for President. But there were liberal Republicans and reactionaries. My family looked at Republicans as the party of Lincoln, dedicated to social reform and devoted to progressivism. My mother and dad loved Teddy Roosevelt. They saw him as a champion of the workingman, and I was raised in an atmosphere and tradition of liberalism on domestic issues that influenced me to cast my first presidential vote for Robert La Follette on the Farmer-Labor ticket in 1924. But nobody really cared much about political philosophy. Political power was all that mattered, and the working people who had taken the political route out of the mills worked within the framework of the Republican Party out of simple necessity.

One such man was Red Welsh—the political big shot in our ward—and he's the one to whom Mark Stanton referred me. But Welsh was far beyond my reach, so I approached him through one of my football friends (Babe Keenan) who knew him. Red, in turn, introduced me to an associate of Murray's who made an appointment for me. He also mentioned casually that the job would pay $225 a month—which sounded to me about one cut below what Andy Carnegie must be making.

I met Phil Murray in the office of Pat Fagan, who was head of the United Mine Workers in Pittsburgh. Murray was thirty-eight then, a handsome, dignified, impeccably dressed man, with a shock of black hair that bent over rigidly horizontal eyebrows. The eyes, brown and cool, regarded me quizzically as my benefactor—a UMW organizer named Dave Hickey—said, "I've found a secretary for you, Phil."

I was scared, and Murray knew it and tried to put me at ease. He leaned back in Fagan's chair and put his hands behind his head in a gesture I would learn to know and said, "Just tell me about yourself."

So I started talking. Murray listened, letting me run down. Then he went back and asked some questions. He seemed particularly interested that I was president of my high-school alumni group and had helped organize the Catholic Alumni Association of Pittsburgh. He questioned me closely about night school, my reasons for going and my feelings about education. I lied a little about my shorthand and typing abilities. Then he looked at me in that pensive way of his and said, "You sound ambitious."

"I am."

And he smiled and said, "You want to work for me?"

I did—for thirty-four years.

There was no breaking-in period. Murray was leaving in a few days for New York, and he told me he would want me along. As I left the office, he said casually that I would need $120 for expenses. I ran down the steps, heart pounding with excitement over my new job and consternation at the thought of raising $120. Mother and Dad accepted my news with some reservations. The immediate trip to New York unsettled them a bit, and Dad called on Murray to see what kind of man he was. He came back satisfied and lent me $20—all he had. When I reported for work on September 10, 1923, Murray somehow sensed my problem and advanced me the other $100 while I was trying to figure out how to tell him I couldn't raise it.

Before that, however, I had to quit my other job with only a one-day notice. My boss was outraged, but he finally calmed down when I found him a replacement. I spent the weekend frantically practicing shorthand. My sister and her friends dictated to me in shifts until I was so tired I could no longer see what I was writing. Then I was on a train headed for New York, in possession of a lower berth I didn't have to share, and launched—a little uncertainly—on a new life that was to carry me into the power elite of the American labor movement.

On the way to New York, Murray and I talked about the death of President Warren G. Harding and the gossip being heard everywhere about impending scandals in Washington. When the Harding funeral train had passed through Pittsburgh a few weeks earlier, I'd gone to the Hazelwood station to see it clank slowly and somberly by. A newspaper photographer had taken a picture of the crowd, and I was in the forefront—a fact which, at that time, excited me more than my observation of this small slice of history. Had someone told me then that I would, a few years hence, become closely involved with six United States Presidents I would no more have believed him than I would have believed that one day my picture would appear in Pittsburgh newspapers more often than any other living American.

Murray also asked me if I knew about the report just published by Judge Elbert H. Gary, then president of the U.S. Steel Corporation, after a year-long study of working hours in the steel industry. I admitted I didn't, so Murray read me part of it, including the flat statement that "abolition of the 12-hour day in the steel industry is not now feasible, as it would add 15 percent to the cost of making steel and would require 60,000 additional workers." I thought of my friends at Continental and their fear of being fired, and I knew they would have to live with the twelve-hour day until someday, somehow, someone organized them into an instrument of power strong enough to stand against working hours that made industrial slaves of human beings.

I was pleased and impressed that Murray spoke to me as an equal, never patronizing me and apparently honestly interested in what I had to say.

After these preliminaries, we began to talk about the United Mine Workers and the directions I could expect my new work to lead me. I found that Murray had been born of Irish parents in

Scotland, worked in the coal mines there as a boy, and continued in the mines when his family emigrated to Pennsylvania in 1902. He had worked his way up in the UMW until he was elected vice-president in 1920. Although he didn't say so, I knew he was now regarded as second-in-command to the miners' new leader, John L. Lewis.

The UMW, at that time, was probably the most powerful industrial union in the world and the only broad-based one to survive the five decades of union-baiting and genocide that followed the Civil War. It had won organized labor's greatest victory in the 1902 strike, when the coal mine owners—threatened with a takeover by President Theodore Roosevelt—had agreed to negotiate with the UMW on the day I was born. In 1912 and 1916, the mine workers had won full recognition and the eight-hour working day, both signal victories. Now, under John L. Lewis, the UMW was seeking higher wages and demanding safer working conditions for the miners—and getting both. The prospect of being close to the power center of such an operation excited me, and long after Murray had gone to bed, I lay in my lower berth, listening to the clacking of the wheels and dreaming about the adventures ahead of me.

They started early. I walked bug-eyed through the labyrinth of tunnels from the station to the Hotel Pennsylvania, where I had a room to myself and a chance to freshen up before joining Murray for breakfast. He told me we would be meeting John L. Lewis after breakfast, and in the haze of excitement at that prospect, I had no idea what I was eating—even though this was my first meal in a big city hotel dining room.

Meeting Lewis was to me—at the age of twenty—comparable to meeting Babe Ruth or Jack Dempsey or Teddy Roosevelt, the three men I admired without reservation. Lewis was in a class by himself as a labor leader who had defied powerful industrial coalitions and even U.S. Presidents to win concessions for his miners. His reputation for toughness and absolute fearlessness had made him a legendary figure. Small wonder, then, that I was shaking visibly as I followed Phil Murray out of the dining room of the Pennsylvania Hotel after breakfast.

In one corner of the lobby, an alcove filled with palm fronds had been screened off. We slipped behind the screen, and there he was, sunk in an overstuffed chair and surrounded by a group of his assistants. Lewis looked up as we entered, then stood to greet us. He was every bit as imposing as I had imagined, broad of shoulder and thick of girth, built rather like an oversized fireplug. He had a shock of thick, wavy brown hair that fell over a handsome bulldog face dominated by piercing gray-blue eyes, shaded by bushy brown eyebrows. The built-in scowl, I learned later, was simply the way his face was constructed. Behind that scowl, he was capable of both charm and softness. He greeted me warmly, saying, "Welcome to the United Mine Workers of America. I hope you have a long, successful career in the labor movement, Dave," while I stood, mouth agape, totally awed for the first time in my life.

The moment passed—but never completely. Although my association with Lewis became quite close in the years that followed, I never altogether lost this feeling of schoolboy awe when I was in his presence. He commanded a room simply by being there, and the second-echelon people around Lewis were always afraid of him. The men I met that day in the Hotel Pennsylvania, however, were top lieutenants, in New York, I presumed, for a strategy meeting with the boss. I settled on the fringes of the group—the youngest by a good fifteen years—to hear momentous events planned. Instead, they talked almost exclusively about the Dempsey-Firpo fight coming up the following night in the Polo Grounds.

When the meeting broke up, Murray motioned for me to follow along upstairs. The three of us went to Lewis' suite, where I was told that his secretary couldn't make the trip and I would have to take over. It was a confusing and frightening day, because the miners who called spoke an idiom I didn't understand, and many of the messages I passed along to Lewis lost a good deal in the translation. He was more amused than irritated, however, and he tried to put me at ease in that great, round voice of his that sounded like distant thunder. He spoke impeccable English that didn't seem pretentious then, although it did later.

Murray told me he would try to get me a ticket to the fight, but there were simply none to be had so he suggested that I go the Polo Grounds in the afternoon and try to buy a general admission ticket. It was my first ride on an elevated train, and I stood in the doorway for three stops to make sure I didn't miss the Polo Grounds. It would have been impossible to miss, because even then—five hours before the fight—the streets and sidewalks for several blocks around were packed with a swaying, sweating mass of humanity waiting to pick up one of the few thousand general admission tickets scheduled to go on sale.

I found the lone ticket window and worked my way into a position close enough to get in when the box office opened. About ten minutes before that was scheduled to happen, a tidal wave of people who knew they had no chance at a ticket simply swept away those who had been lined up in front of the box office. I saw it coming and braced against it, but I couldn't hold my ground, and I bobbed around inside that mob like a cork in a hurricane. Mounted police came down the street, breaking the back of the wave, and when it receded, I found myself clinging to the little house that contained the box office—first in line.

With the police standing by to preserve some semblance of order, the tickets were sold and I got into the stadium. Glistening in the distance was the tiny white square of ring. Surrounding it, as far as I could see, were rows of wooden benches, swarming with people. Jeez, I thought, one day in New York and I've met John Lewis and Jack Dempsey. Dempsey had been a miner in his youth and Lewis was called the "Jack Dempsey of the labor movement" by many news feature writers.

I worked my way into a seat about twenty rows back from ringside. I could see Lewis and Murray and the UMW crowd in front of me, and I shouted but they didn't hear me. Then a little knot of handlers opened an aisle for the fighters to get into the ring, and everybody in the Polo Grounds stood up. I couldn't see a damned thing, so I stood on the bench with one foot and braced my other foot on the backrest in front of me and saw about one minute of wild action in the first round; then the backrest splintered, I lost my balance and fell violently to the ground. Lying there, half groggy, staring at feet, I heard somebody shout, "He's out of the ring."

I clawed my way up, grabbed a husky man beside me and said, "*Who's* out of the ring?" He told me to get up on his shoulders, and I surfaced just in time to see Dempsey pushed back into the ring by the sportswriters at ringside. I'll never forget his face. It was deadly calm. He stalked Firpo, measured him, and then connected with a right hand that simply exploded on the side of Firpo's head. But Firpo got up and Dempsey hammered him down again and again—seven times before the bell finally ended the round.

Dempsey finished it in the second, raining blows on Firpo until the challenger finally crumpled to the floor. As the referee counted, Dempsey turned his back and looked out over the crowd, almost as if he were counting the house. Then, at the sound of "Ten," he rushed to the stricken Firpo, picked him up in his arms, and carried him to his stool. For the second time in two days, I was overcome with awe.

There was no chance for me to ponder such perfection. The next day was one of the most important in my life. Frequently we don't recognize these turning points when they're happening. Only in retrospect do we see their nature clearly. But there was no doubt in my mind about this one. I knew immediately that the whole direction and thrust of my life was being shaped.

The morning after the Dempsey-Firpo fight, Murray told me we were all going to Wilkes-Barre for a speech by Lewis to celebrate the settlement of the 1923 anthracite coal strike. I'd hardly caught my breath when we were on a train headed for the Pennsylvania coalfields. The UMW local had hired the Wilkes-Barre ball park for the event, and thousands of miners and their families were on hand when we arrived there in midafternoon. They were in a holiday mood, back at work after a six-week strike that had brought them a substantial pay raise. Lewis had done it for them. Lewis was their hero, and they received him that way, cheering wildly as our little group entered the ball park. It was only later —after getting to know hundreds of these miners and their families—that I realized Lewis had given them something they prized much more than a raise in wages. He'd also given them dignity as human beings. They wouldn't have put it in those words—one swarthy miner told me, "By God, maybe now they know we're *people*"—but they felt it and they believed Lewis had done it for them and they loved him for it.

When he was introduced from the speaker's platform built over second base, the crowd cheered so long I thought it would never stop. Lewis looked out over them silently, drinking it in, making no effort to stop it. When he did, his gesture was decisive, and they settled back to listen.

He reviewed the purpose of the strike and the achievements and commended the workers for standing fast in the face of all sorts of pressures to compromise the goals they sought—and deserved. Then he paused—so long that I thought perhaps he'd lost his way. But Lewis was a master orator, and this was his way of underscoring what he was about to say.

Thundering the words, he told the coal miners that with the strike over and victory theirs, they must now turn their attention wholeheartedly to producing coal in partnership with the operators who opposed them so steadfastly during the strike.

Throwing his hands to the sky in a gesture Lewis saved for his most impressive moments, he shouted: "We are partners in this great enterprise. We must work together—miners and operators —and we must turn out this product for our own good, the good of the owners and the good of the country."

This penetrated slowly into my consciousness. The idea of labor and management in partnership had never occurred to me before. I had always seen them as blood enemies. Yet, here was a man who could say a few days after a long and sometimes violent strike that the antagonists had to work together, now that it was over, for the ultimate good of both. And this was no company man speaking. This was one of the toughest spokesmen in the history of American labor, a man feared and hated by most of the mine operators.

"We're partners," he was shouting, "whether we like it or not,

and as it is with all partners, we have our fights and our friendships. This is part of a partnership—and a necessity for the successful operation of democratic capitalism. Once a fight is over,
the partnership must begin to function again, and production
must roll. The industry must be successful if the workers are to
earn a decent living, and the workers must produce an honest
day's work for a decent day's pay."

Democratic capitalism. I rolled the phrase around in my mind. I
knew that this concept of partnership between management and
labor had been rejected out of hand by both sides in the violent
years of the late 1800's. I remembered a coal-mine operator who
said publicly, "I would rather have two men killed than one
mule." And one of the Molly Maguires exhorting his fellow miners: "Men, if you must die with your boots on, die for your families, your homes, your country, but do not longer consent to die
like rats in a trap for those who have no more interest in you than
in the pick you dig with."

Was it possible, from the depths of this hatred, to build a viable
partnership? Could men who had etched the lines of battle in
blood and recrimination for so many years actually work together
to a common end? This speaker who fought without quarter for
the rights of his miners but was then willing to start anew, from a
fresh base—this man thought so. And he had the courage to say it,
when he could simply have trumpeted victory.

Democratic capitalism. I was still grappling with the implications of the words when Lewis finished. Suddenly we were sub-
merged in noise and people. They swarmed out of their seats and
surrounded the platform, reaching for him, trying to shake his
hand or just to touch him. I saw dozens of burly, bearded men
kneel and try to kiss his hand, and for an embarrassed instant I
had a mental picture of Christ and the multitudes. Lewis was a
Saviour to many of these people, a concrete, bigger-than-life figure
they could see and touch, and to men of the earth, this was the sort
of substance they could understand. Lewis at first tried to draw
back from the adulation, but finally stood rather helplessly in its
midst, extracting his hands—when he could—to shake those of

miners and their families pressing about him. I was amazed to see him weep, fat, unashamed tears trickling down that bulldog face.

The rest of that day and evening was a haze to me. We went to a dinner given Lewis at a local hotel, and I saw the other side of him—the raconteur, the hail-fellow-well-met, relaxed and expansive among his friends—but these impressions simply bounced off the surface of my consciousness, because I was thinking about what Lewis had said that afternoon, and wondering if it really might work.

I was still wondering and thinking when we got on a train the next morning and headed back to Pittsburgh to settle into an office routine after the three most exciting, rewarding and provocative days of my young life.

3

I was very big in the evenings at McMillan's Drug Store in Hazelwood for the next few weeks, alternately describing the Dempsey-Firpo fight and the Lewis speech to an audience of old school friends who were at first unbelieving and finally—after the hundredth repetition—bored.

At the office, I was getting acquainted with Phil Murray. He was a strange combination of workingman and a scholar. He'd come up a tough road, emerging from the mines to become a check-weighman, an elected union official who stood at the mouth of the mine and made certain the weigh-foreman wasn't cheating the miners when he weighed the cars they loaded. He advanced quickly through the ranks of the UMW, winning the presidency of District 5 when he was in his early thirties and election as Lewis's vice-president when the two ran for the top offices in the UMW in 1920. He had a sharp, penetrating mind, but his style—unlike that of Lewis—was never flamboyant. He wore conservative suits and an air of dignity that could approach stuffiness, and he spoke in a Scottish brogue that I always suspected would have fallen away years earlier if Murray hadn't cultivated it almost as a trademark. Murray's wife was about five years younger than Phil, a quiet, withdrawn woman with a serious hearing problem that got steadily worse as she grew older. When it became apparent to the Murrays that they were not going to have any children, they adopted a son, Joseph, from a Pittsburgh orphanage and took their niece, Mercedes Daugherty, to raise.

Mercedes was very close to her foster parents and later became Murray's private secretary, but Joe was a willful, difficult kid, constantly at odds with his father. The gap grew wider over the years, and Murray was never able to bridge it. A lot of people felt that Murray saw me as a substitute for the son he never had. I was aware of this and thought about it from time to time, but I'm no armchair psychologist and never got that far into Murray's head. All I know is that we liked each other instantly and, until his first heart attack, our relationship was built on a solid foundation of mutual respect and affection.

Within a month we were traveling again, this time to Portland, Oregon, for the national convention of the American Federation of Labor. It gave me my only look at Samuel Gompers, the tiny Manhattan cigar maker who had founded the AFL in 1881. The AFL grew out of the refusal of the Knights of Labor to permit the craft unions special privileges. Many of the craft unions had been around in one form or another for almost a hundred years; they resented this treatment and withdrew from the Knights to form their own national organization. Within a few years, the Knights of Labor were dying, consumed in the fires of public indignation that followed the bombing in Haymarket Square in Chicago on May 4, 1886. After that, the AFL—made up primarily of the elite of skilled workingmen and committed to a program that avoided all participation in political matters and guaranteed the autonomy of each member union to administer its own policies and affairs without any interference from the federation—became the only national labor organization of any significance.

That's the way it was when I attended my first AFL convention. The speeches were long and generally boring until William Green —later the AFL president but then secretary of the Resolutions Committee—delivered a fire-eating resolution condemning Communism and all it stood for. He was answered instantly by a man in the audience who was wearing a flaming red tie ("the mark of Bolshevism," Murray whispered to me). Red Tie denounced the speaker and his resolution and then launched into a long defense of Communism.

Instantly, the whole convention came to life. One after another, union officials from all over the country stood to castigate the Communists, and I could watch the crimson creep up the neck of Red Tie, who was sitting just in front of me. The Speech I remember most vividly was delivered by the president of a UMW District in West Virginia. Looking directly at Red Tie, he said: "The Communists don't give a damn about the workers. In my state, the Communists are working hand in glove with the coal operators to wreck the United Mine Workers of America. They know they have no chance to establish their own union or to take over the UMW, so they have joined with the people they say they hate to destroy the only organization that *really* works for the miners. And why are the Communists doing this?" He paused, then jabbing his finger at Red Tie, said slowly, "I'll tell you why. Because you think that by destroying our union you can wipe out all the gains we've made and then move into that misery and take over for the Communists. You don't care about the workers. All you care about is the party."

The convention cheered, and Red Tie stalked out, glowering. I watched him go and wondered, Could this really be true? It was my first exposure to the concept of Communism. I knew vaguely that the wealthy industrialists in America had been blaming Communism—long before the Russians ever knew what it was —for most of the activities of the labor unions, and I knew this was mostly a lot of hot air, a convenient and emotional tag for the big men of industry to put on any activities that threatened them. But this was the first time I had seen Communism from the other side. Red Tie was an honest-to-God, card-carrying Communist leader, dedicated to the principles of the recent Bolshevik revolution in Russia. And here he was, being ridiculed out of a national labor convention that most Americans would probably have expected to welcome him with open arms.

Murray and Lewis also spoke out eloquently against the Communists, and when the oratory was finished, Green's resolution was carried overwhelmingly. Then the convention returned to tedium, and I had time to ponder my surprise at the conservative —almost stuffy—tone of most of the speeches. I found my own views considerably more radical than the majority of the delegates on almost every position the convention took, and I was struck by the irony of the fact that for years the industrial and business world had been able to shoot down organized labor as a movement of leftists and radicals. These men I was watching—in their high collars and high-blown oratory—were every bit as conservative, even reactionary, in their thinking as a corporate board of directors. And I wondered, How the hell can the public image of these people be so wrong?

It's a question I was no more able to answer then than I can now—except for the obvious observation that industrial propaganda has always been more effective and high-powered than that of the unions. But in 1923, I was less interested in philosophy than in discovery—and there was still much to be discovered.

I was invited to accompany Lewis and Murray on a tour of the West, an awesome experience for a lad who had only been out of Pittsburgh once before in his life. Most of the top functionaries of the UMW were in our party—Elliot Searles, a pince-nez dandy who edited the *UMW Journal*, Kacy Adams, economist, critic and professional cynic, "Judge" Henry Warrum, the world's greatest labor lawyer, and many of the UMW district directors. To all of them, I was "the kid," a lanky, blond, glib and slightly precocious newcomer who had been accepted by Murray and Lewis and was therefore a part of the family.

When we returned from the West, Murray and I dropped off in Indianapolis, where the International headquarters of the UMW was located. Here, too, I was years younger than anyone else on the staff, and I had to put up with the nickname of "The Sheik," the title of a Rudolph Valentino movie then playing around the country. I learned my first lesson in union intrigue in Indianapolis. The UMW offices were surprisingly plush and divided into two very distinct sections, with a threshold that either side seldom crossed. Lewis and Murray occupied one wing, the secretary-treasurer the other. Each section had its own set of telephones, an eccentricity that puzzled me until Kacy Adams explained that neither group wanted the other listening to its telephone calls. I would remember that many years later, when my own secretary-treasurer was plotting my downfall from the next office.

Indianapolis was incredibly dull, at least for a newly emancipated man of twenty who was interested in a little action. A wild evening consisted of a movie and a lobster dinner at the Claypool Hotel, which was how I spent my twenty-first birthday. It was typical of Lewis that he remembered and congratulated me. But most evenings were spent with other UMW staff members in the lobby of the Claypool, sitting in a discreet semicircle around Lewis and listening to him talk. Usually, his topic was the union, but once in a while he would venture into politics or foreign affairs. Lewis was a staunch Republican, and his political views— which he expressed forcefully—would be considered reactionary today and almost were then. But all this talk, this exposure to the great men of labor that so excited me when I first encountered it in New York City finally began to bore me. I longed for some action. And early in 1924, I began to get more than I really anticipated.

4

In 1924, the American soft coal operators in the South decided to break the United Mine Workers and destroy John L. Lewis. And over the next eight bloody years, they came very close to bringing it off.

The action started in triumph for the UMW, even though the miners were in a highly vulnerable position. The demand for coal —to make steel, run the railroads, and export to our allies in Europe—accelerated during World War I. So mine operators looked for new sources of coal and found them in many of the Southern states where there had been a few small mines before.

Production doubled. So did employment and UMW membership. Then World War I ended, and almost as suddenly as it had accelerated, the demand for coal dwindled. By 1924, domestic needs for coal were back to prewar levels, and the country had dozens of active coal mines and thousands of miners that were no longer needed. To complicate matters further, the Southern mines —able to attract cheap Negro labor—were paying wages considerably below their Northern competitors. The Southerners justified this on the grounds that they had to ship the coal farther to markets. As long as all the coal that could be mined was sold, this wage differential was exasperating but not crucial. But when competition became cutthroat, it enabled the Southern mines— becoming almost entirely nonunion—to undersell their Northern competitors literally by taking it out of the pay envelopes of the miners.

In a free economy, an entrepreneur—whether of labor or business—is in trouble when the supply of his manpower or product greatly exceeds the demand for it. And that was the situation facing the UMW negotiators as we headed for Jacksonville, Florida, in February, 1924, to open talks with the Central Competitive

Field (Western Pennsylvania, Ohio, Indiana and Illinois) of the bituminous coal industry. It was my first labor negotiation. I had become expert in shorthand, and Lewis had me at the negotiating table to take down what was said. Sometimes I found the ploys so fascinating that I was caught, pencil poised in midair, listening when I should have been writing.

Both sides immediately acknowledged the serious condition of the industry, which saved a lot of time. The wage scale, negotiated a year earlier by Lewis, was $7.50 a day, quite high for that time. Under the circumstances, Lewis knew there was no chance of getting more money for the miners. His hope was simply to hold the wage line while the industry tried to stabilize itself. The operators argued for a wage reduction, pointing to nonunion operators in West Virginia, Kentucky and several other Southern states who were paying much lower wages and crowding out the union mines. Lewis argued that the freight hauling disadvantage made up for this difference and therefore no reduction could be tolerated.

The arguments—always reasonable, and surprisingly free of rancor—continued for several weeks. Then the owners offered to hold the wage line in return for a three-year contract. Lewis agreed, and a contract was signed continuing the $7.50 weekly rate. The UMW team was elated, and we sang our way home on the train, certain we had won a victory in a sticky situation. Lewis told his miners that the contract would help stabilize the industry, provide a long period of security for UMW members and help bring nonunion miners into the UMW, and they accepted his assessment with a minimum of dissent. Calvin Coolidge's Secretary of Commerce, a stocky, round-faced California engineer named Herbert Hoover, also agreed and commended both the UMW and the coal operators. The country was prosperous and getting more so, and the specter of a coal strike held no appeal to the Coolidge Administration.

This euphoria lasted about one month; then the roof fell in. Efforts to use the terms of the Central Competitive Field contract as a basis for contracts with union operators in West Virginia and

Kentucky got nowhere. These producers said they couldn't compete with nonunion mines and continue to pay the $7.50 rate. As
these arguments raged, some of the Central Competitive Field
operators had second thoughts and decided they couldn't live
with the contract they had just signed. Lewis could probably have
settled with both groups at this point for $6 a day, but he knew
that if he did nonunion Southern mines would simply cut prices
and wages and the whole miserable cycle would start all over
again. So he refused to move from the $7.50 previously negotiated
and the coal operators—including some who had signed and all of
those who hadn't—refused to pay it. In this impasse, the UMW
had only one choice: strike. So in mid-1924, Lewis pulled his men
out of the union mines that refused to meet the $7.50 figure.

The temper of the country in 1924 was almost totally antagonistic to labor strife. Even labor leaders were caught up in the golden
glow of prosperity. William Green, by now president of the AFL,
was saying that strikes were outmoded, and the head of the Loco-
motive Engineers made a speech in which he said: "Who wants to
be a Bolshevik when he can be a capitalist instead? We have
shown how to mix oil and water; how to reconcile capital and
labor."

While Lewis had expressed some of these same views in the
past, he was now caught in a box. The coal industry was definitely
not prospering, and he saw the root of the trouble as a cutthroat
competition that was open-ended. If he went along with it, by permitting his miners to accept lower wages from a depressed industry, there was no telling where it would stop. So he dug in his
heels, said, "this far and no farther," and we had a strike on our
hands in the midst of the greatest prosperity the United States of
America had ever known.

To complicate matters further, the UMW had its annual convention about this time, and Lewis' enemies within the union—
there were always people who strongly objected to his authori-
tarianism and who sought to limit his power—decided Lewis was
in trouble and this was a good time to go after him. They chose to
attack him on the issue of the "appointive power" of the president,

insisting that all of the miners' representatives should be elected by the membership instead of some being selected by whim of Lewis. It was the first time we had used a public-address system at a convention, and there was one microphone on the floor and one on the stage. The argument became louder and angrier, with the floor faction trying to outshout Lewis at the podium. All of his enemies—from Communists to union rivals seeking his job to people who just plain didn't like him—banded together for this attack, and it finally got out of control.

I was sitting on the stage, damned nervous, when that happened. Still fresh in my mind was the adulation at Wilkes-Barre, and I couldn't really believe what I was seeing here. I wasn't yet able to distinguish the difference between the gratitude of men and their families who have just been handed a substantial raise in pay and the greed and vindictiveness of men seeking power at whatever cost to the organization. But I saw it here, first simmering, then—as the argument heated up—boiling over into the aisles of the convention hall.

A few men in the rear poured out of their seats and began to move menacingly down the two aisles of the rickety upstairs auditorium we were using. As they came forward, they picked up conscripts by the dozen who knocked over chairs in their eagerness to get out and join the mob. Their target was Lewis, and instinctively those of us who were on the stage stood and moved to his side. He pounded the gavel in a series of mighty thwacks that were lost in the swelling noise of the mob.

I don't know what would have happened if they had reached the stage. There would have been some heads bloodied, at least. But they never got there. Our chief Sergeants at Arms had been chosen well, thank God. The insurgents came down the left aisle first, and our man on that side was "Whiskers" Smith, a giant coal miner from Tennessee whose trademark was a scraggly black beard. He didn't stop to debate with the mob. He planted himself firmly in the center of the aisle and pointed a pair of six-shooters at the leaders. They stopped. He was prepared to shoot, and they knew it.

On the other side, the ringleader was Alex Howat, the head of the UMW in Kansas and a longtime enemy of Lewis. "Bush" Mc-Cormick, another giant of a man, met that charge. He simply picked up Howat bodily and threw him into the ranks of the crowd behind him. Howat's flying body knocked over a half-dozen men, and the rest of the mob piled up on the prone figures of their fallen comrades. They might have regrouped, but McCormick gave them no chance. He waded into the pile picked up Howat and carried him, struggling, to the stage for a direct confrontation with Lewis.

Lewis seemed remarkably calm. He measured Howat with those icy eyes, then said to him in almost conversational tones: "You goddamned son of a bitch, you are a disgrace to this union and to the whole labor movement. You would destroy this union and all we've gained to satisfy your own personal ambitions." He went on to excoriate Howat in that great, booming voice that needed no loudspeaker, and the delegates began to cheer. The moment of revolt had passed, and the insurgents—still milling about in the aisles—crept back to their seats. They never mounted another attack, but the entire convention was filled with turmoil. Lewis had a clear majority and won the day on every point, but never without bitter denunciations from the floor. Lewis accepted the challenge as one of the prices a man in his position has to pay for power. If he ascribed it to anything more than the normal processes of rivals seeking that power, he never said so. But I found it hard to believe that adulation could turn so quickly to recrimination. And many years later, a former coal mine owner told me that a group of coal operators had collected many thousands of dollars to bribe Howat and his cohorts to mount a rebellion against Lewis.

The tempestuous convention was being matched in the coal-fields. The reaction of the unionized coal operators to the strike was immediate and decisive. They went into the South and imported workers—mostly Negroes—at starvation wages and brought them through picket lines under the guns of company cops and state and local police to work the mines. Southern Negroes who had nothing before were willing to do this backbreaking, dangerous work in the coal mines for as little as a dollar a day. They had no concept of strikes or of any social issues or moral principles involved. They simply wanted work at whatever wage they could get it, so they poured into the mines—particularly in West Virginia—by the thousands. (The union Negroes stood shoulder to shoulder with their white brothers.) This was probably the first mass migration of Negroes to the North, a migration that never really stopped. But the responsibility for this one, and for the bloodshed and misery that followed, rested squarely on the mine owners who imported them.

At first, both Lewis and Murray made an effort to resolve the strife in the only way it could have been resolved at this point: by a liaison of the coal operators to resist cutthroat competition. Even the $6 rate—which Lewis wasn't about to concede—wouldn't have settled matters now. The operators had found a source of cheap labor, and they were out to break the union once and for all. Lewis and Murray made dozens of speeches urging operators—in their own self-interest—to band together to resist the destructive effects of continued price cutting, but there were too many producers caught up in it to make it possible for the others to be effective.

Finally, in desperation, Lewis turned to the Republican President he had helped elect. Calvin Coolidge's theory of government was quite simply to get the hell out of the way and let business run unimpeded, as far and as fast as it could. He was given to taking two-hour naps in the afternoon, and if the turmoil in the coal mines disturbed his slumber, he never indicated it. Lewis and Murray were able to arrange an audience with him. Murray told me later that Lewis turned on all his eloquence to try and persuade Coolidge to call a conference of coal operators and UMW officials to reach some sort of *détente* that would prevent further bloodshed. The President listened impassively, brooded out the window for several moments, then turned, looked at Lewis and said, "Mr. Lewis, our country must have its coal." That was all. The audience was finished. Coolidge never explained what he meant, and he never called the conference. (The only other time the UMW gained Coolidge's private ear was a breakfast conference Van Bittner had with him. Van talked throughout the meeting, while Coolidge ate and said nothing. When the meal was over, Coolidge dismissed Van without comment, leaving him only with the vivid memory of a President of the United States finishing off his breakfast with apple pie smothered in catsup.)

Meanwhile, in the West Virginia coalfields, conditions—according to reports pouring into our headquarters in Indianapolis—were approaching anarchy. Most of the workers lived in "company towns"—houses erected by the company near the mines and rented to the workers—and traded at the "company store."

As strikebreakers poured in from the South, the miners and their families were moved, forcibly when necessary, out of their company-owned homes. They were without money and had no place to go, desperate people, hungry and embittered. These were the men who walked picket lines. Small wonder that when they saw a scab or a company cop, they attacked blindly. The cops were armed and fired into the pickets, and miners were being killed and maimed by the dozens. And the United States, caught up in prosperity, jazz and bootleg booze, couldn't care less.

Sitting in Indianapolis, hearing these horror stories, I had a feeling of unreality. Things couldn't be *that* bad, could they? Even though I had known labor strife in my own family and had spent many hours around our kitchen table listening to tales of violence, it always had something of a dreamlike quality to me because it had never really been a part of my own life. The stories coming back from the coal towns affected me in much the same way. Then I saw one firsthand—and I grew up, almost overnight, to the realities of the hatreds and commercial excesses that could lead to this degree of inhumanity.

Van Bittner was a tough man in a tough spot—a squat, balding, iron-willed man of great intelligence and an ironic wit—who headed the UMW in West Virginia. He needed help badly, and in mid-1925, Murray went abroad on union business and Lewis sent me to help Bittner. I was glad to get away from Indianapolis, a rookie eager to shake the tedium of training camp for the excitement of combat. Like the trainee, I had no concept of the real nature of combat. I found out quickly. West Virginia was virtually an armed camp.

Bittner met me at the train in Fairmount and drove me to his office in the local hotel where the rest of his troops were quartered. Our job was to offer what encouragement and comfort we could to the striking miners who, with their families going hungry, were under terrific pressure to capitulate to the mine owners, leave the union and go back to work for whatever wage the owners chose to give them.

Have you ever tried to tell a man whose kids are starving to death that he must stick by a principle that offers him no bread now, and only an elusive security somewhere in the future? I tried, and the words would stick in my throat, and I would turn away, confused and bewildered that this could be happening at all. Each morning, at dawn, we would set off in a car with a batch of handbills, announcing a mass meeting of miners for that night. We would tack them on fence posts and telephone poles and trees, and then we would backtrack and find that the coal and iron cops had been trailing us and ripping down the handbills as fast as we posted them. But the news of the meetings got around anyway, by word of mouth, and the miners would show up by the hundreds—often with their wives and children—to sit among cowslips on a grassy hillside and listen to Bittner or one of his assistants exhort them to stand fast. We had so little to offer them, and they knew it, and would listen with the empty eyes that come with hopelessness. At first, they found heart in the speeches. They would cheer and go away emotionally recharged, but as the strike dragged on, the cheers tailed off, hope was harder to come by and more and more miners turned their backs on the union and returned to work.

We had a tremendous obligation to those who didn't, and we did our damndest to meet it. We used our diminishing funds to build flimsy wooden barracks to house the families thrown out of their homes. The barracks were a poor excuse for living quarters;

they were cold and crowded and without running water or toilets. But they offered a roof over the heads of people who would otherwise have been living in the open, like animals, and they were tangible assurance—such as it was—that the union was doing everything it could to help.

When I was able to slip past the coal and iron cops, I would help these families move their belongings to the barracks. Sometimes the husband was walking a picket line and was forcibly prevented from returning to his own home; then his wife would have to do the moving alone, often with small children clinging to her and crying. In the fuzzed memories of those awful days, one family haunts me.

It was raining, hard, and the streets of the company town were ankle deep in mud when I arrived. The first thing I saw in the mist was a young-old woman, frightened and bedraggled, standing in the rain in a cotton housedress holding an infant in her arms. Around her, in the mud, were a few pitiful pieces of furniture. A few yards away her husband, gaunt, wild-eyed, with a stubble of beard on his face, stood with fists clenched and the rain trickling down his face. It sounds like a scene from a Grade B movie, but it was West Virginia and the United States of America in 1925, and these were very real people.

As I hurried through the ooze to help, a pair of coal and iron cops, neatly uniformed, came out of the house carrying a settee which they put down with the other furniture. And the husband, sick wth rage, shouted unintelliigible things at them as they moved implacably back into the house. I did what I could. I was honestly afraid he would attack them the next time they came out and they might kill him. So I persuaded him to take the baby and help his wife to the barracks where it was at least dry. He looked at me a few seconds as if he didn't really see me at all, then he took the baby, put his arm around his wife and I followed, carrying a wet chair.

Scenes like this were repeated hundreds of times. When such men got on picket lines, they were violent, and when scabs (usually Southern Negroes or immigrants just off the boat who had no idea of the issues) were moved forcibly through these lines, there were fights—with fists, with rocks, with guns. Many nights I lay in bed at the Fairmount Hotel and listened to the distant crackle of gunfire and wondered which families would be without a home *and* husband when I got to the mine site in the morning.

In an effort to prevent open warfare, the companies began erecting high fences around the mine properties. The scabs would live and work inside these walls, fearing to emerge because they knew they would be attacked by the picketing miners who marched day and night outside. When new scabs were brought in or a group would want out to go to town, company cops would form an armed phalanx to escort them.

There was little distinction made between the coal and iron cops, the local police and the state police. They were all in evidence and all working for the coal operators, breaking union heads at every opportunity. Everywhere we went, we were harassed by police, sometimes in uniform, sometimes deputized civilians with hard eyes and itchy trigger fingers. Whenever we held a meeting, it was surrounded by police, standing just outside the perimeter of the miners in attendance. It's damned uncomfortable conducting a meeting under the muzzle of machine guns, manned by guys who would like your scalp and know they have authority squarely behind them. They would set up searchlights to sweep the meeting, and mounted officers would sit in the shadows behind the lights, the silhouette of their guns plainly visible and their horses neighing and stomping restlessly. It isn't an atmosphere conducive to winning or holding converts, and we were doing neither. It's a miracle, really, that as many miners stood fast as did.

Sometimes, after a day and night of this, I would think about Lewis' speech at Wilkes-Barre and wonder how he must be feeling now. I found myself beginning to hate, and I didn't like it. Lying in bed, I would stare at the ceiling and think, Tomorrow maybe I'll kill one of those bastards and I'll feel better for it. And the thought shocked and embittered me, because it was all tangled up with twenty years of hope and optimism that suddenly seemed pretty shallow, and I wondered what was real and what was right.

Were these people living in absolute degradation, women and children with no place to go and no clothing to wear, men with souls so scarred by hatred and violence that they would never be able to think rationally again—was this the *real* world that I had never seen and must now accept and meet on its own terms? Or was this a shadow world, a fringe world, that I must keep in perspective so it wouldn't destroy the frame of reference I had built for twenty years, one that enabled me to look on my fellow humans as basically decent and capable of reforms that would make this country wholesome and habitable for all of its citizens? I honestly didn't know. I was confused and angry, and the longer I stayed in West Virginia, the greater became my anger and the smaller my hope.

I don't know what might have happened to me, finally. My whole attitude was hardening dangerously, and the philosophy I had embraced at Wilkes-Barre—the idea of democratic capitalism—might well have been extinguished forever in an unreasoning sort of hatred for all management because of what the management was doing to the coal miners of West Virginia. But I never quite fell into that mental chasm. As I balanced on the edge, Murray returned from Europe, and I was sent to Pittsburgh to resume my duties as his secretary and administrative aide. Even that might not have saved me had I known several things then that I know now. Because, behind the scenes, the coal operators were using vast amounts of money to buy union-busting allies wherever they could find them, even among Communists whom industrial leaders continued to insist publicly were actually running the union and fomenting the strikes. The best measure of the operators' hypocrisy is the fact that, while they were damning the UMW leadership as subversive, they were hiring *real* subversives to destroy that leadership.

Two examples will illustrate. Frank Farrington, a UMW official in Illinois and an archenemy of Lewis, in 1926 signed a backdoor agreement with the producers to send his men to work for $6.00 for

an eight-hour day. Kacy Adams was later able to prove that Farrington was in the hire of The Peabody Coal Company and had
been bought off by them to shatter the UMW front in Illinois. A
year later, a group calling itself the "Save the Union Committee"
surfaced, embracing every Lewis-hater in the UMW, including a
number of known and admitted Communists. This group, well ad-
vertised and supported by *The Daily Worker,* called a convention
in Pittsburgh to organize a union in opposition to the UMW.
Lewis could play rough, too, and he and Murray decided the committee should be uprooted before it had time to gather sustenance
and grow.

And so I learned another lesson in the exercise of power. In
Pittsburgh—an industrial city where the votes of workingmen
elected public officials—*we* had some official muscle. Murray and
Pat Fagan, President of the Pittsburgh District, met with Mayor
Herb Kline of Pittsburgh, explained the situation, and asked him
and his police force to look the other way when the "Save the
Union" convention came to town. The mayor agreed.

About five hundred delegates met in a hall a mile from downtown Pittsburgh. The meeting had just been called to order when
an equal number of striking miners, imported for the occasion,
broke in the doors and invaded the hall. There was one hell of a
fight that ended with the delegates scattering and the UMW holding the hall. Not a single cop turned up to interfere. The police,
however, didn't know it was to be a doubleheader. The delegates
reassembled in an old waterfront hotel, but UMW spies reported
their location and once more the meeting was invaded. The delegates took off through corridors of the hotel with UMW men chas-
ing them and guests crawling under beds. Dave Hickey, a union
staff man in charge of the Workmen's Compensation Department,
posted himself at the front door of the hotel and picked off a dozen
delegates as they flew out. Police patrols came roaring up and the
cops were taking on everyone until they got the word from somewhere that there were Good Guys and Bad Guys; then they concentrated on the delegates, hauling several dozen of them off to
jail for inciting a riot and leaving our men alone.

The "Save the Union Committee" never recovered from this rout, and when the sound and fury had abated, Murray charged publicly that the Pittsburgh Coal Company had given the Communist Party $50,000 to finance the "committee's" effort to overthrow Lewis and the UMW. The company denied the charge, and there the matter stood until twenty years later when a San Francisco butcher identified himself to me as a former treasurer of the Communist Party in Pennsylvania who had been involved in the committee's activities. He told me that the actual amount that had changed hands was $100,000, and that it had been given to him in cash by an emissary of Pittsburgh Coal to spend in whatever way was necessary to crush the UMW.

But the union was resilient, and Lewis seemed to be downright indestructible. No one else could possibly have held such a group together against the forces that conspired to wipe out the UMW throughout the 1920's. While the soft coal miners straggled back to work on their employers' terms and the union crumbled in West Virginia, the paralysis moved north and the aristocrats of the industry also reneged on their union contracts and began employing scabs. Pittsburgh Coal's defection in 1925 was the most destructive blow of all, because the company was owned by the Mellon family, and Andrew Mellon was Coolidge's Secretary of the Treasury. The example of a man in his position deliberately abrogating a labor contract, signed in good faith, gave heart to all the Philistines, and soon the entire soft coal industry was at war with the UMW. And Mr. Coolidge continued to take his afternoon naps.

All the misery of West Virginia and Kentucky was now transmuted to the North. I found myself back in the refugee business, sorting out homeless people and assigning them to barracks. I would line them up and ask, "How many kids?" and a woman with tired, downcast eyes would whisper, "Five," and I would say, "Okay. Two rooms. Next." And they would come to me and say, "The walls are full of cracks and our kids are cold," and I would tell them, "Stuff the cracks with newspapers." I was a tough son of a bitch at twenty-two.

I thought we'd seen it all in West Virginia, but there were still some surprises left in Pennsylvania. For example, there was the case of the tiny Slav miner named John Barkoski who was pulled off a picket line by a half-dozen coal and iron cops and taken to a shanty they used for a hangout. There they amused themselves for an afternoon by beating him to a bloody pulp. One cop would ask him why he was striking and the Hunky would try to answer in his halting, heavily accented English. Then the cop would beat him to the floor with the butt of a rifle and another would take over the questioning. They had the kindness to carry him to a hospital when it was over, and I saw him there before he died, toothless, black-and-blue from head to toe, barely conscious and totally bewildered. The late Michael A. Musmanno, who later became a Supreme Court justice in Pennsylvania, wrote a book called *Black Fury* based on this tragedy, and the book—later a movie was made from it—helped bring about the abolishment of the coal and iron police in Pennsylvania.

But that happened much later, and in 1926 only one segment of the coal industry seemed to be safe for the union. This was anthracite, in northeastern Pennsylvania, made up of a tightly knit group of producers not afflicted with suicidal price cutting and therefore able to stand apart somewhat from the rest of the industry. Here, it appeared, the UMW could survive and rebuild its strength, because anthracite miners required skills, dictated by state law, that made it difficult for the producers to import scabs to do the work.

There were times when the anthracite miners' special position proved to be an irritant as well as a blessing. During the worst of the bituminous miseries, we asked the UMW members in the anthracite industry—who were still earning the $7.50 contract minimum—to send us some money to help keep their brothers in the soft coal industry alive. They didn't believe things were that bad, so we invited a committee of anthracite miners to take a trip with us to one of the struck mines. We arrived in the middle of a shooting fray that couldn't have been better timed if someone had written a script. The committee went home convinced and began to generate some badly needed relief supplies. Before they began arriving, however, we got hit with what seemed, at the time, a real knockout punch. The anthracite producers refused to renew their contracts without a wage cut, and the whole industry was shut down.

Lewis, smelling disaster, set up headquarters in Wilkes-Barre to supervise the strike personally, and he took me along as his aide. Within a few hours after we checked in at our hotel, I took a phone call for Lewis from a man who identified himself only as a "Wall Street agent" and who insisted on talking with Lewis directly. I cupped the mouthpiece, told Lewis about the call and he took it. Lewis' end of the conversation consisted mainly of affirmative grunts. When he hung up, he packed a bag and told me to leave the hotel with it in a few minutes and meet him at the railroad station. Then he disappeared. Following his instructions, I dropped the bag at his feet in the railroad car and walked on by without showing any signs of recognition.

The next day—after I had thrown a couple of newspapermen off the scent by telling them Lewis was out taking a walk—he phoned and asked me to join him in Philadelphia. There I found that the anthracite operators, with no stomach for the bloodletting and strikebreaking going on in the soft coal industry, had hired a New York attorney to settle with Lewis and get the mines back in operation. I helped draw up the formal agreement, and by preserving the wage line, it probably saved the life of the union and the career of Lewis, whose enemies were waiting for the opportunity to move in on him and pick up the pieces of the UMW.

With the anthracite producers safely out of his hair, Lewis had one more try at the bituminous industry. Meeting with what was left of the Central Competitive Field producers, he pleaded, threatened and cajoled them to get together, stop price-cutting, stabilize the industry and take back their union miners at the wage rate renewed by the anthracite producers. It was an impossible quest, and Lewis knew it. The disarray in the soft coal industry was so widespread that there seemed no way out of the violence and hatred except through the attrition of time.

There was, however, one other avenue open to Lewis, and he took it, even though it involved a route he had always viewed with deep suspicion and confided to me now would "probably mean the end of the free enterprise system." The UMW registered a group of lobbyists in the halls of Congress and turned them loose on Senators and Representatives involved in interstate commerce. Since the Federal Government was the union's last recourse and President Coolidge was obviously not going to act, Congress offered the only remaining possibility. And Congress, caught up in the general fever of prosperity, proved to be unbelievably ignorant about what had been going on in the coal mines.

Simple dogged persistence finally brought some results. A Senate subcommittee made up of Frank Gooding of Idaho, Burt Wheeler of Montana, Bob Wagner of New York and William Pine of Oklahoma toured the coal fields and returned to Washington considerably shaken. I was with Gooding when he got his first look at a barracks camp of dispossessed Pennsylvania miners. He was a stiff-necked, hard-rock conservative with damned little love for unions, but he was also an honest and a compassionate man, and the conditions he saw there and in Ohio and West Virginia shocked him. He returned to the Capitol determined that the Senate must know about this tragedy and the Federal Government must do something about it. He made a speech saying: "Conditions which exist in the strike-torn regions are a blotch upon American civilization. It is inconceivable that such squalor, misery and distress should be tolerated in the heart of one of the richest industrial centers in the world. The committee found men, women and children living in hovels which are more insanitary than a modern swine pen. They are breeding places of sickness and crime."

Then he called for a full-dress hearing and subpoenaed many of the nation's industrial leaders, including R. B. Mellon, John D. Rockefeller, Jr., and Charles M. Schwab, all with extensive coal properties. I attended all of those meetings with Lewis, Murray, our chief counsel, Henry Warrum, and Kacy Adams. My function was to have the right paper at the right time for the UMW official who happened to be testifying.

The industry representatives offered no solutions—only problems, along with warnings that the Federal Government must not meddle with the workings of a free economy. The union came up with a suggested piece of legislation later introduced by Senator Tom Watson of Indiana as the "coal control bill." Among other things, it recognized officially for the first time "the rights of labor to organize and bargain collectively." In 1927, it got nowhere, killed summarily in a Senate committee. But six years later it became a cornerstone of the National Industrial Recovery Act.

During those long, hot Washington summer evenings, I would walk with Henry Warrum and he would point out statues of long-dead American heroes and tell me about them. His grasp of history was profound, his insight was anything but stereotyped and his range of profanity was colorful. We also talked endlessly about the need of the Federal Government to protect the rights of the workingman in America. The coal control bill was his idea, and—oddly enough—he had to sell it to Lewis, who felt as strongly as the industrialists fighting him about keeping government the hell out of business. Warrum regarded this view as outdated, and he spent many hours bouncing off on me the ideas and arguments that he planned to put before Lewis. It was fascinating to me later to realize that Warrum had to talk Lewis into endorsing the legislation that—during the Roosevelt Administration—was to be called the "Magna Charta of Labor."

In 1927, however, all these efforts got exactly nowhere, and the 70th Congress adjourned, leaving the coal miners and coal operators exactly where they were before—in armed camps boiling with hatred, hunger and heartbreak. But time, that great equalizer, was already beginning to stabilize the situation. Thousands of miners were packing off to Detroit to man the production lines of the booming automobile industry, where unskilled workmen could still find a place to earn a living. And slowly—very slowly—the disparity between the supply of miners and the demand for them was closing.

This was the time Coolidge did "not choose to run" and the first political cracks in the leadership of the UMW began to appear, cracks that were to widen, years later, into open enmity between Lewis and Murray, in which I was finally caught up, too. Lewis knew Herbert Hoover quite well, had once served on his Labor Committee and found Hoover's political views closely paralleling his own. Now he strongly supported Hoover for the Presidency. Murray, Tom Kennedy, Van Bittner and some of the other top men in the UMW had seen enough of Republican administrations. They wanted a President who might at least be aware of the problems of the workingman. Al Smith seemed to be such a man, and they supported him privately. In 1928, this political division never came into the open in UMW councils. Lewis knew it existed, but it was never discussed—at least not in my hearing.

Al Smith, of course, never had a chance. The country wasn't ready then to elect a Catholic President and an enemy of prohibition. When Hoover was swept into office, a lot of us hoped that Lewis had some sort of private understanding with the new President that he would intercede in the coal war, which was now almost six years old. But nothing changed. Both Hoover and Congress ignored the situation until 1930, when Lewis paid a formal call on Hoover and asked him to convene a joint conference of coal miners and operators to work out a collective bargaining arrangement and end the strife in the mines.

I accompanied Lewis to the White House; this was my first visit to the Oval Office that in later years would become a familiar place to me. But in 1930, I was so overcome by awe at being in the presence of a President of the United States that I was hardly aware of what was happening. It happened quickly. Hoover glanced at Lewis' petition, referred it to his Secretary of Labor, William Doak, who was also present, said, "Thank you, gentlemen," crisply, and we were back outside on the steps. Lewis—red-necked and a little stunned at this brush-off—said bitterly: "We ask for a gold watch and we get a wooden leg."

And that's precisely what it turned out to be. No action was taken on the petition. By this time, Hoover had other problems. Not only the coal industry but the whole nation was in a shattering business depression. We had once hoped to bring the coal industry up to the prosperity of the rest of the country. What had happened, instead, was that the rest of the country was now in the same chaotic condition we had lived with since 1924.

5

We were back in Pittsburgh. In the midst of the coal war, the UMW moved Murray and me to Pittsburgh so we could be closer to the main arena of action. I was living at home again and wondering if my future was with the United Mine Workers after all. I was making a good salary—$225 a month—for Depression days and my dad was running the Ancient Order of Hibernians in Pittsburgh, so we were well off financially. But the UMW was in shambles, teetering on the edge of extinction. And even if it had been healthy, my prospects there were limited. Under UMW by-laws, a man had to work in the mines for at least five years in order to qualify for elective office, and I was already holding what was probably the best appointive job in the union. So where could I go?

Brooding about this, I decided to return to school. I still remembered those days with Father LaValle when he had forced me on a stage. I'd enjoyed it tremendously—and, I was told, done well at it. So I enrolled in the night school Drama Department of the Carnegie Institute of Technology in Pittsburgh. Being in drama served two purposes: it was an area that interested me deeply and also enabled me to adjust my night class schedule to the frequent trips I had to make to Washington with Murray. So throughout the Depression years, I was learning acting, directing, playwriting and economics at night and working for the UMW during the day. And in 1932, I received a Certificate of Graduation from the Carnegie Tech Department of Drama.

It was beginning to look then as if I would need some other vocation, very soon and very badly, for the dark years were continuing in coal, and internal dissension was growing to alarming proportions within the UMW. For the first time since he took over the union, Lewis had to run against an opposition slate in 1930. It was headed by John Brophy, president of the UMW's Central Pennsylvania District; two years earlier, Brophy had tried to form a competitive union that died from lack of funds when the anthracite districts decided to remain loyal to Lewis. They stayed with Lewis in 1930, too, and their solid support was enough to vote him back into office in the only serious challenge he ever faced for the presidency of the UMW.

But in the early thirties, Lewis was constantly beating out brush fires that threatened to consume what was left of the UMW. Almost every soft coal district had gone nonunion by now, and the workers who once resisted the mineowners with such courage had either capitulated and gone back to work in the mines without a union contract, had moved elsewhere, or were slowly starving. Potluck unions challenging the UMW were popping up everywhere but particularly in Illinois, where anarchy seemed to be the order of the day. In Kentucky, miners driven beyond human endurance by the deplorable wages and safety conditions walked out spontaneously, then were driven back to the mines by hunger. A shroud of fear overlay the country.

Washington, once an exciting place to me, became incredibly boring. Murray and I had to spend a good deal of time there, and lobby sitting no longer held much appeal. The routine was still the same as it had been, years earlier, in Indianapolis. Lewis and Murray would always go out to dinner together, usually early, come back to the hotel, sit in the lobby and talk union affairs—or occasionally baseball—and then go to bed. They wore somber clothes and somber manners and it was all pretty damned dull. These were the days of Prohibition, and neither of them would drink publicly. Lewis—as far as I knew—drank very little or not at all. He always went first class, though, even when the union was at its lowest. He was earning $9,000 (and Murray $7,000), which wasn't a lot of money, even then, but Lewis stayed in the best hotels and picked up the dinner checks. He would talk about this sometimes, telling me: "Dave, this is a first-class union, and when you are representing it, I want you to go first-class, too." I remembered that, and I lived by it in later years without apologies.

But picking up dinner checks couldn't save a union, and in 1932 the UMW needed saving. So did the country. The national morale was as low as the economy. It needed a massive transfusion of spirit as well as prosperity if it were to survive. The prosperity took awhile in coming, but the spirit was launched that year from the banks of the Hudson River in Albany, New York.

I first met Franklin Delano Roosevelt in the summer of 1932. We had just concluded negotiations with the anthracite coal producers. They had demanded a reduction in wages but had finally agreed to continue for one year at the current level, and Lewis and Murray were pleased with this small triumph.

I was serving as secretary to both Lewis and Murray, which caused some complications the following morning. First Murray called me in and asked me to try and arrange an appointment for him in Albany with Governor Roosevelt—the Democratic nominee for President—through a mutual friend in the AFL. Then Lewis asked me to sit in on his meeting with the head of the Carpenter's Union—Big Bill Hutcheson—to make plans for a labor committee to reelect Herbert Hoover.

I kept my mouth shut, but my sympathies were decidedly with Murray. How Lewis could continue to work for a Republican Administration after the kicking around we'd had for the past eight years was more than I could understand. Murray and I were both registered Republicans, but in Pennsylvania this was a simple political necessity—like being a Democrat in Alabama. We were both totally disenchanted with the Republicans and had voted for Al Smith in 1928. Now Murray was ready to throw whatever weight he had into an effort to elect a Democratic President who might breathe new life back into our union, our economy and our country.

The appointment with Roosevelt was made, and six of us—including Murray, Tom Kennedy, secretary-treasurer of the UMW, and Henry Warrum—were received at the governor's mansion in Albany the following week. An aide took us into a living room where Roosevelt was seated at the end of a long divan. He didn't attempt to get up, and we all filed past him, giving our names and shaking hands. We had been briefed in advance about his infirmity. I remember he had huge hands and a strong grip.

Tom Kennedy was the only one who knew the governor, and there were some wisecracks about the rest of us being Republicans. Then we got down to business. Murray was our spokesman, and he sketched the problems in the coal industry briefly and graphically. Roosevelt would interject an occasional question that went right to the meat of Murray's argument, and it was quite clear that the governor had briefed himself thoroughly before our arrival.

Roosevelt became impatient toward the end, and when Murray finished, the governor said brusquely, "I'm well aware of this situation. Our family used to have some interests in Pennsylvania mines. I know the problems that confront you and I'm familiar with the dire needs of the miners. The question, of course, is: what can we do about it?"

"We want you," said Murray, "to call a meeting—a collective bargaining conference—between the coal operators and the United Mine Workers so we can get a labor agreement and bring peace and prosperity back to the coalfields."

Roosevelt mused for a few seconds, then said, "If that's what you want, that's what I'll do."

Murray pressed on. "Governor," he said, "what if you call the coal producers and they refuse to come?"

Roosevelt threw his head back and roared with laughter.

"Gentlemen," he said, "when I call them, they'll come."

I believed him. It was a bravura performance and I left Albany impressed and encouraged for the first time in months. Roosevelt was a man of wealth, culture and breeding who carried it easily and with little ostentation. He made no effort to talk down to us, to patronize us or—as far as I knew then—to kid us. I had a powerful feeling as our train clacked out of Albany that I had just witnessed the rebirth of the United Mine Workers of America.

That feeling finally made a difficult decision easier for me. My work at Carnegie Tech and with a Pittsburgh amateur theater group brought about an opportunity to change the whole direction of my life. Through a Pennsylvania state Senator and theater owner named Frank J. Harris, I was offered a job as an assistant director at Warner Brothers Studio in Hollywood. I had almost made up my mind to take it when I met FDR. But after that meeting in Albany, I knew he would be elected and there would be new and greatly expanded opportunities for the workingman in America. I decided I wanted to be a part of that growth and so—with great reluctance—I turned down the Hollywood offer.

Murray and I joined Roosevelt several times during his campaign to remind him of his pledge to the coal miners. His audiences were huge and enthusiastic, and almost overnight there was a Democratic Party again instead of the feeble organ that had been humiliated in national elections for the past twelve years and shredded in the infighting over the candidacy of Al Smith. In the familiar Claypool in Indianapolis, we visited FDR in his suite and he renewed his promise "not to forget the coal miners." Two weeks later in Pittsburgh, he promised in a campaign speech to bring peace to the mines through collective bargaining if he was elected. Although he had heavy braces on both legs from his polio affliction and walked with a cane, he always gave an impression of great physical strength and vigor.

He took the country by storm—and just in time, because we were perilously close to anarchy. The signs were all around us. In northeastern Pennsylvania, a group of unemployed miners broke into a locked and shuttered mine property and began mining their own coal. No one stopped them. Other miners would band together in groups of three or four and open up a hole on an abandoned property. Their only thought was to scratch enough from the earth to feed their families. The mines that were still open were off limits to the union. All of them posted signs saying, "No Organizers." They meant it. Organizers were shot on sight by company police.

The UMW's remaining bastion of strength—the anthracite locals—was wracked by internal dissension. Rivals for district leadership were mailing bombs to one another—live bombs. One district leader was shot to death at his desk by supporters of another faction. I remember Murray receiving a bomb-sized package by messenger at our hotel in New York during this period of anarchy. Such was our collective state of mind that he took one look at the package, dropped it in the bathtub, turned on the water and called the police. It turned out to be books.

The Communists were preaching revolution and making headway, particularly among groups like the Workers Alliance—unemployed workingmen who met on street corners and listened to talk of sedition looking bewildered and angry. In a tinderbox like this, there continued to be large corporations like Pittsburgh Coal that would use the Communists to break up legitimate trade unions. The Communists would, in turn, use the companies for the same purpose. And both would expect to emerge alone on top, over the prostrate body of the union. The United States of America has never remotely appreciated the function that trade unions served during the 1930's in standing off the inroads of domestic Communism that was often aided and abetted by the industrialists who professed to hate it the most.

Social reforms to ease the distress of the workingman and turn his gaze away from exotic solutions like Communism didn't stand a chance with the Republican administrations of the 1920's. Long before the New Deal took office, Phil Murray proposed that the State of Pennsylvania put aside $50 million for the relief of its poor and hungry. He was ridiculed—and some of the ridicule came from union friends who were appalled at the idea of government "meddling."

This political and philosophical division among union people in 1932 continued right up to election time—and it continues today. It always makes me angry to hear people talk about the "labor vote." There is no labor vote, and there never has been. Labor walks no carefully delineated political line. In the coal industry, for example, the anthracite workers have long been traditionally Republican. They didn't even vote for their own secretary-treasurer, Tom Kennedy, when he ran for Lieutenant Governor of Pennsylvania. Franklin Roosevelt was elected in 1932 by an overwhelming mandate of *all* Americans, not just workingmen. Relatively, there was probably no higher percentage of labor for

Roosevelt than any other segment of the society, and that situation still holds generally today.

But the important thing is that he was elected, and overnight there was new hope for the American workingman. I heard the returns in a bar in Pittsburgh where I was drinking beer with a group of my Republican friends from the old neighborhood. They lost hard, and I told them they'd better be damned glad to see this man in the White House. Three months later, most of them agreed with me.

Those first hundred days of the Roosevelt Administration produced the most far-reaching labor legislation in the history of the United States. Roosevelt gathered around him the nation's best brains in labor matters, among them the UMW attorney, Henry Warrum, who got out and dusted off the proposal he had offered the Gooding Committee in 1926. This time, the country was ready for it, and Section 7(a) was written into the National Industrial Recovery Act. The crucial paragraph guaranteed "that employees shall have the right to organize and bargain collectively through representatives of their own choosing and shall be free from interference, restraint or coercion of employers of labor or their agents in the designation of such representatives or in self-organization or in other concerted activities for the purpose of collective bargaining or other mutual aid for protection."

A law, an honest-to-God law telling coal operators they can't beat us up or shoot us if we try to organize their employees and negotiate for a living wage and a chance to become human beings again. For the first time in American history, we had more than courage and brute force on our side. We had specific law. And if Lewis ever pondered the curious fact that it came from an administration he'd tried very hard to defeat, he never said so. All he cared now was that FDR had put the bit in his teeth and he was ready to run with it. All of us were.

In 1933, more than 600,000 workers went on strike for union recognition and wage increases—three times more than the previous year—and almost a million workers poured into labor organizations. But we were much too busy to worry about the big picture. We had a union to rebuild and a decade of the most brutal and inhumane sort of treatment to redress. And we had legislation and Federal support on our side.

No one really knew, at this point, exactly how far 7(a) would carry us, but Lewis took it as a mandate to reorganize the mines, and he wasted no time in getting started. Our treasury was down to $150,000, and Lewis decided to go for broke and blow it on a single, massive organizing effort. He called us all together and handed out organizing assignments. Murray was in charge of the northern part of the country, and I was to assist him; Van Bittner was to run the southern campaign, Tom Kennedy was to handle the finances, and Lewis would supervise all operations.

Back in Pittsburgh, Murray and I rounded up the district presidents and told them to seek out all the old UMW organizers who had been laid off during the lean years and put them back to work. Then we printed hundreds of thousands of enrollment cards designating the UMW as the official representative of the miner signing. These cards were distributed to the districts and, through them, to the individual organizers. We were back in business.

Within a few weeks, UMW organizers were appearing at the pit gates of coal mines all over the country. Six months earlier, they would have been shot. Now, coal producers didn't know how to deal with them, and they reacted in many different and ambivalent ways. Some realized the game was up and made no further effort to resist. But others—particularly in the South—had no intention of letting this wild man in the White House tell them how to run their mines.

Fairly typical was the experience of a young organizer named George Pennington who was sent by Bittner to a mine in Kentucky where there was no union. The owners were known to be very tough operators and the miners totally cowed by the iron rule imposed by the company police.

"I'll get killed," protested Pennington.

"You'll be a martyr," Bittner told him, "the biggest hero in the history of the union."

Pennington went reluctantly and discovered a bridge crossing a creek that led to the entrance of the mine. He stood in the predawn darkness at the head of this bridge, watching the miners' lights come bobbing over the hill as the men trudged to work. When they approached the bridge, Pennington stood in the entrance and declared with more conviction than he felt: "This mine is on strike."

"Who says so?" the leading miner asked.

Pennington made up a number hastily. "Local 1234 of the United Mine Workers," he answered.

"We got no union, boy. Get outta the way and let miners go to work or we'll all be in trouble."

Pennington stood fast, produced his pack of membership cards and began telling the miners why they should organize. In the midst of his speech, a platoon of company police hurried across the bridge from the other end and ordered Pennington off the property. He refused to go and had started to cite the new Federal law as his authority when one of the cops clubbed him in midsentence. He came to in a hospital with Bittner at his side.

"Good work, boy," the elated Bittner told him. "Those miners got sore at the way you were treated, they organized a union on the spot and refused to go to work. Now we're in business there, and you're a hero."

Some of the company countermeasures were more subtle. They spent a great deal of money trying to find out what was going on at union headquarters so they could prepare their defenses in advance. Sometimes, these company spies were turned up in peculiar ways. I had a caller one day in Pittsburgh who turned out to be a coal and iron cop. Sickened at what he was asked to do to striking miners, he had quit. He stood away from the window and told me: "Pull down your shades. There's a guy across the street with a pair of field glasses looking in here all the time, and I don't want him to see me."

Then, with the shades drawn, he told me: "You've got a Polack working in the District 5 office who is being paid by several of the coal companies. He's reporting everything you do to them. I'm getting out of this lousy business, and I wanted you to know this before I leave Pittsburgh."

I told Pat Fagan, and he called the man in and laid the accusation before him. His reaction gave him away, and he didn't even bother to deny it. Trembling with rage, Fagan said: "You spying son of a bitch, I should kill you. Now get out of here before I do."

But there was a different undercurrent to these conflicts. We were winning again, and there's a feel and a smell to success that is infectious and feeds on itself. Membership cards poured in by the thousands. Our boys were signing up anybody who could write his name or make an X, and God knows how many barbers and saloonkeepers were represented in that cascading tide of signatures. While I stockpiled them in a stack of old shoe boxes, Roosevelt came through on his campaign pledge to Lewis and Murray; he called a conference of coal operators and union leaders to discuss collective bargaining and labor peace in the coal industry.

That first meeting—held in an auditorium in the Commerce Building in Washington—was chaotic. A few of the coal operators had met previously with Lewis to draft a "Code of Fair Competition" for consideration at the meeting. But a substantial number refused absolutely to take part in any meeting where union officials were present; they came just to raise hell with Roosevelt. Some shouldn't have been there at all. The job of sorting them out fell to the NIRA Administrator, General Hugh Johnson, whose nickname of "Ironpants" was honestly come by. Alternately shouting and cajoling, he sifted out the legitimate leaders of the coal industry and got them to a meeting with Roosevelt. The President insisted they sit down with union officials and reach some sort of agreement on a "coal code" that would bring stability back to the industry. Reluctantly, they agreed.

I sat in on those meetings, and they were tense and antagonistic. Facing each other were men who had been at war for eight years and were still absolutely certain of the justice and ultimate victory of their own cause. Hatred overlay that conference and threatened to stifle it. But not entirely. There were bits of sunlight admitted by a few coal operators who really believed that the only way to eliminate suicidal price-cutting and restore profits and stability was through a solid labor agreement with the UMW. Slowly and painfully, these chinks of light were expanded in that dreary auditorium.

Behind the scenes, the President was working through his extensive Wall Street connections to induce the bellwethers of the coal industry to meet with the UMW and hammer out some sort of labor agreement. When we went as far as we could go at the Commerce Building, this summit conference was arranged. It was typical of Lewis' style that he sent Murray to feel out the four coal industry representatives whom we met in a suite at the Shoreham Hotel. Or maybe he knew in advance what was going to happen. At any rate, the meeting lasted one hour and was damned discouraging. Murray told the operators we were there to initiate collective bargaining and negotiate a labor agreement.

Ralph Taggart, president of and apparently the spokesmen for the southern coal group, tipped back in his chair, surveyed Murray, and asked: "What's your big interest in this, anyway? What do you get out of it?"

Murray bristled. "Not a goddamned thing but my salary."

Taggart said: "You're kidding. That's hard to believe."

Murray's Scotch burr hardened. "It happens to be the truth. Now let's get down to the business we're here for."

Taggart looked him directly in the eye and said: "We're not prepared to negotiate a labor agreement, now or any other time."

"Then what the hell are we here for?" Murray asked him.

And Taggart said, "That's what I'd like to know."

On that note, the meeting broke up. Taggart stood at the door and told us as we departed, "It was nice to have known you, gentlemen."

This was my first close experience with the power politics and psychology of high-level labor negotiations, and I was shocked at the cavalier way we'd been treated. The others shrugged it off. They'd been down this track before. Bittner told me in the hall as we left, "Don't worry, they'll change their tune before the summer is over."

They did. A month later, Hugh Johnson had us back in the same room again, this time for some serious negotiating. Somebody had gotten the word to the coal operators in the interim. They weren't exactly bubbling over with goodwill, but at least they were ready to talk. Lewis was now working on an NIRA code for the coal industry, and he turned over the negotiating job to Murray. I sat in with him throughout the negotiations—to help with visual aids, make quick computations and take down in shorthand anything important enough to preserve. This time the spokesmen for the coal group were two ex-miners, Duncan Kennedy and Charley O'Neill, who now headed a pair of coal operators' trade associations. Both men were tough, but fair. Prospects looked better.

They just *looked* that way. We met fifteen hours a day, every day for several weeks, mostly to hear alternating speeches by the two sides. When the speakers started repeating themselves, we broke off the talks. The next morning, Lewis called us together and said Johnson wanted to see all of us. When we got to his office, Johnson was closeted with the coal operators and we were told to wait. An operator's aide was pretty high-handed about it, and Lewis' fuse those days was short. They had some words in the waiting room that ended with the aide calling Lewis a "loud-mouthed son of a bitch." Lewis drew back to hit him, and I grabbed his arm and we hustled Lewis into an empty office across the hall. When we let go of him, he picked up an office chair and threw it through a glass door. It made a hell of a crash and seemed to satisfy Lewis.

When Johnson called us in a few minutes later, he made no reference to Lewis' temper tantrum. He was red in the face and agitated. The conference was short. "I'm going to tell you," he said, "the same thing I just told the coal operators. The President wants an agreement and I want an agreement. Now get back to that meeting and give me one."

So we went back and began to tackle the problem on which the negotiations always foundered: wage differentials in various parts of the country. The Northern operators now seemed willing to sign and get it over with, but the Southerners—led by P. C. Thomas of the Koppers Coal Company—were adamant in insisting on a substantial wage differential. In the midst of this impasse,

Murray began to recite the extent of our success in signing up miners all over the country. He threw out some startling figures that the coal operators obviously didn't believe. So Murray sent me back to Pittsburgh to collect my shoe boxes full of cards. The operators were impressed. A spot check of those names might have turned up some interesting results, but they never bothered.

Then, when the opposition seemed to be cracking, two events broke it wide open. General Johnson appeared at the Shoreham one morning, threw out everyone but the four principal negotiators—two for each side—and shut himself in a room with them. The rest of us waited in an adjoining room, and I found myself sitting next to Warden, chairman of the board of the Pittsburgh Coal Company. As we made small talk, there was a phone call for Warden and I could hear both ends of the conversation clearly. The caller was Andrew W. Mellon, head of the Mellon financial empire, which owned Pittsburgh Coal. The conversation went something like this:

Mellon: What's holding up an agreement there?

Warden: P. C. Thomas is arguing for big wage differentials for the Southern producers.

Mellon: Who the hell is P. C. Thomas?

Warden: He's vice president of the Koppers Coal Company.

Mellon: I've just talked with President Roosevelt. I want an agreement, and I want it immediately. Now goddamn it, I want you to tell this Thomas for me to cut out the delaying tactics or he's going to be out of a job.

And there was a click on the other end.

Warden didn't look at me. He got up, rapped on the inner door and was admitted. A few minutes later, the group emerged and announced they had reached an agreement. Thus was the United Mine Workers reborn.

It took weeks to work out the details of the "Appalachian Agreement and Code of Fair Competition," but fundamentally, it did six things:

—established miners' wages at $4.60 per day in the North and $4.20 in the South;

—provided for an eight-hour working day and forty-hour week;

—eliminated all racial distinctions in wage rates;

—established grievance machinery;

—regulated company stores and wiped out the use of scrip payments in lieu of wages;

—and, most important of all, firmly established the United Mine Workers as the representative agent for the coal miners of the United States.

To men who had been working for $1.50 a day, often in fear of their lives and always on the thin edge of starvation, this was a victory of such incredible proportions it was almost beyond belief. It would also mark a resurgence of John L. Lewis and the United Mine Workers that was to continue until the UMW—almost without help—could underwrite the organizing of millions of American workers whose lack of industrial skills had prevented them from representation for many years. The largest group would one day be known as the United Steelworkers of America, and the idea began germinating almost as soon as the treasury of the United Mine Workers was restored to vigorous health.

6

My only regret during those early Roosevelt days was that my father couldn't be around to share them with me. He died of cancer early in 1932, believing that his dreams of social security, medical insurance, accident compensation and the opportunity for the workingman to live in respect and dignity might never be realized in this country. He was ahead of his time, and he died without any real confidence that his time would ever come.

But it came much earlier than any of us could have imagined. And with it came a remarkable upturn in the fortunes of the UMW; Lewis' $150,000 investment paid off handsomely and with surprising speed. Once the bituminous mines—the real troublemakers of the 1920's—were in the fold, Lewis turned his attention to the anthracite producers and the so-called "captive" mines. These were the mines owned by the steel companies to provide them fuel to operate their plants. Anthracite was no problem, but the captive mines kicked up quite a fuss.

This time the trouble came from the miners instead of the owners. From nowhere, a loudmouthed, fire-eating demagogue named Martin Ryan surfaced and began making stump speeches to the captive miners in Western Pennsylvania. His theme, always the same, was that Lewis and Murray were sellout artists who were plundering the union and had no real feeling for the miners. He didn't offer much evidence, but his hell-and-brimstone delivery was so convincing that he talked a lot of miners into resisting our agreement and closing down the mines until they got a better rate. It took us almost six months to persuade the captive miners that Ryan was full of hot air and get them all back to work. In just one year, we had grown from a low point of less than 100,000 to a membership of 400,000, and we finally had a chance to draw a deep breath. But when Lewis breathed deeply, he had a tendency to swallow something.

Lewis had now become an outspoken convert to FDR and the New Deal. Roosevelt had another sweeping labor project he wanted undertaken, and Lewis was probably the only man in the country who could hope to bring it off successfully. The first hint I had of it came a few weeks after the captive mines were brought to heel. Lewis and I were walking down a Washington street when he stopped suddenly, looked at me, and said, "Dave, can you tell me the difference between a horizontal and a vertical union?"

It was an odd question, and I suppose he put it to me simply because it was on his mind and he wanted to articulate it. If I didn't know the answer, I had no business in the job I was performing. But I played it back to him anyway, explaining that vertical unionism stratifies the men and women in a factory into various craft unions while under a horizontal system, everyone would belong to a single organization, similar to the UMW. He seemed satisfied, and as we resumed our walk, he told me he had been talking with General Johnson—which, by interpolation, meant President Roosevelt—about industrywide unions, and some ideas were beginning to take shape in his mind.

This was a complex question that offered as many interior problems as exterior. The AFL leadership, nurtured in the craft unions, historically showed little enthusiasm for industrial unions of unskilled or semiskilled workers. As a result, some of the craft unions tended to be as exclusive as a college fraternity with about the same degree of social consciousness. And outside of the union movement, business leaders assuredly didn't want any industrial unions. They had fought such unions with guns and clubs, with hired thugs, with political pressure and even with bribes to the Communist Party for more than a hundred years. My dad's old Amalgamated Association of Iron, Steel and Tin Workers foundered equally on the refusal of the AFL to consider bargaining on anything but a craft basis and the refusal of the steel industry—frequently backed up by violence—to deal with an industrial union. As a result, some three-fourths of the workingmen in the United States were still not represented by a union.

Roosevelt's primary interest in industrial unions was to build a powerful political force among workingmen to counter the strong opposition he expected from big business. Even though the NRA price stabilization features had been dictated by business leaders, the reactionary ranks were in disarray at the moment. But Roosevelt knew that when they regrouped, they would fight his planned economy measures right down the line. He wanted a counterforce to throw at them, and labor offered the best possibility. The AFL craft unions weren't enough—not nearly enough. So there had to be a strong effort to mobilize the unskilled industrial workers of America.

During these early days of the New Deal, the UMW headquarters was moved from Indianapolis to Washington, and Lewis and Johnson became close friends. They spent many hours discussing the concept of industrial unions with the President and some of his chief advisers. Small wonder then that when the UMW convened in January, 1934, Lewis prodded through a resolution urging the officers of the AFL to begin organizing such basic industries as steel, glass, rubber and automobiles on a horizontal basis. It was a deliberate needle in the thin-skinned hide of the AFL leadership, although Lewis—at this juncture, anyway—was very careful to phrase the resolution so that it implied no threat to the existing craft unions.

Meanwhile, my personal fortunes began to rise a bit. The original Appalachian Agreement had been for only six months, and we had to meet with the operators again to extend it. This time, there were relatively few problems. The two main accomplishments of that negotiation were to reduce the workday to seven hours and establish a joint commission to explore means of eliminating forever the sticky problem of wage differentials by region. I was named secretary of that commission (which, incidentally, got nowhere) and my salary was boosted from $225 to $350 per month, which was almost luxurious for a bachelor in those Depression years.

That summer the first skirmish in the war within the high councils of labor over the concept of industrial unions took place. The UMW sent a large delegation to the AFL convention in San Francisco, and Lewis—as its spokesman—again urged the AFL to get on with the organization of industrial unions. The AFL president, William Green—a mild-mannered, soft-spoken compromiser who had once been a preacher—avoided an open clash by supporting a resolution that industrial union charters should be issued on approval of the AFL Executive Council. That sounded like a dead end, since the council consisted of eight craft union disciples. Lewis managed to get the size of the council increased to fifteen and a seat on it for himself. And there the matter stood for the moment. Everyone involved knew this was merely a delaying action. But Lewis was willing to see if the AFL really meant business, and Green—the eternal optimist—was hoping that somehow during the next year the problem would go away.

It didn't. Local unions began popping up in all the basic industries, free-lance collections of workers without roots or muscle but determined to find some sort of collective voice. Lewis and Murray and I watched this restlessly, waiting for some sign that the AFL was moving into these ripe fields to harvest the manpower crop. Nothing happened, nothing at all.

In Washington, however, things were happening. Roosevelt's enemies had finally recovered and regrouped and launched an all-out attack on the National Industrial Recovery Act and the sweeping social reforms it encompassed. While the legality of the NIRA was working its way up through the courts, Hugh Johnson resigned as its head and Roosevelt replaced him with an Administrative Board that included representatives of both industry and labor. Murray was appointed to the board, and I was named as his assistant. Sidney Hillman, president of the Amalgamated Clothing Workers of America, was the other labor representative. We had just located an office in Washington when the Supreme Court declared the NIRA was unconstitutional, and we were out of business before we ever really got started.

In subsequent years, of course, almost ever feature of the NIRA —except the price fixing power—was restored through individual bills, and one of the first was Senator Robert Wagner's National Labor Relations Act. Our beloved 7(a), for which we had sweated so long and so hard, was incorporated in the Wagner Act, and once more the American workingman had a solid position in law to organize unions without interference from his employer. Labor was united in backing the Wagner Act, but once it was passed, there was no longer any way to avoid a direct clash within the ranks of labor over the problem of industrial unionization.

The AFL had done nothing to implement the resolution of its 1934 convention to encourage and admit industrial unions to the national family of labor. It was clear, weeks ahead, to even the most sanguine that there was going to be one hell of a battle on this point at the 1935 convention. I doubt if anyone would have predicted the degree of violence that actually took place, however.

The convention was held in Atlantic City at a rambling old frame hotel called the Chelsea. About a thousand delegates, seated at tables according to the unions they represented, were crowded into the low-ceilinged auditorium. The UMW delegation—by design, I suspect, since we were regarded as distinct troublemakers—was seated at the extreme rear. Just in front of us was the Carpenters' Union—the largest in the AFL—headed by Big Bill Hutcheson.

After the usual preliminaries, Lewis took the podium and asked for immediate implementation of the 1934 resolution on industrial unions. In an eloquent speech, he said: "The organization I represent has an interest in this question. Our people work in a great base industry, basic in its service to the American people and the economic and commercial processes of the nation. They struggle against great odds and against greater influence, and the intensity of their struggle and the weight of their burden is greatly increased by reason of the fact that the American Federation of Labor has not organized the steel industry and a few other industries similarly situated.

"We are anxious to have collective bargaining in the steel industry and our interest is, to that degree, selfish because our people know that if the workers were organized in the steel industry and collective bargaining there were an actuality, it would remove the incentives of the great captains of industry to destroy and punish and harass our people who work in the captive coal mines throughout the country, owned by the steel industry."

Lewis was answered immediately by several of the craft union leaders who made it very clear they weren't about to be crowded into bringing just anybody into the AFL. They didn't attempt to obtain an official AFL stance against industrial unions; they were too clever for that. Rather they indicated by a lot of double-talk that nothing was going to be done under the pretext of doing something.

Lewis listened to this for several hours, then asked for the floor again. This time he wasn't polite. He made a clear, forceful argument on behalf of industrial unions, then put it directly up to the convention either to fish or cut bait in this matter. He was in great form, and when he stepped off the stage, the delegates knew they could no longer beg this decision. Lewis had put them on the spot. He left the stage to a mixture of cheers and boos that pretty well indicated the division of the convention on this question.

Murray, sitting beside me, was uneasy; I could feel him shift in his seat as Lewis came striding down the aisle. Just before he reached us, Lewis found his way blocked by Bill Hutcheson, who stood up and stepped into the aisle. Hutcheson weighed three hundred pounds, and when he stepped into an aisle, it was full. Lewis stopped. The two men said something I couldn't hear, but the tone came through, and I didn't like it. I was half on my feet when I heard Hutcheson, his face a few inches from Lewis', shout: "You're nothing but a dirty bastard."

Lewis didn't debate the point. He hit Hutcheson with a solid left hook to the jaw. He had to reach up to do it, since Hutcheson towered over him. But the blow landed with a solid *thwack* that resounded throughout the hall, and within seconds a thousand chairs were being pushed back and the hall was one vast brawl.

In a biography of Lewis, written some years later, Saul Alinsky says Lewis told him he had deliberately provoked the incident in order to dramatize the differences between the two factions in the AFL. "An act of some kind, an act dramatic to the degree that it would inspire and enthuse the workers of this country was necessary," Alinsky says Lewis told him. "Did I say necessary? It was essential."

Maybe so. Lewis never told me this, and from my vantage point, it looked like an act of spontaneous combustion. Although the explosion was spectacular, I remember staying rather calm. I recalled Father LaValle's advice from my boyhood that if I ever got caught up in a gang fight, the best way to stop it was to get to the leading opponent and hang onto him. Getting to Hutcheson was no small problem. Beside me, somebody grabbed Murray by the tie and pulled him across the top of the table. I debated briefly going to his aid, then decided to concentrate on Hutcheson. I was young and strong and I vaulted the table and shouldered my way through the crowd around the two principals. Hutcheson was drawing back to hit Lewis when I grabbed him from behind and held on with all my strength.

Someone else was holding Lewis, and I thought maybe we had things under control. But while I tightened my hold on Hutcheson, a burly miner who had been sitting at the foot of our table came charging through the mob like a water buffalo and hit Hutcheson full in the face. The force of the blow sent him flying backward across a table, with me under him. We slid off the table and hit the floor, and I managed to roll far enough so that the whole three hundred pounds didn't land directly on top of me. While we lay there, dazed, a couple of Hutcheson's assistants collected him and took him to the men's room for first aid. Green, with a fine sensitivity for the moment, adjourned the meeting. And the delegates picked themselves up and filed out to make repairs before the afternoon session.

It turned out to be an anticlimax, thank God. A lot of the delegates had used the lunch hour to arm themselves. I could see bulges under a good many coats, and it made me damned uneasy. It wouldn't have taken much of a spark to ignite that convention again, and this time the explosion might have been lethal. Fortunately, no one lit a match. There was more debate in the afternoon, but neither Lewis nor Hutcheson participated. Then someone called for the question and Green, no longer able to avoid it, put Lewis' resolution that the AFL embark immediately on an aggressive recruitment program of industrial unionization to a vote. It lost. Thus was the CIO born in strife.

7

After his defeat on the AFL convention floor, Lewis had two choices open to him: he could accept the setback as temporary and work behind the scenes to convert a majority of the delegates to industrial unionization by the next convention. Or he could strike out on his own. Lewis' temperament was not conducive to low-key persuasion. He was also probably getting considerable heat from Washington. Nevertheless, he decided to have one more try at going through channels.

Still in Atlantic City, he called a meeting of AFL leaders who agreed with his position on industrial unions (Charles P. Howard of the Typographical Union, Sidney Hillman of the Amalgamated Clothing Workers, Thomas McMahon of the United Textile Workers, Thomas Brown of the Mine, Mill and Smelter Workers, Harvey Fremming of the Refinery Workers, David Dubinsky of the Garment Workers and Max Zaritsky of the Millinery Workers). They decided to form an organization within the framework of the AFL to be called the Committee for Industrial Organizing. Lewis was elected chairman and Charley Howard, secretary. The stated objectives of the CIO were to educate workers on the advantages of organizing industrial unions and to build up support within the AFL for this effort. Green and his Executive Council didn't like this show of independence and said so, but Lewis resigned from the council, ignored Green and started making plans for a massive effort to organize the industrial workers of America.

At the UMW convention in Washington the following January, Lewis pulled a grandstand play. He invited Green to address the miners and present his arguments on why the AFL should stay out of industrial organizing. When he finished, Lewis asked those who agreed with Green to rise. There were two thousand delegates and two of them rose. As Green slumped dejectedly into his seat, Lewis delivered an emotional speech in which he told the miners that their own survival depended on the aggressive organizing of industrial workers. He singled out the steel industry, declaiming: "The citadels of the steel barons must be assaulted and the steel-workers provided an opportunity to share in industrial democracy. They must have the right to organize, and I'm prepared to put up $500,000 from the Treasury of the United Mine Workers to get that job done."

It is some measure of Lewis' spellbinding that the delegates stood and cheered this announcement that a half-million dollars of their money was going to be used to benefit a group of workers which—in spite of Lewis' oratorical embrace—was of marginal interest to the individual miners.

Every time Lewis spoke thereafter, he moved himself and the CIO farther away from AFL policy. And every day converts appeared at the UMW office in Washington to enlist in the CIO cause, some of them hat in hand—like Lewis' old enemy, John Brophy, whom Lewis put in charge of organizing for the CIO—and others, Sidney Hillman and David Dubinsky for example, from seats of power as great or greater than Lewis' own. The labor news was being made in the UMW office in those days, and the place was always swarming with reporters and photographers.

Lewis frankly enjoyed this attention and growing power. He had never been troubled with humility, and he now—on occasion—became arrogant. I remember two UMW district leaders who made an early-morning appointment with Lewis, then came in from several hundred miles away to see him. He kept them waiting until late afternoon, and when he finally admitted them, one said, rather mildly, "We've been out here since ten o'clock." And Lewis pinioned him with those bushy eyebrows and cold eyes and snapped: "You were drawing your pay, weren't you?"

For a year, all of us wore two hats, and there was not much doubt which one was the more exciting. The UMW problems were routine, for a change, and the challenge of the CIO was vast and provocative. Although I didn't yet know it, that challenge was about to become a very personal one for me.

Murray and I continued our commuting between Pittsburgh and Washington, and as we were approaching Pittsburgh along the Monongahela after one of these junkets on a dismal February day in 1936, Murray pointed out of the train window at the billowing smoke and ugly sprawl of the steel mills that fronted the river and said, "David, you see those mills? You and I are going to organize them this summer."

I was incredulous.

"What do you mean?" I asked him.

"Lewis just told me this afternoon he's going to appoint a committee to organize the steelworkers. I'm going to be chairman of it, and you'll be the secretary-treasurer."

Once again I had reached a decisive point in my life, and once again the decision was made for me by forces beyond my control. The offer from Hollywood had just been renewed. I was weighing it carefully against my prospects with the UMW, and I was leaning toward Hollywood. But this was something else again, the challenge—and the opportunity—of a lifetime. Here was a chance to move back into the industry that had held my dad and my uncles and my friends subservient all these years, that had treated its workers with contempt and arrogance when they tried to make common cause. For fifty years, steelworkers had been forced to live by the precept, *Do as you're told and no back talk or we'll have your job*—even when the back talk involved a living wage or the most basic kind of plant safety or a work week that would enable the worker to spend at least a few hours with his family. Now they were about to be offered the machinery that would make it possible for them to stand up for the rights they had been denied all these years—another dream my dad had carried to his grave. I *had* to be a part of that effort.

Murray and I kept quiet and waited, and Lewis came through as promised. Three weeks later, he put his plan for organizing the steelworkers before the CIO board. It agreed unanimously that we should proceed immediately and also approved the choice of

Murray and me to head the drive. After thirteen years in Lewis' shadow, Murray and I would now step out on our own. The steel industry was to be our reservation; Lewis had other things on his mind. The mandate was clear and unequivocal.

For the first time in a good many years, I took a hard look at Phil Murray. Although we had worked together rather closely for well over a decade, our relationship had vacillated back and forth between two rather unsatisfactory extremes. On the one hand, he still tended to regard me as the son he'd never had. As father figure, he was kind, generous, sometimes slightly patronizing and often rather stuffy. At the other extreme, although I was now thirty-four years old, there was still an inclination to regard me as "the kid" who had joined the UMW entourage back in the days of Warren G. Harding. Granted I was still by some years the youngest of the top-echelon people in the UMW, but I wasn't "the kid" anymore and didn't want to be regarded this way. My new role with Murray seemed to offer immediate possibilities of changing my status from administrative do-it-all to administrator, period. And that was all right with me.

On June 11, 1936, Murray and I met in Washington with the leaders of the 4,000-member Amalgamated Association of Iron, Steel and Tin Workers of America, the only representative labor union in the entire steel industry. Although it had neither size nor power, we couldn't just steamroller this group. So after I came up with a name for our new operation—the Steel Workers Organizing Committee—that was acceptable to the CIO board, we drew up an agreement, which I wrote, between the CIO, the Amalgamated, and the just-created SWOC. The agreement, signed that afternoon, officially put us in business.

On June 17, 1936, the Steel Workers Organizing Committee opened up shop on the twelfth floor of the Commonwealth Building in Pittsburgh. Some of those present were old, familiar faces: Van Bittner, Pat Fagan, John Brophy. Others who would soon be just as familiar included Clint Golden, former Pittsburgh regional director of the National Labor Relations Board, Lee Pressman, as attorney for the Rural Electrification Administration, and Vincent

Sweeney, labor writer and Sunday editor of the *Pittsburgh Press*. Golden was put in charge of organizing the Eastern part of the country (Bittner had the West and Canada and Alabama's UMW district president, Bill Mitch, the South), Pressman was named general counsel and Sweeney, publicity director. This group was destined to go a long way together.

Our first order of business was to draw up a set of policy guidelines. There were four, and they were simple and direct:

—to establish a permanent organization for the purpose of bargaining collectively with management;

—to avoid industrial strife and strikes if at all possible;

—to meet with management in a reasonable spirit after a sufficient number of employees had been organized;

—to insist that local unions conform to the national plans and policies of the SWOC.

That was it. Murray turned his team loose, then looked around him and decided he didn't like our temporary quarters. He asked me to search out something more suitable, and as I was leaving he stopped me and said firmly, "Nothing but the best, David." That's exactly what I found. The suite I selected on the thirty-sixth floor of the Grant Building—Pittsburgh's tallest at that time—looked out splendidly over the industrial heart of the city. It also topped by several floors the offices of some of the steel companies we hoped to organize and left no doubt of our permanence and stability. Psychology, I had learned at Lewis' knee, is nine points of negotiating.

Lewis had given us a check for $25,000 that barely got our office open. The task of putting together an effective group of organizers was the heart of our effort. It was also expensive, and Lewis knew it. Within a few weeks, he sent us a second check, this time for $500,000. We established an account and credit at the Commonwealth Trust Co., and the word got around quickly in the right places that this was no fly-by-night effort but a well-financed movement of labor union professionals who knew what they were about and meant business. Which was exactly right.

Apparently on the theory that the best defense is a good offense, the Iron and Steel Institute tried to beat us to the draw by running full-page advertisements in several hundred newspapers across the United States which stated flatly that the steel industry would fight the unionization of its workers. They supported this position by three arguments we were to hear many times in the months ahead: that we were "outsiders" interfering with the chastity of their employees; that our aim was simply to bring on a rash of strikes and strife; and that this effort would severely hamper the industry—and, by implication, the country—just as it was pulling out of a six-year recession.

Actually, this was pretty mild stuff compared to what industry in other sectors was doing to prevent growing unionization. The La Follette Senate Committee—which conducted a searching investigation into industry's purchase of violence and espionage—estimated that American corporations spent $80 million a year during the mid-thirties to fight unions. They hired 100,000 spies who penetrated almost every union local and sometimes became union officers; thus they were able to finger the union activists so they could be fired. General Motors admitted spending $419,000 with the Pinkertons alone between January, 1934, and July, 1936. A company called Federal Laboratories, Inc., made a fortune selling tear gas during this period; its president testified that he considered himself a humanitarian because it was "better to gas a striker than kill him." Much of this was justified on the familiar grounds that the corporations were fighting Communism, an argument we'll examine in some detail later, since it was directed more at the CIO than the SWOC.

The Iron and Steel Institute ad was a mistake, and I found out later that some of the steel corporations opposed the idea from the beginning. Murray welcomed it with joy and thanksgiving. Nothing could possibly have given us a better send-off. It provided us stature through the industry's recognition of the threat we posed. It gave us a chance to point to the vast sums of money that were being spent by the steel industry to fight the "little people" who worked in their mills. And—best of all—it enabled us to tell the men we hoped to organize that the industry had drawn a line and forced their workers to choose up sides. Are you with *us*, we could now ask, or are you with *them?*

So the two hundred organizers we sent out into the field now had a theme, provided to us thoughtfully by the Iron and Steel Institute. But neither Murray nor I were happy with a purely negative approach. We wanted the organizers to carry a positive message to the steelworkers and to the communities in which they lived, and the rallying cry we hit on was the one Lewis had stated so emphatically so often: the concept of "industrial democracy." Our recruiting refrain always emphasized this theme—the bringing of industrial democracy to the individual steelworker and to the steel towns where the worker often was denied political democracy, too.

Aliquippa, Pennsylvania, provided an excellent example of a feudal company town. Its 40,000 residents were controlled absolutely by the Jones & Laughlin Steel Corporation, which operated a dirty, dingy, dangerous mill that provided the bulk of the town's employment. The company owned the town officials and, through them, the police force by two simple expedients: fear and bribery. The workers lived in constant fear of losing their jobs, and because the company controlled the election officers in the precincts, it knew how its employees were voting. The instructions were unwritten but explicit: vote for the company candidate or look for another job. On the infrequent occasions when this iron discipline broke down, the company simply bought the people it needed. No humanitarian instincts were ever permitted to get in the way of the system; the slightest concession might be used as a wedge to break apart this absolute tyranny. That's why companies like J & L and towns like Aliquippa and Weirton, West Virginia, and Massilon, Ohio, and Bethlehem, Pennsylvania, began to run scared as soon as we announced our organizing campaign. And that's also why our organizers ran into big problems with local police almost everywhere they decided to operate.

But the time seemed ripe and the situation ready, and we were convinced that nothing could stop the tide of industrial organization. For the first time, we had legislation on our side, and the employers who attempted overtly to prevent our organizers from talking to their employees were now breaking the law. This didn't dissuade a good number of steel companies—particularly in the South and in small, captive mill towns—but it did serve to confuse and diversify their efforts to resist organization. We were no longer dealing with a monolithic corporate front, and this made it possible for us to divide and conquer.

Strangely enough, once the major steel companies accepted our existence and made some sort of peace with the realization that we were probably going to organize their workers, the biggest problems we had were with the workers, themselves. Contrary to union propaganda—some of which I helped to write—the steelworkers did not fall all over themselves to sign a pledge card with the SWOC.

There were a good many valid reasons. In the first place, we were bucking a fifty-year tradition of nonunionism in the steel industry. Since my father's generation had been beaten down by Andy Carnegie's troops at Homestead, the steel industry had been able to resist every effort at unionization. As a result, the men we approached had very little understanding of what trade unionism was all about and what it could do for them. All they knew, really, was what they had been told by their employers about these dangerous subversives who would try to take advantage of them. Then, too, these were still depression years, and the steelworkers were frankly afraid of losing their jobs if they flirted with the union. They couldn't understand that the union would protect those jobs for them once it was established; they were afraid of what would happen to them before it was established; and in most instances, those fears were fully justified by threats passed down to the workers by word of mouth in the mills. Then—let's face it—in some of the more enlightened companies—especially those where company unions had been established—the individual workers were as apprehensive about dictatorship from an international union as they were of arm-twisting from their employer.

So all of these things combined to make organizing the steelworkers a very different sort of project from the UMW campaign. The miners were union oriented, they were angry and they eagerly sought a collective voice. The steelworkers were deeply infected with antiunion propaganda and were generally passive. So our problems of persuasion and education were multiplied many times as the SWOC organizers scattered out over the country.

Once again, we printed hundreds of thousands of pledge cards for individual steelworkers to sign. An organizer would take a stack of cards to a plant, meet the workers as they came off a shift and tell them about industrial democracy. He would explain that the union would get them more money, better and safer working conditions and secure for them the right to talk back to a boss when he was wrong, to file grievances and to be assured of protection against arbitrary firing for personal reasons. Then he would pass around the cards and ship those that were signed back to me in Pittsburgh.

What we hoped would be a torrent turned out, instead, to be a trickle. Under our arrangement with the Amalgamated, it would charter a local union as soon as we had enough men signed up in a plant to form the nucleus of an effective organization. Oftentimes the locals consisted of the half-dozen men daring enough to sign the charter application. When these skeleton requests straggled in, we assigned impressively high lodge numbers in the hope that outsiders would think we had that many locals. Only Murray and I knew how thin the tally was, although Lewis would insist on the truth whenever I visited Washington, then would shake his head in wonderment at the lack of progress.

Money was also a growing problem. Even in those plants we had organized, we were unable to get the members to pay their dollar-a-month dues. Recruits would pay their original dollar, then we would never hear from them again. The dues checkoff was years in the future then, so we would have to scratch for the money. Somehow these new members in the steel industry never associated the payment of their dues with the services the union could offer them.

I recall having a little Slav worker pointed out to me at the mill gate by one of our organizers.

"See that guy?" he asked bitterly. "Last month I won a grievance for him that got him $700 back pay. And the very next time I tried to get one buck for his union dues from him, he wouldn't pay."

I hit the road often to work with the organizers, and I usually came back depressed from these junkets. The hotels were terrible, the working hours impossible and the results negligible. On a typical day, I would meet with the local organizers at 5 A.M. to pass out handbills for distribution at the plant gates. The handbills would urge the steelworker to "join the SWOC for better hours, pay and working conditions." We would arrive at the plant about 6 A.M., usually to a reception as cold as the raw morning wind. While our sound truck made a union pitch nearby, we would pass out our handbills and try to collect a group of workers to listen to our arguments and ask us questions. In a discouragingly few minutes the gate would be deserted and the ground littered with our handbills. Sometimes we would pick up those that hadn't been too badly mangled, drive downtown, have breakfast, discuss strategy, pick up a new set of handbills and meet the next shift. Three times a day we repeated this process, usually ending up in a bar where we would set up drinks for workers and invite them to a meeting that evening. We usually had to pack it with miners to give some illusion of excitement and interest.

Towns began to look the same to me. There was Warren, Ohio, where the local charter signers had promised me a big audience and four people showed up in a hall that seated five hundred. In Birmingham, there were more people on the stage than in the audience. In Weirton, we promoted a "mass meeting" of twelve people. And I was never quite sure whether it was apathy or fear that kept them away.

The only thing that saved us during this period was the overreaction of the steel companies to our modest efforts. In spite of their extensive spy system, they apparently believed the figures we were putting out and had no idea how really badly we were doing. So the companies would counterattack—often in stupid ways like the national newspaper ad or charges that we were all a bunch of Communists—and we would turn their own ammunition against them.

Sometimes, we gave them ammunition, too. Vin Sweeney had started a monthly SWOC magazine called *Steel Labor*, but he was busy with other matters and turned the paper over to a publicity man on loan from the Amalgamated Clothing Workers. This clown chose for the picture on the front cover of the first issue a dramatic shot of smoke pouring from a series of mill stacks with a huge hand emerging from the smoke giving an unmistakable Communist salute. While the steel corporations were saying, "we told you so," I hurried back to Pittsburgh, found the temporary editor in conference with a local reporter from *The Daily Worker* and told them both to keep to hell out of our business. Murray backed me up and ordered Sweeney to take over immediate supervision of the magazine.

The Communist Party of America was at its high-water mark about this time, and it unquestionably did manage to plant some organizers in the SWOC. We routed them out when we found them, but some were pretty smooth operators. One of the smoothest was a rugged, charming man named William K. Gebert, who showed up in Murray's office one day saying he had been sent out from CIO headquarters in Washington to help us in our organizing efforts. He knew all the right names, was damned persuasive, and we took him on.

Shortly afterward, Gebert and I shared a platform at a meeting of Pittsburgh steelworkers. I spoke first, and, in the course of giving my union pitch, I also tied into the Communists for interfering in our efforts to set up a democratic union to operate within the framework of a free society. The workers in the audience were almost all of Slav extraction, and when Gebert got up to talk, he addressed them in a Slavic language I couldn't understand. I saw the men in the audience eyeing me with increasing antipathy during his talk, and I was certain he was tearing down what I had said, but I could get no proof afterward because no one would talk to me.

The whole incident made me suspicious of Gebert, and I checked with the CIO in Washington and discovered they hadn't sent him to us at all. Then I asked an FBI friend for a confidential rundown on him and was told he was one of the chief organizers for the Communist Party in the United States. Before we got rid of him, I made a middle-of-the-night exploration of his office, found a notebook of his contacts within the SWOC and copied them down for future reference. One of those names was Gus Hall, then a SWOC organizer in Warren, Ohio, and today the secretary of the Communist Party of America.

About the same time, I got a complaint from a group of steel-workers in Minnesota saying they would like to join the union but they were being told they would also have to join the Communist Party. I hurried to Minneapolis to look into that one and found—incredibly—that it was true. SWOC organizers were carrying three pledge cards, one for the union, one for the Farmer-Labor Party and one for the Communist Party of America. I collared one of our organizers and asked him why. He said the state governor refused to permit them to operate any other way.

I met Governor Carl Olson at a dinner that night and asked him if he knew anything about this. He said he did and added: "If you are going to organize the steelworkers in this state, this is the way it will have to be done."

I said: "Governor, beginning tomorrow morning, my men are going to be carrying just one card—the union card. And if you try to stop them I'll expose you to all the people of the United States."

He answered, "If you do that, you'll be making a big mistake."

The next day I rounded up our organizers and told them hence-forth they were to carry a single pledge card. And that's what they did—without interference or harassment.

We had other internal problems. Periodically, we would call in all of our organizers for a progress report and a pep session. Most of them told us what they thought we wanted to know instead of the facts that existed in their districts. This was pleasant, but not very enlightening, and we usually knew from other sources when they were lying. We played these little games for months. The organizers would report signing four or five times as many men as they really had, we'd put them through an inquisition to get the facts, then we would turn around and report publicly the first figures they'd given us.

And the steel companies, apparently believing the published figures, would escalate the fight—often unnecessarily. In Portsmouth, Ohio, for example, we organized the workers at Portsmouth Steel. The company refused to recognize the union, which then called a strike. The company tried to bring in strikebreakers, and the workers set up picket lines surrounded by gun emplacements to cover the lines if the pickets were attacked. I hurried down there and found the strike leader, a handsome young man named Carmen Newell, in a foxhole wearing a steel helmet and carrying a rifle. I rented a truck, mounted the back of it, told the assembled workers a lot of lies about how fast the union was growing, and convinced them they were spearheading a movement that was sweeping the country. We had no money to offer them, only moral support, and if the strike had dragged on, the workers probably couldn't have held out very long. But when the company saw that the strikers meant business, it capitulated and recognized the union. Most of our victories came painfully, in just this way; and they came very slowly.

They came so slowly that all of us were despairing, secretly if not publicly, when an incredible stroke of good fortune came our way. At the lowest ebb of our organizing program, with money running out and additional funds doubtful, the United States Steel Corporation fell into our lap.

8

While we were having our troubles organizing the steel industry, John Lewis and the CIO were reaching out in many other directions with considerably more success. Lewis would use his top lieutenants interchangeably, which meant that Murray and I would sometimes be sent to help out with organizing efforts in other industries.

Murray was deeply involved, for example, in the Ford negotiations with the United Automobile Workers. After the worst of the sit-in-violence had subsided there, Lewis sent Murray to Detroit to talk with Henry Ford. Murray got on well with the old man, and after a lengthy tour of the plant, Ford demonstrated to Murray how he would rebuild his energies by catnapping on the thick carpet in his office. He stretched out and fell sound asleep for an hour while Murray watched helplessly.

When he awoke, he asked Murray what the union wanted. Murray told him, "A union shop," and Ford said, "What's that?" After Murray explained, the old man said it all sounded sensible to him, and he instructed his assistants to proceed. Negotiations foundered—as Ford knew they would—on whether or not to include Harry Bennett's plant protection "army" that had been breaking union skulls. The union didn't want them in, and Ford insisted that if a union shop meant everybody belonged to the union, it would have to include Bennett. Lewis finally settled the matter personally with Ford in Detroit; Bennett and his men were excluded as representatives of management—which was certainly the understatement of the year.

I was also dragged into a hairy episode in Michigan. Two of our organizers—both tough, experienced men—were sent to Flint to lend a hand to the beleaguered UAW troops during the General Motors sit-in strike. Two days later, Murray called me in and said our two boys had "disappeared" and I'd better go to Flint and see if I could find out what had happened to them. Through a connection in Governor Murphy's office, we got the state police on the job. They finally found our organizers being held incommunicado in a hotel room. Their captors were General Motors' police who had spotted our men as "outsiders," followed them from a picket line to their hotel room, kidnapped them and planned to hold them until the strike was broken. They were turned over to me, and I persuaded them to return home; they wanted to go back to the picket line and fight it out with the GM cops.

There were dozens of similar incidents taking place almost daily in the tidal wave of CIO organizing that was sweeping across the country. Unhappily, by late 1936 the wave was beginning to recede in basic steel, which was hard to explain. The average wage of steelworkers was only sixty-six cents an hour, about the same rate I'd been paid in the mills eighteen years earlier. And there were no fringe benefits of any kind.

Murray put his finger on the weakness of the steel industry's position in refusing wage increases early in 1936 when he responded to an announcement of the payment of back stockholder dividends by asking publicly: "If it is just and fair to pay back dividends, why isn't it just and fair to pay back wages? Your own charts show that weekly earnings for steelworkers dropped 53.6 percent between June, 1929, and June, 1932. Don't you think it is fair and just that these men who suffered such wage reductions in the dark years of the Depression are entitled to the wages they lost in the same fashion as the stockholders are entitled to back dividends?"

But the steelworkers continued to be dubious that we could improve their lot and fearful that, if we tried and lost, they would lose everything. We used every gambit we could imagine. The only one that achieved much success on a broad basis was a campaign of boring from within the company unions of U.S. Steel. We persuaded them to call meetings of U.S. Steel workers—which were called Employees Representation Committees—in various parts of the country to demand that the steel industry establish a $5 daily minimum wage, a forty-hour week and time and a half for overtime. We then tied in this movement with our own organizing effort and managed to make some headway with leaders of company unions. But we were still a very long way from significant inroads into the ranks of the 600,000 workers in basic steel. By the end of 1936, we had enrollment cards in hand for 82,000 members, and plenty of those couldn't stand close examination.

Then the miracle. It was passed in February, 1937, in a Park Avenue home in New York City. Lewis requested Murray, Sidney Hillman and me to meet him in a Manhattan hotel. He didn't say why. Lewis' prestige as head of the CIO was—at this point— massive. Leading the striking automobile workers in person, Lewis had forced General Motors—after a bloody 44-day sit-down strike during which GM was losing its market to its unsympathetic competition—to recognize the UAW and agree to negotiate with it. This was probably the most important single triumph in the history of American labor. But Lewis didn't bask in it. Less than two weeks later he was summoning us to New York, this time—we were to learn in a few hours—to break open the whole steel organizing campaign.

Lewis was waiting for us impatiently at the Essex House on Central Park South. He told us that he, Murray and Hillman were going to have dinner that evening with Myron Taylor, chairman of the board of U.S. Steel. The invitation had been phoned to Lewis the day before, and Lewis had no idea what Taylor had on his mind. I was to stand by at the telephone in Murray's hotel room to await developments.

There was no call. I paced the floor most of the evening, wondering what was going on. About 11 o'clock I heard a key in the door and Murray entered. He looked dazed.

"For God's sake," I asked, "what happened?"

He shook his head. "You're not going to believe this," he said, "but we've got an agreement with U.S. Steel. They've recognized our union and have agreed to negotiate with us on behalf of their workers. *The whole damned company.*"

The way he said it, it sounded almost like a benediction.

Hillman came in then, and the two of them told me the story, savoring it all over again in the telling. Taylor had just returned from a diplomatic visit to the Vatican for President Roosevelt. He had come back by ship through the Mediterranean and had done a lot of thinking—a hell of a lot of thinking.

When the three labor men arrived at Taylor's home, he met them at the door. At the end of a long entrance hallway, Taylor showed his visitors an ancient carving of a ram's head, mounted on a pedestal. "That," Taylor told them, "is from Babylon, one of the few authentic artifacts of Babylon in existence today. And Babylon is what I want to talk with you about tonight."

Then, over drinks and dinner, Taylor said: "When that ram's head out there in the hall was carved, Babylon was the mightiest fighting nation of her time. She could put an army of 10,000 chariots and 100,000 men in the field. But Babylon doesn't exist today. She's been dead and gone for many centuries, and that ram's head is one of the few things remaining to remind us of her days of glory.

"Babylon traded throughout the known world and she had all kinds of businesses. She even had labor unions, and there were strikes and people fighting, just as there are today. As I crossed the same waters that the Babylonian ships used to sail, I did a lot of thinking about what you fellows are doing back here in trying to organize my employees into a union. And it occurred to me that one day we will be just as extinct as Babylon, and a thousand years from now, nobody is going to know or care about the decisions we make today. I have to make a decision about you. I either have to fight you or bargain with you. I have no desire for a fight. I don't want a strike and I don't want to see people hurt and killed on picket lines. So on that ship, I made up my mind. I want to make a labor agreement with you men for the employees of U.S. Steel."

I was incredulous. We were a long way from being able to put together enough muscle for a meaningful strike at U.S. Steel. I could see many bitter months of the hardest kind of organizing activity ahead before we would approach that point, then many more months of strife before we won recognition—if we won it at all. And here, tonight, in a few minutes at a dinner party the head of the biggest steel corporation in the world called off the war, pulled down his barricades and invited us in.

I didn't really believe it until I saw it in writing. That happened a week later in Pittsburgh, on March 2, 1937, when Lewis and Taylor each put his name at the bottom of a single page of the most encouraging prose I'd ever seen written. In addition to providing recognition of the union as bargaining agent for the men it enrolled, the agreement also provided for a daily minimum wage of $5, a forty-hour workweek, seniority protection rights, establishment of grievance machinery and vacations with pay. Details were filled in over the next two weeks and on March 17—nine months from the date of the original meeting of the SWOC—our first major victory was formally signed by Phil Murray, myself and Benjamin Fairless, who was then president of Carnegie-Illinois, U.S. Steel's largest subsidiary.

The rest of the steel industry was outraged. They would have been apoplectic had they known how little we had to bargain with at the time Taylor capitulated. When the U.S. Steel agreement was signed, we had enrollment cards from about 7 percent of U.S. Steel employees, and only half of those were paying dues.

The U.S. Steel agreement had a perverse affect on the steel industry. It actually hardened resistance elsewhere, particularly among the independent producers known as "Little Steel." That battle was to be joined later. But in the immediate aftermath of the signing of U.S. Steel, our efforts were concentrated on the other members of the family of "Big Steel." Of these, probably the most intransigent was Jones & Laughlin, which had a long history of terrible working conditions and almost total insensitivity to the problems of its employees.

I asked Murray to put me in personal charge of the J & L campaign, and he agreed to give me a free hand. I felt strongly that we had been diffusing our manpower too much, so I pulled in the best organizers we had and concentrated them on Jones & Laughlin. For several weeks, our organizers swarmed all over J & L. They weren't signing a hell of a lot of people, at first, but they put on an impressive show.

One of the best was a Serbian named George Medrick, a coal miner who was recruited to help in the steel organizing because he could talk with the Slav workers in their own language. I happened on George one day when he was surrounded by steelworkers with questions and obviously out of his depth. He finally threw up his hands and said: "I don't know nothing about ignuts or pig nuts. I know about hard coal and soft coal and bony coal—and the only other thing I know is, join the union."

We made enough of an impact that J & L's board chairman H. B. Lewis asked for a meeting with Murray. While they talked, we stepped up the action at the J & L mill gates, and fights began to break out between the workers who wanted to organize and those who didn't. As the word spread that J & L was refusing to make any concessions in its talks with Murray, our organizers began to sign more workers. By mid-May, with no indication of progress in the talks, our new members asked permission to strike J & L and we granted it. For the first time in almost a year and a half of strenuous effort in the steel industry, we were operating from strength, and we knew it from the enrollment cards we had in hand. But once again, the steel industry misjudged us. Where they had overestimated our strength before, this time they underestimated it. Within thirty-six hours, J & L ended the strike by suggesting a government-supervised election. If a majority of the J & L workers voted for the union, the company was willing to give us exclusive bargaining rights.

Murray and I went to see the Pirates play baseball on election day. There was nothing more we could do at that juncture, and our enrollment cards foreordained the results. They were accurate within a few percentage points. About 70 percent of J & L employees voted for SWOC, and we were fast solidifying our position as the bargaining agent for the basic steelworkers of the United States.

With the first and fourth largest producers signed up, we began to pick off the other major producers and dozens of smaller steel fabricators by the handful. Only one powerful pocket of resistance remained, a group of independent steel manufacturers who accounted for about one-fourth of the nation's steel production and came to be known in the bloody months ahead as "Little Steel." Led by Tom Girdler of Republic Steel, allied with Youngstown Sheet and Tube, Bethlehem and Inland Steel, this group insisted they had been betrayed by Myron Taylor and the other steel companies that had signed with SWOC. Girdler said publicly several times that he would quit the steel business and grow apples before he would sign with the CIO because he wanted to play no part in handing the United States over to the Communists. And to back up this kind of talk, he and his cohorts—according to figures assembled by the La Follette Committee—spent $44,000 for machine guns, rifles, revolvers, tear gas and bombs in April, 1937.

9

I was married in the late summer of 1937. The timing probably could have been better. It was a year when the infant Steelworkers Union wavered between life and death, and those of us who were doctoring it had to spend about twenty hours a day rushing blood plasma to the expiring parts. It wasn't a time for paying the proper amount of attention to personal matters, and those frenetic months set an unhappy pattern neither my wife nor I was ever able to check and reverse.

At thirty-five years of age, I had been married to the labor-union movement for seventeen years. I paid court to a dozen different girls during those years, and in my early twenties came very close to marrying a high-school sweetheart. But always, the demands of my job took me off somewhere and the moment passed, never to be recaptured.

I met Emily Lou Price in the spring of 1937, shortly after Lewis had hired her as one of his secretaries. She was a striking beauty, blonde and slim, and I asked her for a date the first time I saw her. After that, whenever I came to Washington on union business— which was quite often—I pursued Emmy Lou. She encouraged me at first, then abruptly turned cool. When I pressed her for an explanation, she finally told me that John Lewis' daughter, Catherine, who ran the UMW office in Washington for her father, had forbidden Emmy Lou to go out with me on penalty of losing her job.

Cathy Lewis had, unhappily, inherited her father's looks, which were extremely effective for a labor leader but didn't rest too well on a girl. She was strong-willed, fractious and something of an intellectual, and she ruled her domain with an iron fist strongly reminiscent of her father. By this time I was in love, and I went to

Cathy and asked if there was anything personal in her edict to Emmy Lou. She told me that none of "her girls" were permitted to date men in the organization. The rule, it turned out, was her idea, and when I told her if she didn't relax it in Emmy Lou's case, I would take it up with her father, she relented and I resumed my romance. Emmy Lou and I were married on August 4, 1937, in her family's palatial lakefront home in Cleveland.

When I married Emmy Lou, I couldn't divorce the union. I thought she knew this. Perhaps she did intellectually, but emotionally she was never able to accept my long absences. We both thought, in those early years, that this might change when the steel industry was finally organized and there could be some stability in our lives. Our first year of marriage was marked by almost total chaos in the steel industry, ending, finally, with the violent eruptions in Little Steel.

Before that battle was joined, however, I had to deal with a much more practical but almost as devastating problem: money. In the first glow of the U.S. Steel and J & L victories, it seemed that our financial problems were finally at an end. Dues from our new members in these companies would make us solvent and perhaps even permit us to put a little aside to apply on our debt to the United Mine Workers. All of this would have been true if the steelworkers had paid their dollar-a-month dues. But once in, the great majority of them simply ignored their dues. We were suddenly rich in members and starved for funds.

This problem had been solved among the coal miners by instituting the checkoff, in which union dues were collected along with other routine deductions from the paychecks of the miners. But the steel industry wasn't ready for the checkoff. There had been enough trouble simply winning recognition, and insisting on a checkoff system at this juncture would have been pushing too far and too fast. So we were faced with the problem of coming up with some method of collecting dues—in quantity and in haste. This was serious but not crucial before the strikes that accompanied the Little Steel crisis. Then, faced with the problem of feeding thousands of strikers' families, we had to divert our attention from solving the dues-collection problem to breaking through the defenses of the companies that made up Little Steel.

Although Girdler had been making a great deal of noise, we didn't suspect, at first, how far the Little Steel companies were prepared to go to fight us. I wanted to single out Bethlehem, the largest remaining unorganized company, and apply the same strategy that had worked so well with Jones & Laughlin. Then, once Bethlehem was in the fold, we could pick off the other members of Little Steel one by one.

I proposed this plan to Murray and he turned it down on the grounds that Bethlehem plants were scattered from coast to coast and such a technique would be unwieldy. I backed up my argument with a careful breakdown I'd compiled, showing that we had signed almost half of the Bethlehem steelworkers and only a fourth of the other companies. A concentrated effort at Bethlehem, I insisted, would put us over the top there and enable us to win an NLRB election easily. But Murray had made up his mind, and he brushed me aside, saying, "I don't pay a damn bit of attention to your figures anymore." I tore them up in front of him.

He then told us to go after recognition agreements from the other three members of Little Steel. We hit Republic first. Clint Golden and I met with their director of industrial relations and general counsel, and they listened to our arguments in silence. When we finished, they said they had been instructed by Tom Girdler to tell us that Republic Steel would not recognize the union under any circumstances. End of conference. Bittner got the same answer from Youngstown Sheet and Tube and Inland Steel in Chicago.

Murray then called a meeting in Youngstown of the officers of the union locals being organized in these three companies. I had with me a tabulation of the number of members enrolled in each local as reported by our organizers. Murray called on the presidents for a progress report, and each one, in turn, read off figures that were fantastically exaggerated. One president reported more members than there were workers in his plant. Suddenly Murray became intensely interested in my figures, but by now it was too late. We were committed to a course of action with these three companies, and the local officers present weren't about to let us off the hook. Murray tried to leave himself some maneuvering room by telling the assembled group that we were seeking only one objective: union recognition. It was of basic importance, he told them, that we step up our organizing campaign until we enrolled enough members to get some action like that of U.S. Steel. But this group was ready for a more militant step. Organizing campaigns held no more appeal to them; they wanted action. So a motion was made, seconded and shouted through that the mills of all three companies be shut down until the union was recognized.

Murray accepted the verdict of the Youngstown meeting and sent out a call the next day to start the shutdown. Girdler, who was really fight happy, tried to beat the union to the punch by firing thousands of his workers at the Canton and Massilon, Ohio, plants in order to scare hell out of the rest and keep them on the job. It didn't work. The Little Steel plants were closed and the picket lines began to form at midnight on May 26, 1937.

The companies immediately shifted into a plan of action developed by the Remington Rand Company and circulated widely by the National Association of Manufacturers. This called for the branding of any strike as a Communist plot, the use of full-page inflammatory newspaper advertisements, attempted domination of the local police and the formation of "citizens' committees" that might be more aptly described as vigilantes. Little Steel was ready for war, and it implemented its battle plan immediately and aggressively. The result was armed skirmishes at dozens of steel plants. But in East Chicago, Indiana, it was tragedy on a scale reminiscent of Homestead and the coalfields of the 1920's.

There, a group of about one thousand steelworkers and their families met on Memorial Day for a mass meeting to build morale and generate enthusiasm for their cause. When the meeting ended, they formed ranks for a protest march to the gates of the Republic Steel plant where they worked. The marchers never arrived there. About halfway to their destination, they were attacked by a force of two hundred East Chicago policemen, armed with rifles and tear gas. There was no parley and no warning. The police fired the tear gas into the marchers; then they fired their guns into the mist and confusion. When the clouds of gas lifted, ten marchers were dead and scores of others wounded.

We don't have to speculate on what happened after that. A Paramount newsreel cameraman was on hand and filmed the entire affair. His film showed police clubbing fallen marchers, many of them women and children. It showed police dragging a grievously wounded man feet first out of a car where friends had laid him for a trip to the hospital; the man died on the street. It showed an old man battered to death on the pavement by a half-dozen husky cops. It is some measure of the temper of the times that these films were never released for public showings. And Tom Girdler, in the superheated atmosphere that followed the Memorial Day Massacre, said cheerfully, "Sure, we got guns."

He meant it, too. The La Follette Committee Report noted that "the Republic Steel Corporation has a uniformed police force of nearly 400 men whom it has equipped not only with revolvers, rifles and shotguns but also with more tear and sickening gas and gas equipment than has been purchased by any law-enforcement body, local, State or Federal in the country. It has loosed its guards, thus armed, to shoot down citizens on the streets and highways."

It looked like the coal wars of the 1920's all over again. There were a half-million steelworkers and their families who needed to be fed. There were armed forces drawn up against one another. There was hatred, deep and violent. Yet, there were basic differences, too. A major segment of the steel industry had signed with us and was operating peacefully, so the opposition was divided. And most of the steelworkers had a roof over their heads. They were often hungry, but seldom without shelter.

The Little Steel companies flagrantly violated both the word and the spirit of the Wagner Act, and the workers often responded violently. By the time the National Guard had been called out in a half-dozen states to stand between the strikers and the plant police, eighteen workers were dead and more than two hundred injured. The Guardsmen brought an uneasy end to the shooting. Then the strike settled down into a long, acrimonious battle of wills and patience. And that's where we began to hurt.

The flimsy financial base on which the SWOC was operating simply dissolved. We needed to set up soup kitchens, and we couldn't even buy the pots. We couldn't get dues from our members, and when we went to other—more solvent—unions for help, we got a lot of high-blown rhetoric but very little money.

I was charging around the country, trying to keep morale up and hunger down and not succeeding very well at either one, when I got an emergency call for help from the SWOC man in Youngstown. About five miles from the city limits, I was stopped by a police roadblock that had been set up to prevent "outside agitators" from getting into town. I told them I was a salesman for Whiz Products—a company I created on the spot—and got away with it. I could smell the tension in the town as I drove through; all the people I saw looked angry and fearful. I hurried out to the Youngstown Sheet and Tube plant, where I found several hundred pickets milling around one end of a 150-foot steel bridge that led across a railroad track to the entrance of the factory.

The temper of the crowd was measured by one stocky, bull-shouldered picket who told me grimly, "No goddam scab is going to get across *this* bridge." Company guards were massed at the other end of the bridge, and occasionally they would lob a tear gas shell into the massed pickets who would scatter for a few minutes, then return to their posts, usually in greater strength. Between the tear gas assaults, I mounted a car and exhorted the workers to "hang in there," assuring them of support from the SWOC that was almost nonexistent by that time.

From the plant, I hurried to strike headquarters on the twelfth floor of the Ohio Hotel. There I got several nasty shocks. From the window of the room, I could see hundreds of armed men, apparently well equipped with tear gas, rifles and even a few machine guns, stationed on the roofs of downtown buildings. They looked as if they were expecting an invasion.

I turned to our district director, John Mayo, and asked, "What the hell is going on here?"

He told me he had lost control of the strikers and at that moment a meeting of steelworkers was taking place to organize a march on the power centers of the city. I asked him why the hell he wasn't down there stopping it, and he said it was hopeless because a fire-eater named Shorty Steuben had convinced the strikers that the whole city stood against them and only by a massive show of force—backed with arms, if necessary—could the workingmen prevail. And they were hungry enough and angry enough to believe him. Mayo also told me that Steuben was the head of the Communist Party in the state of Ohio and had been trained in China, both facts he had discovered only after Steuben had shouldered him aside and taken over leadership of the strikers.

Strike headquarters was full of staff men who had remained loyal to Mayo, and they corroborated his story. Some of them were still red-eyed from a tear gas attack at the bridge the night before. They were a sorry, dejected lot, and I didn't help their state of mind any by climbing all over them for not being at the mass meeting or on the picket lines instead of hanging around headquarters.

We got in Mayo's car, then, and drove around the city, talking with pickets and townspeople. At one plant, there were several dozen management people and a few scabs still inside, trying to make psychological points by keeping smoke coming out of the stacks. The men in the plant had to be supplied, and the picket line, led by a tough and determined man named Hugh Carcella, wasn't letting anything through. The company finally solved this impasse by dropping food inside the plant gates from the air. Two light planes appeared while I was standing on the back of a truck, talking to the pickets. The first pilot ignored the food drop, and took a run at me instead, flat-hatting across the pickets just a few feet above the truck. I dove for the truck bed, then got up and had just resumed my talk when a second plane dive-bombed me. Again I hit the deck. Then for the next fifteen minutes, I bobbed up and down, making my speech between bombing runs while the pickets cheered. Finally the pilots dropped their food and headed home, unaware probably that they had helped build the morale and determination of the strikers at that plant.

Feelings were just as strong—if a little less flamboyant—all over the Youngstown area. My early impressions were, if anything, too conservative. Youngstown was a pyre of combustibles to which Shorty Steuben was about to set a match. All during that day, I pictured what perfect targets the Youngstown workers pouring through the streets would make for the machine guns on the rooftops. All the elements of a bloodletting infinitely worse than the Memorial Day tragedy were present in Youngstown, and the town seemed to be waiting for its coming with an almost resigned air of anticipation. I couldn't sleep at all that night, knowing I had to do something and wondering—sometimes praying—what it should be.

As early as I could call Mayo the next morning, I told him I wanted a staff meeting at strike headquarters, and I wanted *everyone* there—including Steuben. An hour later they were assembled, two dozen grim, silent men divided almost equally between anticipation and antagonism. I knew I was going to have to be tough. If I gave any quarter, Steuben would elbow me out of the way, just as he had Mayo.

I looked them over slowly, then said, "This meeting is going to last one half hour, and I'm going to talk for the first twenty-five minutes."

Then I reminded them of East Chicago, told them what I had seen on the rooftops of Youngstown and heard on the streets of the city, and asserted flatly that there would be no march on downtown Youngstown. I didn't use any qualifiers. I said that hundreds of people would be killed and maimed in such a demonstration to no positive end; the union would be blamed and our cause would be hurt instead of helped. We were not in the business, I told them, of inciting violence or deliberately provoking situations in which innocent citizens would be injured or killed. Then I let my eyes roam that circle of quiet men and said deliberately: "This strike can only be won on the picket lines, by keeping strikebreakers from entering the mills. If that brings violence, it's *their* responsibility, not ours, because we are operating completely within our legal rights. Your job is to man those lines and keep out the strikebreakers. Now God damn it, get back out there and do it."

As they stared at me, absorbing this, I looked directly at Steuben. "That goes for you, particularly," I told him, "and if you don't like it, I want your resignation right now."

Our eyes locked and held for a few seconds. Then he said: "The Youngstown City Council is going to vote $30,000 for ammunition at its meeting tonight. Can I go down there and speak against it?"

I knew, then, that I'd won, and I told him to forget it, that Mayo and I would handle *that* situation, too. Then I looked around the group again and said, "If there's anyone who isn't ready to follow through on what I've just told you, I'll take his resignation now."

Again, a long silence. Then somebody muttered, "I've got to get back out to the lines," and the tension broke and so did the meeting. Quickly they all filed out, and I tried to smother a deep sigh because I didn't want Mayo to know how relieved I was or how apprehensive I'd been.

I spent the afternoon seeking local citizens with no union ax to grind who might appear at the City Council meeting to talk against the arms resolution. Many of them were ministers, and I had a hell of a time persuading them that the leaders of the CIO and the SWOC were good Christians who weren't trying to overthrow the country. Several showed up at the council meeting and argued strongly against the City of Youngstown laying in arms to shoot down its own people. Again, it's a measure of the times that while thousands of local citizens were going hungry, the City Council appropriated $30,000 to buy armament with only one dissenting vote.

That was too much for some of the strikers who were sitting in the audience. Before I realized what was happening, one of them had elbowed his way to the microphone, pointed his finger at the council president and shouted, "If Youngstown wants violence, then, by God, that's exactly what Youngstown is going to get."

In the uproar that followed, I stumbled to the microphone, put a football shoulder in the chest of the man standing there, shoved him out of the way and began to talk as fast as the words would come out.

"This man," I bellowed, "doesn't speak for the CIO or for the steelworkers of Youngstown who are on strike for the redress of legitimate grievances. We not only don't seek violence but we'll go out of our way to avoid it. If there is to be violence in Youngstown, it will be because the steelworkers are attacked and forced to defend themselves."

I don't remember what else I said, only that I knew I had to keep talking until that crowd quieted down. And the council members, sensing the situation, let me talk. I used all of the dramatic devices I'd learned in college, all the arguments, all the oratorical tricks I knew until I had the complete attention of the audience and the Council Chamber was relatively quiet again. Then, in as conversational a tone as I could muster, I suggested that the steelworkers disperse quietly and either go home or return to their picket lines. They hesitated a moment, then a handful of them stood up and filed out, and the rest began to follow. The council adjourned instantly.

Outside, I found another brush fire blazing. The steelworkers who left the meeting had gotten only a few steps away from the entrance to City Hall. There, they had gathered around a young, curly-headed man named Burke I'd seen at the meeting that morning, a man identified to me by Mayo as one of Steuben's chief assistants.

I stood on the fringe of the group, listened long enough to learn that Burke was urging them to go through with the original plan to march on the city, then pushed my way through the crowd, put a foot on a fire hydrant, looked long and hard at Burke and said, "Just what the hell do you think you're doing?"

He shoved out his jaw and said, "I'm giving these men their instructions for the march tomorrow."

I have powerful lungs and I drew on them totally to shout, "Burke, weren't you at my meeting this morning?"

"You know I was there," he said.

"Then you heard me say there would be no march on Youngstown, and there won't be. Is that clear?"

He looked at me and didn't answer, so I went on: "Now I want you to tell these men to disregard what you just told them. Either you tell them that or you're fired, right now."

He chewed his lip and hesitated while I held my breath. Then in a low voice, he turned to the group around him and said, "Okay, you heard it. No march. Break it up."

And for the third time that day, a group of sullen, angry steelworkers dispersed slowly and reluctantly. I watched them go, speculating on how many other blazes would have to be beaten out that night. If there were others, I didn't know about them. I spent an uneasy night, wondering if the marchers were collecting somewhere without my knowledge and I would be wakened by machine guns chattering from the roofs nearby. But it never happened, and slowly—very slowly—over the next few weeks, the citizens of Youngstown began to accept the fact that the strikers were seeking recognition, nothing else, and were not a part of a Communist conspiracy to take over the City of Youngstown.

By that time I was long gone, trying to keep SWOC fences mended in other strike centers. Although the potential for widespread violence had probably been greatest in Youngstown, I found company police and local vigilantes attacking pickets almost everywhere I traveled. All of this was, of course, illegal, but Little Steel generally had local police in their pocket, and the corporation attorneys had found an alleged loophole in the Wagner Act that was being argued endlessly in Federal courts. In this impasse, Lewis—still profoundly suspicious of government interference and angry over a strike he didn't want—finally turned in desperation to President Roosevelt. And the President, unexpectedly and inexplicably, brushed Lewis off with "a plague on both your houses" wisecrack that hurt Lewis' pride and sensibilities deeply and kindled an antagonism that was to turn into hatred over the years.

So once again we were in trouble. We had a strike on our hands we couldn't resolve, thousands of hungry steelworkers we couldn't feed, and a Federal Government that had given us the tools to forge our freedom, then told us to go to hell when those tools were turned against us.

Congress made a pass at resolving the dispute by starting a series of interminable investigations and hearings, but all of its testimony led exactly nowhere. There were charges and counter-charges and lawsuits and accusations, but none of this brought bread into the homes of the striking steelworkers, and that's where we were really hurting. In the kind of money that buys staying power, the Little Steel companies held a clear advantage over the SWOC.

This was illustrated by an incident in Canton, Ohio. Our people there were running a soup kitchen for the families of striking workers. They needed money to keep it going, and they called me for help. I went to Canton to tell them we didn't have any money and they would have to close down the kitchen.

It was one of the most difficult things I ever had to do. Our district director, Frank Hardesty, took me to the union hall where the food line had been set up. It was filled with people, mostly women, and they had a beaten, hopeless look about their eyes. They were waiting for food to arrive. What they got, instead, was a very short speech from headquarters, delivered in a voice that quavered unmistakably. "How can I tell you," I said, "that we have no more money and we're going to have to close down the kitchen?" They never changed expression. They just looked at me.

If an epitaph is ever written for the Little Steel strike, that would have to be it: "We have no money and we'll have to close down the kitchens." It was as simple as that. We couldn't collect dues and we couldn't get help and we couldn't keep the kitchens open. So over the months, the men slowly drifted back to work without the recognition they sought and without return on the high price already paid—the months of hunger and privation and the dead and wounded from a dozen different fronts.

Tom Girdler and his associates in Little Steel laid the groundwork well for an effective move by the Communist Party of America into the ranks of the steelworkers. The credit for beating it back belongs entirely to the union leadership—and to the workers who suffered from the inhumanity and intransigence of their employers on the one hand and the inflammatory excesses of the Communists on the other. The workers who survived and went on to build a strong, progressive union of steelworkers are legitimate labor heroes. Neither they nor the nation owes any thanks to the Tom Girdlers or the anarchists, both of whom used every resource at their disposal to prevent orderly, legitimate, democratic processes from functioning. But the processes and those of us who stood by them proved too strong in the end. The victory of Little Steel was short-lived. Though it hurt like hell when it happened.

10

As Europe threshed about on the edge of war, there were three pieces of unfinished business monopolizing the attention of Lewis, Murray and me. Little Steel was still not organized. The problem of dues collection within the SWOC had still not been solved. And the split between the CIO and AFL was widening almost daily.

The latter problem was the most easily resolved, since the AFL did all the resolving in a series of actions that began on August 4, 1936, with the suspension of all CIO unions and ended in January, 1938, when the CIO charters were revoked. At that time, the CIO included thirty-two national and international unions and hundreds of directly affiliated locals; it had a membership of more than four million workers with some 30,000 collective bargaining contracts in effect. The AFL actions caused scarcely a ripple in CIO headquarters. Lewis had mentally long ago divorced the AFL; the granting of the decree was a mere formality, accompanied by changing the name from "Committee for Industrial Organizing" to "Congress of Industrial Organizations."

The other two problems, however, couldn't be solved quite that easily.

Without money, we couldn't function effectively in organizing the rest of the steel industry, so dues collection became primary. It was the main order of business at the first convention of the SWOC in December, 1937, but about the only thing that came out of that meeting was a hassle at the front door when Lewis—our featured speaker—tried to enter without a badge and was stopped by a pair of very tough steelworkers who took their duties seriously. Howard Hague rushed to him and escorted him to the stage.

We did manage to establish some bylaws for the SWOC and

then discussed our financial plight at great length. It was clear when that meeting ended that if anything was to be done about dues collection, it would have to be conceived and directed from our headquarters.

Murray handed me that job. I did a great deal of exploring and talking, and the best solution I could find was a modification of a plan that was already in operation in the Monongahela Valley area. We called it visual education, which was a high-sounding label for a practice much more accurately described as dues picketing.

It worked very simply. A group of dues-paying members, selected by the district director (usually more for their size than their tact), would stand at the plant gate with pick handles or baseball bats in hand and confront each worker as he arrived for his shift.

A member of the committee would ask: "Let's see your dues card."

That gave the worker three choices. He could show an up-to-date card and pass on into the mill. He could detour to a nearby table, pay his back dues and go to work. Or he could tell the committee to go to hell. Reaction to the third course varied by mill, but usually the worker was simply barred from entering the plant until he paid his dues. It was a remarkably effective system that could be challenged successfully only by a group large enough to force its way past the committee; and this really didn't solve anything since there would be a larger "committee" there the next day. The weakness, of course, was that as soon as the committee disappeared, the dues slacked off again, but we could bring our treasury up-to-date whenever it was necessary by putting the committees back on the plant gates.

If all of this sounds like extortion, that's your word, not mine. This money was owed us, and we were in trouble, fighting for our life. We were also providing a growing range of services and benefits to the steelworkers without the minimal contributions we required to survive. Dues were our only source of income. Our line of credit with the UMW had just run out. Our relief work for the

Little Steel strikers had exhausted our funds. Dues picketing was the only effective answer we could find.

The steelworkers didn't accept it passively. Most of them were strong individuals with no background in unionism, and they were convinced that the money they contributed was put in a paper sack and divided between McDonald and Murray every Saturday night. A dollar to these men meant ten stops at the local saloon after work; it also often meant talking their wives into turning it loose for a purpose the wives didn't understand, either. And so we had trouble at the plant gates whenever the dues committee showed up to put its bite on the workers.

The problem was aggravated by some of our own officials who objected publicly to dues picketing. Clint Golden was major complainant, and I finally called him in to headquarters for a showdown. Bittner was there, too, and we argued it out in front of Murray. I told Golden it was one thing to be philosophically opposed to the dues picketing technique but it was something else to try and meet a payroll every week and keep the union functioning. I said that until he came up with a better system, we were going to have to continue dues picketing or close up shop, and I would rather see the union killed right now than die slowly of financial dry rot. Bittner agreed with me, and Murray just listened. When it was over, he said he wanted to think about it; then he called me in later and told me to proceed as I thought best. This was typical of Murray. Philosophically, he probably agreed with Golden—hell, so did I, for that matter—but he recognized the practical problems, too. He could get himself off the philosophical hook by throwing the problem back to me to take the practical steps that were distasteful to Murray.

I took them. I had no choice. And slowly we built up our treasury. There were some bad moments. Our Donora, Pennsylvania, district director, Jack McGarry, came into my office one day when I was about ready to chuck the whole business. He read it on my face, asked me what was wrong, and I told him I didn't have enough money to meet the payroll on the next day. He asked how much I needed, and I told him $12,000.

"I can get it for you," he said, "if you'll let me do it."

I thought it over. After our session in Pittsburgh, Golden had accepted dues picketing grudgingly but had also issued an order in the Eastern Region that there could be no more than five pickets at any gate for dues inspection. He was acclaimed as a labor statesman for this move, but the practical effect was to increase the fighting at mill gates by making it easier for workers who wanted to resist to force their way in. McGarry had been a UMW leader and there were plenty of coal miners in his district he could call on for help. I knew this was what he had in mind. I looked at our checkbook, pondered the high hopes and purposes we had for this union, then told him, "Go ahead."

"Golden might fire me," he said.

"Don't worry about that," I answered. "I'm over Golden, and if he fires you, I'll put you back on the job."

The next day, McGarry showed up at the plant gate with two dozen miners wearing their mining helmets and carrying pick handles. A dues inspection was carried out. There was no rough stuff. It wasn't necessary; the implication was plain and the steelworkers weren't stupid. They paid their dues. That evening, McGarry showed up at my office with a paper bag containing $14,000 in cash, and we made our payroll.

There were a good many payrolls we didn't meet, however, during this period, and for almost six months our staff people drew only half their pay of six dollars a day, and sometimes not that much. We had long since moved from our plush offices to a dreary set of quarters in another building. The dues picketing kept us alive, but obviously we needed stronger medicine to bring us back to health.

I had one bit of leverage I hadn't used, and—on reflection—it seemed to me to offer the only possibility of a permanent solution. Whenever the dues picketing committees appeared at the plant gates, production fell off to about 25 percent of capacity because of absenteeism while the men either paid their dues, tried to fight their way into the plant or went home to sit it out. Consequently, the companies didn't like the system but they were also reluctant to involve themselves directly in the internal problems of the union. It seemed to me that I could use corporate desire to get rid of dues picketing to evolve a better system requiring their cooperation. So I came up with a plan that would permit one dues committeeman for each twenty-five workers to collect dues inside the mill on one payday each month. I took this plan to U.S. Steel and they turned it down. The dues picketing continued.

About a month later, Ben Fairless—now the president of U.S. Steel—called Murray and asked for a meeting. Present with Fairless was John A. Stephens, an industrial-relations expert with whom I would negotiate many times in the years ahead. Fairless was agitated, pacing the floor as he told us that the dues picketing was beginning to hurt production badly and it would have to be stopped. We told him we didn't like it either but we needed money to operate the union, just as he needed money to operate U.S. Steel, and we would be happy to listen to any suggestions he might have. He then made a strong pitch for the Golden plan of five men on a gate on payday to collect dues.

Murray looked at me and said, "What about it, David?"

I said: "No, sir. I won't settle for less than four hundred men on a gate."

Fairless was appalled. "My God," he said, "that will mean riots."

"It might," I said, "and we don't want riots any more than you. But we do want our dues collected, and I told you a month ago how it could be done without trouble for anybody."

Then occurred one of those fortuitous bits of luck that always seem to affect momentous decisions. The phone rang, Stephens answered it, said, "Oh my God," and handed it to Fairless. He listened silently for a few seconds, cradled the phone and said to Murray, "Our Donora plant is down because of a dues picket line."

Murray was caught unprepared. He didn't know that McGarry and I had arranged for a dues inspection that day. He looked at me and said, "David, can you get it called off."

"I can get *this* one called off," I said, "but it's going to happen again until we get the whole matter solved."

While they thought that over, I picked up Fairless' phone, called McGarry and told him to withdraw the pickets. When I finished, Ben thanked me. This was a psychological play on my part. It worked.

The next morning, Stephens appeared at my office, the first time a U.S. Steel official had ever made that pilgrimage. He declined to sit down, standing, instead, before my desk, shifting a brown Homburg from one hand to the other.

"About those dues collectors," he said. "We can't agree to one for every twenty-five men. But we *will* go along with one for every thirty-five."

I stood up, we shook hands on it and he left. Thus was the Steel Workers Organizing Committee finally put on a solid financial footing. There were still problems—mainly finding dues committeemen, since the job was voluntary and nonpaying—but the machinery now existed and it began to function, wheezing a bit, almost immediately. At my insistence, we hired the accounting firm of Main and Company to set up a completely integrated accounting and internal office control system. One-fourth of the dues money was to go back to the local unions to pay their expenses, and I wanted to leave no doubts that they were getting their share. When the big money finally began to pour in, we were geared to handle it. From that day our books were always open, and no charge of mishandling funds was ever proved against us. In 1942, we would become the first international union to make public the semiannual audit of its books, long before this was required by law.

As we slowly built our financial strength for a concerted campaign to organize the remainder of the steel industry, Tom Kennedy of the United Mine Workers added to labor's growing prestige by running successfully for the lieutenant governorship of the State of Pennsylvania. Since the Pennsylvania governor can't succeed himself, Kennedy should have been governor four years later, but the political establishment in Pennsylvania couldn't quite swallow him. David Lawrence, later to be Pittsburgh's mayor, was the power in Pennsylvania Democratic politics, and Lewis and Murray met with him to push Kennedy's candidacy.

Lawrence resisted, insisting, "Kennedy can't win and we can't risk losing the State House by running him." Lawrence also resented this interference from "meddling Republicans," and Lewis angrily told Murray and me to set up a statewide campaign and run Kennedy anyway. We lost in the primary, but I learned some valuable lessons that were decidedly useful twenty years later when a young Senator from Massachusetts carrying the same name made a run for the Presidency.

Murray and I were still officers of the UMW, drawing half our pay from the miners, so we had to make periodic trips to Washington, even during the crises in the steel organizing campaign. On one of these trips, Lewis asked me to look into a union pension program. I spent several months working out a plan with Metropolitan Life and presented it to Lewis. He didn't like it because he felt the union should administer it. I contended that union administration would work under the present leadership, but if the union ever got into the hands of crooks or incompetents, the miners' money could be lost overnight. We argued for almost two hours, exploring every facet of the plan, before Lewis said, "Okay, you win. Set it up."

Then he leaned back in his chair, looked at me from under those hooded eyebrows and said, "You know, we haven't really talked for a long time, and there are some things I'd like to discuss with you."

He told me that the future of the labor movement was in the hands of people like me and he had great confidence in my ability to handle whatever responsibility came my way. But, he said, and his voice took on an edge, it was important that I not become too deeply ingrained with the "socialist philosophy that hangs around the Pittsburgh office of the steelworkers."

I asked him what he meant, and he reached in his desk and pulled out a clipping from a Philadelphia newspaper reporting a speech I'd made there. I was constantly backstopping Murray who would accept speaking engagements he had no intention of fulfilling, then send me as a substitute at the last minute. This one had been to a Junior Chamber of Commerce, and I remembered it well. My remarks had been taken out of context by the reporter and sounded considerably more leftish than they really were. I explained this to Lewis and said, "If you like, I'll tell you the conclusions I offered in that speech."

He leaned back in his chair, said "Go ahead" and listened intently as I expounded the same basic principles of democratic capitalism I had heard him set forth to thousands of coal miners in Wilkes-Barre fifteen years earlier.

He heard me out, then asked, "Is *that* what you believe?

I said, "Yes, sir."

He stood, shook my hand and said: "Maybe as we get older we're inclined to resent you young fellows coming along. Keep up the good work, Dave."

The good work that summer became routine enough so that I was able to get away for my first vacation in five years. Emmy Lou and I spent more than a month driving about the country, mostly in California. In Los Angeles, I was urged to take over an organizing campaign for motion-picture actors and workers and form an industrial union, and Emmy Lou was offered a screen test. We turned down both opportunities, soaking up sun, instead, until it was time to return to Washington for the opening of new contract talks with the coal operators.

We were seeking a union shop and a substantial wage increase. The operators resisted both, and the talks droned on with no appreciable progress. (It was during one of these sessions that Lewis got ponderously to his feet, looked around the negotiating table and intoned: "Well, gentlemen, shall we repair to our respective lairs and gnaw the bones of discontent?") When the contract expired without a new agreement, the miners—faithful to their "no contract, no work" pledge—shut down the mines.

President Roosevelt, who had been needling the negotiators through various aides, now took a personal hand. He summoned both parties to the Cabinet Room, then entered with that expansive smile of his, leaning heavily on a pair of canes. It was the first time I'd been close to him since his election, and the years of turmoil hadn't appeared to age him. He still looked youthful and vigorous. He chose to be low key, telling us affably but firmly that the country couldn't afford a coal shutdown and he wanted us to stay in continuous negotiations until we reached an agreement.

It was clear we were going to have to give on one of our major points, and we finally—at Phil Murray's suggestion—traded a wage increase for a union shop agreement with the entire coal industry. It was something less than a smashing victory (although this was the first industrywide union shop), but we were glad to be out of the negotiations because we had another—more serious—problem plaguing us, and a coal strike would have been a distinct liability in dealing with it.

For fifty years, the focal point of the argument of the more reactionary American industrialists—particularly the National Association of Manufacturers—against labor unions had been the red herring of Communism. Organized labor, so went this argument, is a socialistic concept being directed by hard-core Marxists who would take over the unions and eventually the nation. This argument was so widely believed—it still is today, in some quarters—that it enabled industrialists to keep their workers in virtual servitude until the Wagner Labor Act gave organized labor a legal platform from which to operate.

As with most big lies, there were enough grains of truth in these charges to provide the people who made them ammunition to perpetuate the lies. This was particularly true in the 1930's when a concerted, well-heeled and thoroughly professional attack was launched on the CIO as a nest of Communists, carefully spawning subversion for the ultimate take-over. This attack was aided immeasurably by the notorious Dies un-American Activities Committee of the U.S. House of Representatives and by angry AFL officials who resented the withdrawal of the CIO and never missed an opportunity to tear down its leaders.

President Roosevelt called the Dies Committee methods a "sordid procedure" and Cardinal Mundelein of Chicago warned in 1938: "We must not let others use communism as a cloak to cover corrupt practices when they cry out against communism and they, themselves, practice social injustice."

Conference of the United Mine Workers and William N. Doak,
Secretary of Labor under Hoover, in Washington, D.C., July 14,
1931. McDonald and Philip Murray (*left*) and John L. Lewis
(*right*). (*Manuscript Collection, Carnegie Library, Syracuse
University*)

Reading election results at
the 1st Constitutional
Convention of the United
Steelworkers in Cleveland,
1942. (*Manuscript
Collection, Carnegie
Library, Syracuse
University*)

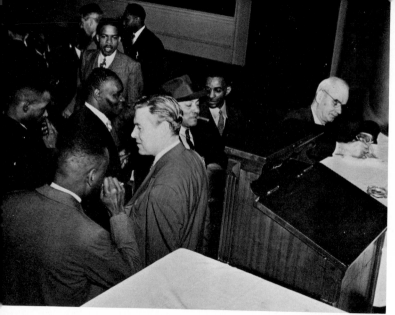

Meeting with delegates at the same convention.
(*Manuscript Collection, Carnegie Library, Syracuse University*)

With Eleanor Roosevelt in Pittsburgh, March, 1948.

At the 10th Constitutional Convention of the CIO in Portland, Oregon, November, 1948. (*Front row, left to right*) Jacob Potofsky, president of the Amalgamated Clothing Workers, McDonald, Allan Heywood, Philip Murray. (*Manuscript Collection, Carnegie Library, Syracuse University*)

With Arthur Goldberg (*back turned*) and Philip Murray in the William Penn Hotel, Pittsburgh, 1950. (*Associated Press Wirephoto*)

ABOVE. With Nelson Rockefeller at the National Conference for Human Rights, in New York City, 1955. (*Manuscript Collection, Carnegie Library, Syracuse University*)   BELOW. Meeting workers at Great Lakes Steel Corporation USW meeting, August, 1955. (*Manuscript Collection, Carnegie Library, Syracuse University*)

ABOVE. With New York Mayor Robert Wagner and ex-President
Harry Truman, celebrating Truman's 75th birthday at the
Waldorf-Astoria Hotel, New York City, 1959.   BELOW. A meeting in
Los Angeles, August 19, 1960, following the Democratic Party
Convention. (*Left to right*) Harry Boyer, president of
Pennsylvania AFL-CIO; David Lawrence, Governor of
Pennsylvania; Vice-Presidential nominee Lyndon B. Johnson;
David J. McDonald, Jr.; McDonald; F. N. Hoffmann; Presidential
nominee John F. Kennedy; Senator "Scoop" Jackson. (*Manuscript
Collection, Carnegie Library, Syracuse University*)

TOP. A meeting of the Steelworkers Executive Board in the Cabinet Room of the White House February, 1961. BOTTOM. R. Conrad Cooper, chief negotiator for the steel industry, and McDonald prepare to sign 1962 basic steel agreement in Pittsburgh, June, 1962.

Owen "Buck" Jones
swearing in McDonald
as USW president, in
Pittsburgh, March, 1963.

With President Kennedy and United Nations Ambassador Adlai
Stevenson going into the Americana Hotel, New York City,
November 15, 1963.

Rosemary McDonald meets President Kennedy the same evening, a week before the assassination.

George Meany, president of the AFL-CIO, and McDonald presenting a contribution from the United Steelworkers for the John F. Kennedy Memorial Library, at the Robert F. Kennedy home in Virginia, September, 1964.

But somehow comments like these were lost in the widespread publicity given to such inflammatory statements as the testimony of John P. Frey, president of the AFL Metal Trades Department before the Dies Committee. He said flatly that the CIO was Communist-dominated, then offered a secret list of 248 CIO leaders he contended were Communists.

Was there any substance to these charges? Of course there was; to deny them totally would be to deny the evidence of my own senses and experience over two decades of fighting Marxist elements within the trade-union movement. What is needed is to put them in perspective, to understand the forces that were at work and the relative effectiveness of those forces.

Lewis said that those who accused the CIO of being Communist-dominated "lie in their beard and they lie in their bowels." And he was exactly right. The CIO was dominated by John L. Lewis—a conservative Republican politically and philosophically most of his life and unquestionably one of the strongest, toughest and most articulate proponents of democratic capitalism ever to live. It was always incredible to me that anyone who had ever listened to Lewis or read any of his public statements could have been anything but amused at charges that he ran a Communist union.

At the CIO convention in 1938, he said: "Our people in this movement know how hard it is to preserve their rights and their liberty—even within a democracy. They have battled against violence, brutality and calumny. The forces of public order have been perverted against them. And yet, our people have not faltered in their conviction that they have rights which must not be destroyed. The agencies of public information have boiled with jeremiads against the CIO. On no other occasion of modern times has the American ideal of a free press been so sullied. The loyalty of the members and friends of the CIO through these storms of falsity shows again that American people will not be misled by cynical untruths and bitter misrepresentations. . . ."

But the American people *were* being misled. Large numbers of them were accepting these charges as dogma. Why was this true?

On reflection, it seemed to me there were two reasons. Many citizens were confusing desperately needed social reforms—labor unions, workmen's compensation, social security—with Communism. And—under the prodding of organizations like the NAM—they were also projecting the handful of legitimate Marxists who had surfaced in the labor movement to a take-over of the whole movement by the Communist Party.

How serious was the threat of Communism to the American labor movement? On several occasions, notably in the early 1930's, it might have been very serious indeed. One thing kept it from becoming serious: the absolute dedication to the precepts of democratic capitalism of most of the people heading the labor movement. And this is where the broadside accusations of people like Girdler and Sloan of General Motors hurt the most. By accusing these labor leaders of Marxist leanings, the Sloans and Girdlers were weakening the nation's strongest line of defense against just the developments these industrialists said they feared.

During most of my years as a union official, I read *The Daily Worker, New Masses* and other Communist publications regularly. I knew the party line and the current thrust of party activities. I saw and heard this line in union meetings frequently, and I fought it wherever and whenever I saw it. For this reason, there was considerable pressure put on Murray by some of the leftist members of the Steelworkers Union to get rid of me. He laughed off these efforts, just as Lewis laughed them off in the CIO.

It was natural and normal that domestic Marxists would be attracted to the labor-union movement in the United States. During the years that movement was being organized, it certainly offered the best possibilities in American society of a foot in the door for the Communists. Lewis and Murray knew this, but they didn't get hysterical about it. Girdler and Sloan and the NAM knew it and did. At no time was any union with which I was associated even remotely close to being taken over by Communists. The same holds true for John L. Lewis and the CIO. Lewis was quite aware of the Marxists who sought a home in the CIO. He attacked them periodically in speeches, and it always sounded as if he were giving them hell. The music was terrific, but when you read the words later, they didn't mean anything. He wasn't giving them hell at all; he was using them to help the CIO organize. When it was building, he accepted them as an unpleasant but relatively insignificant fact of life. When it was built, the CIO threw them out. It was as simple as that.

It is my firm conviction that our troubles with the Communists would have been much more profound in the desperation days of the Great Depression if the CIO had not come along. Lewis was a massive figure to the American workingman, who was being starved, beaten and humiliated during those years. Had Lewis not been there to carry on the fight for their dignity as human beings, great masses of American workers might quite well have turned their loyalties elsewhere. But they didn't, and Lewis and the American labor movement have never received the credit due them for preventing it. That time of danger has long since passed, and about the only function the feeble coalition of domestic Communists serves today is to provide a rationale for the fearful people who inhabit the John Birch Society and some hippie college students. But the Communists who were with us in the days when there *was* some danger needed very badly to be put into some sort of perspective—then and now.

The lack of public perspective toward John L. Lewis was clearly illustrated by an incident at the fiftieth anniversary convention of the United Mine Workers in 1938. Lewis was making his major address, which was being carried over a national radio network. I was sitting about ten feet to the side, watching him, when I saw something begin to descend slowly from the stage drops above and behind him. Almost transfixed, I watched a huge soviet flag begin to take form. Hurriedly, I scribbled a note and thrust it under Lewis' eyes. By this time the miners had seen the flag and were surging angrily toward the stage. While the ushers held them back and Lewis gestured to them to stay calm, several of us raced backstage to try and catch the culprits. In the midst of that frantic search, I was served with a lawsuit summons for seven and one-half million dollars, filed by Republic Steel against the SWOC. By the time I resumed the search, the others had given it up. Whoever dropped the flag made a clean getaway, and we never solved the mystery. Out front, our ushers tried to get the film from the cameras of news photographers who had been on the scene, but they weren't altogether successful. Several got out with their pictures and they were widely printed, probably convincing a lot of people who needed very little convincing that Lewis was, indeed, a Soviet agent.

11

On July 1, 1939, my son and only child, David, was born. In the months before that event, cracks began to appear in a relationship I'd always regarded as monolithic: that of John Lewis and Phil Murray. There were little things at first. Lewis and Murray had always eaten together when we were in Washington. They no longer did, but it was easy to ascribe this to Lewis' growing position as a Washington social lion; Murray, by contrast, was rather shy and withdrawn and avoided social affairs whenever he could. Lobby sitting was also a thing of the past; Lewis was seldom at his old stand in the Carlton lobby, and Murray was thus left to his own devices.

Then *The New York Times* did a story on Murray and the SWOC. The reporter talked with Vin Sweeney and me and asked us a lot of questions about Murray. I lauded Murray's negotiating ability, and when the story came out, it sounded as if we were depreciating Lewis in an effort to build up Murray. Phil came to Vin and me, quite upset, and asked rather sharply if we were trying to get him in trouble with Lewis.

About this time, Lewis, in one of his rare aberrations, decided he would like to have his daughter, Catherine, become secretary-treasurer of the CIO. Jim Carey was doing well in the job, and we thought that Lewis was joking at first, but he persisted and the word began to get around. So many people called Murray and Sidney Hillman to find out if it were true that Murray finally went to Lewis and told him he didn't think it was a good idea and neither did the CIO members who had been calling in. Lewis gave it up and Carey was reelected, but Lewis resented Murray's interference and another note of irritation was added to the Lewis-Murray relationship.

The irritation surfaced several months later when Lewis re-

neged on a promise to address the second convention of the
SWOC meeting in Chicago. In a rather childish display of bad
manners, he waited until opening day of the convention to send us
a wire saying that the press of business in Washington would keep
him from attending. We had one major accomplishment to report
to that convention: Inland Steel, always something of a maverick,
had broken from its Little Steel partners and indicated it would
sign a U.S. Steel-type of contract with us. This was the first tangible sign of progress with Little Steel, the first fruit of almost three
years of controversy and conflict.

Balanced against this hopeful sign of peace, however, was growing evidence of dissidence within the SWOC. Murray was being
given the silent treatment by Lewis from above and a highly vocal
working over by rivals seeking control of the SWOC from below.
The primary issue they chose to attack Murray on was a demand
that the locals get a larger proportion of the dues dollar. Both
Murray and I were compelled to get tough with the delegates.
After explaining for the hundredth time how the SWOC used its
funds, why it needed three-fourths of the dues dollar and inviting
the doubters to come in and look over our books, Murray and I
finally offered to resign and let them draw up a new set of bylaws,
if that's what they wanted. It wasn't. The vast majority of the
delegates supported Murray, and the fuss subsided temporarily.
But it would come up again, and we knew it.

Meanwhile, an issue that would split Lewis and Murray irre-
vocably and eventually drive Lewis from the leadership of the
American labor movement was beginning to come to a head. In
1939, Franklin D. Roosevelt announced that he would be a candidate for an unprecedented third term as President of the United
States. By this time, Lewis' antagonism toward FDR had swollen
to an almost implacable hatred. Publicly, he simply didn't mention Roosevelt, but in our private councils, he would berate FDR
for failing in his pledge to put the unemployed back to work and
for seeking personal aggrandizement and power beyond the
spirit, if not the letter, of the U.S. Constitution.

Neither Murray nor I shared these views. There would have

been no clause 7(a) that first gave us our freedom, no Wagner Labor Act, no reorganization of the miners, no social legislation had it not been for Roosevelt. As a matter of fact, there would have been no CIO without FDR's urging and support. The differences between Lewis and Roosevelt were mainly a matter of clashing personalities. Both were strong, arrogant, purposeful men who would deal directly—and sometimes ruthlessly—with obstructions once they were set on a course of action. It was understandable to Murray and me that two such men might react violently when and if they found themselves on a collision course. But it wasn't comprehensible to us that Lewis should permit a few such collisions to submerge so completely his recognition of the massive contributions Roosevelt had made to organized labor.

But Lewis was adamant, reacting angrily to any effort—particularly by Murray—to present the case for Roosevelt. Meanwhile, the Republicans, in a dramatic last-minute surge of votes, had nominated an Indiana attorney and amateur politician named Wendell Willkie to oppose Roosevelt. Lewis expressed lavish admiration for Willkie, and our only hope at this juncture was that Lewis would keep out of the contest publicly.

He not only didn't keep out, but he characteristically painted himself into a political corner from which there was finally no escape. On the morning of September 1, 1940, Lewis passed the word that he was going on nationwide radio to make an important announcement that would affect the future of the CIO. He gave no indication of what the announcement would be.

I planned to attend a football game that evening, and I took a small portable radio with me—one of the first to be manufactured. At half time, Lewis came on the air and a knot of people gathered around me in the stands at Forbes Field, straining to hear what he had to say. As always, it was said with extravagance of style and abiding conviction. I sat on that wooden bench and my heart sank slowly to the concrete beneath my feet as I heard that familiar, booming voice say, "I think that the reelection of President Franklin Roosevelt for a third term would be a national evil of the first magnitude. He no longer hears the cries of the people. Therefore, I strongly urge the election of Wendell L. Willkie as the next President of the United States."

Having made himself quite clear on this point, Lewis was simply unable to stop. His massive pride and ego compelled him to stake his own future against that of the man he was opposing. Incredibly, I heard him say, "It is obvious that President Roosevelt will not be reelected for the third term unless he has the overwhelming support of the men and women of labor. If he is, therefore, reelected it will mean that the members of the Congress of Industrial Organizations have rejected my advice and recommendation. I will accept such a result as being the equivalent of a vote of no confidence, and will retire as president of the CIO at its convention in November. This action will save our great movement, composed of millions of men and women, from the embarrassment and handicap of my leadership during the ensuing reign of President Roosevelt."

I clicked off the radio and stared unseeing at the marching bands in front of me. However Lewis assessed his own importance, I had no doubt, then or later, that Roosevelt would be swept back into office. I knew that there was no "labor vote," that the men and women of organized labor were perfectly capable of putting their loyalty and gratitude to John L. Lewis in a compartment totally separate from their political loyalties. It was true that when Lewis scowled, his associates usually had to go to the bathroom, but they could vote in private. I knew that Lewis had overstepped himself and that come November his massive pride would permit him no turning back from the position he had just taken.

Before that happened, however, more and serious wedges were driven between Lewis and Murray. And for the first time, I became directly involved in a rather devastating way. In the aftermath of Lewis' speech, Murray asked me to call a number of CIO and UMW leaders and solicit their opinions on what he'd said. I did as I was ordered. Of some three dozen men I polled, about one-third were shell-shocked and unable to form any specific opinion, one-third were loyal to Lewis' position and the remainder were outraged and angry. I turned over my notes to Murray, and he accepted them without comment.

A few days later, business took me to Washington and Lewis saw me in the hall of the UMW building. He commanded me peremptorily to step into his office, then turned his back as I found a chair. When he faced me, the thrust of his jaw and the icy temperature in his eyes belied the conversational tone of his voice.

"What's this I hear, David," he said, "about you calling the members of our Executive Board to try and get them to disregard my recommendation on Wendell Willkie?"

I knew then I was in for big trouble. I started to tell him that I was doing nothing of the sort when he interrupted, his voice and the red in his neck both rising visibly. He berated me for meddling in his private business and for trying to turn his own union against him. He accused me of being a turncoat and ingrate, and every time I would try to explain the reason for the phone calls, he would start on me again. It was a bitterly disappointing half hour, and although he cooled off and listened to me, finally, before I left his office, I knew that our relationship could never be the same again. That saddened and depressed me because I considered Lewis a genuinely great man and regarded my association with him as a rare and privileged experience.

I brooded often about that conversation during the presidential campaign, wondering how I might restore our relationship and knowing, deep down, that it was beyond my reach. By early November, Lewis was virtually incommunicado. He must have known, by then, what was going to happen; Roosevelt won easily and the moment of truth had come for Lewis.

As I knew he wouldn't, he never flinched. Before he faced the CIO convention in November, however, Lewis called Murray and me to Washington and told Murray—in my presence—that he wanted him to take over as president of the CIO. Again it is a measure of the stature of Lewis that, in spite of his growing personal disenchantment with Murray, he considered him the best man to lead the CIO and therefore offered him the job without reservation. Murray resisted at first, insisting that he didn't want it and the CIO would prefer Lewis, anyway, regardless of whatever rash pledges he might have made. But Lewis persisted, and Murray began to waver.

Lewis was very cold to me during these sessions, accusing me once of trying to create trouble between him and Murray. I was hurt and bewildered, and I remember blurting out to him, "I never make a speech, even today, that I don't hold you up as the greatest labor leader in our history."

And he pierced me with his eyes and said coldly, "I don't need you or anybody else to praise me."

Murray and I would spend hours talking over his decision after these sessions with Lewis. Originally, I'm sure that Murray was genuinely reluctant. But as the convention approached, I could see him being torn between loyalty to Lewis and a powerful ambition. And ambition won, although Murray still hadn't given Lewis a definite "Yes" when the convention was called to order.

But no human being alive could have resisted Lewis at that time and under those circumstances. When he stepped to the podium for the first time, the delegates literally went wild. Watching them, I was once again reminded of Wilkes-Barre, but this time I knew how fickle adulation could be, that it was a response to the moment and could be turned around a week or a month or a year later. There was no doubt, at *this* moment, of its legitimacy or intent. The delegates wanted Lewis to forget his pledge and stay on as president of the CIO. For almost an hour, they chanted "We want Lewis," as he stood, immobile, at the podium, his head slightly downcast, his ample brows furrowed, his eyes inscrutable.

If ever a man could—with honor—have backed off a position taken on impulse, Lewis could have done it that day. But it was simply not in him. He had staked his reputation on a political contest, had lost and now he must punish these people by showing them that if they followed him at all, they must follow him all the way. They had made their choice; they preferred Roosevelt as a national leader to Lewis as a union leader, and that was that. He told the convention that his decision was irrevocable and he would like to see Philip Murray named as his successor as president of the CIO. He left no doubts, no loopholes. And so Murray —who had been given absolute assurance by Lewis of his support and that of the UMW—was elected by acclamation and an era had ended. Lewis would not retire from the labor scene—far from it. But by renouncing this position of ultimate power in the labor movement, he marked his own apogee and began a slow descent from public view.

In the aftermath of that dramatic moment, several delegations came to my room and promised me support for Jim Carey's job as secretary-treasurer of the CIO if I would make a run for it. I turned them down. I really didn't want the job. I knew that Murray's new responsibilities with the CIO would throw a considerably greater burden on me in the day-by-day operation of the SWOC. That was by far the more important task and I wanted to be free to do it well. In the years that followed, I was to be grateful many times for making that decision. I had no idea, then, how much of the responsibility for the steelworkers would shortly be mine.

12

In the aftermath of Lewis' withdrawal as head of the CIO, one question troubled Murray and me deeply. Was this just a ploy on the part of Lewis, and did he intend to continue to run the CIO from behind the scenes, regardless of his protests to the contrary? Or was he really capable, at his zenith, of turning over the controls of this instrument of power to another man?

The first suggestion of an answer to these questions was not comforting. A few weeks after Murray's ascension, the Pennsylvania CIO held a state convention in Harrisburg, Pennsylvania, and invited both Murray and Lewis to attend. They drove up together from Washington, apparently on cordial terms. It was a crucial moment because it was their first joint public appearance —and therefore the first real indication of whether or not Lewis was willing to permit Murray the spotlight into which Lewis had virtually forced him.

They entered the room together, and, of course, the delegates stood and cheered. I know a little about theater and the techniques of upstaging, and Lewis applied them magnificently. He held all the cards anyway. He dominated any gathering in which he appeared simply by being there, and to permit another man the center stage would have required a conscious act of deference and unselfishness on Lewis' part. He simply wasn't capable of it. He stepped forward and took all the bows, made all the responses, milked all the attention. I saw Murray's eyes darken and the lines around his mouth set, but he made no effort to fight Lewis for attention. He knew it was an uneven contest from the beginning.

Afterward, he was more hurt than angry. And I was more angry than hurt.

"It was a dirty damn trick," I told Murray, "and it looks to me as if he's going to keep on trying to run the show."

Murray wouldn't rise to my anger. He just kept repeating, "We'll see, we'll see."

But once again forces beyond our control dictated the succession of events. Lewis, always a remarkably healthy man, became desperately ill early in 1941 and convalesced much of that year. When he resumed work, he seemed to have scaled down his desires and his activities. He was still president of the UMW, and some rather serious problems had developed in the coal industry. Lewis directed his attention there and Murray became head of the CIO in fact as well as in name. Lewis never again seriously participated in the administrative affairs of the CIO.

While Murray was firming up his CIO lines of command, I was coordinating the SWOC organizing program that was running into some new and exotic problems. Racketeers, deprived of bootleg booze as a source of income when Prohibition was repealed, had been looking around for other fields of action. One that seemed attractive to them was organized labor, and they tried to strong-arm their way into a number of unions—including the steelworkers. But they made a big mistake in the points of attack they selected in the SWOC.

Two snap-brim hoods called on Van Bittner in his Chicago office one day and told him they had been investigating business opportunities and had decided they would like to go into partnership with Van in organizing the steelworkers. Bittner tipped back in his chair, puffed calmly on his pipe and heard them out. When they finished, he said, "Thank you very much for your offer, but we have the situation well in hand and don't need any partners."

Then the hoods got tough. Hitching their chairs closer to Bittner, one of them said, "You're wrong, mister. You *do* need partners. You just don't know it. And we're here to make a deal with you."

Bittner, who had lived through the horror of the coalfields and the brutalizing of strikebreakers and company cops for twenty-five years, wasn't impressed. He looked over his two visitors and then said, very distinctly: "Okay, boys, if you want to play this game, let me tell you about my team. I can get 10,000 very tough and well-armed miners and steelworkers here within a week, and they might resent taking you or anybody else in as partners."

The hoods looked at each other, one of them said, "Thanks, Mr. Bittner," and they left.

In the Deep South, it took the same kind of straight talk to keep our organizers out of hospitals; only the cast was different there. Southern red-necks, accustomed to putting on sheets and lynching people they didn't like, were threatening to apply these same tactics to union organizers who were telling working people—including a good many Negroes—that they were being short-changed.

I was taking a swing early in 1941 with our most effective Southern organizer—a charming, soft-spoken member of a prominent Birmingham family named Noel P. Beddow—when he halted incipient violence with a frontal approach. Beddow was scheduled to make a speech in the town square to the steelworkers of Gadsden, Alabama. The day before we arrived, Sherman Dalrymple—the international president of the Rubber Workers—had been badly beaten by a gang of thugs while attempting the same thing. Local police were somewhere else at the time.

A committee of frightened steelworkers suggested to Beddow that he delay his speech until the town cooled down a bit. Beddow didn't see it that way. Instead, he called on the manager of the local Republic Steel plant. We were kept waiting for several minutes, then ushered into the manager's office where we were invited to take a seat.

"That won't be necessary," drawled Beddow. "This won't take but a minute. I just came here to tell you that if any of my boys or I am beaten up—as Dalrymple was—I'm going to kill you."

The plant manager's mouth dropped open.

"You're *what?*" he asked incredulously.

"I'm going to kill you if you either use or condone strong-arm tactics," said Beddow calmly. Then he turned on his heel and marched out of the office, with me tagging behind about as startled as the plant manager.

The speech was made and no steelworker organizers were beaten up in Gadsden.

These episodes were sidelights to an administrative routine I'd settled into in Pittsburgh, where most of my time was now spent. In the early part of 1941, Murray was involved in taking over the leadership of the CIO, leaving the day-to-day direction of the steelworkers to me. Although we didn't know it then, this provided both a training ground and a transition for responsibilities I was forced to assume much more quickly than any of us expected.

Early in June, Murray was enjoying himself at a family picnic. Suddenly, in the midst of a badminton game, he collapsed, clutching his heart. He was rushed to a hospital where he wavered between life and death for several weeks. Then, very slowly, his rugged constitution asserted itself and he began to mend. But it was clear that it would be many months before he could return to active direction of the steelworkers. Although it was never formalized, I took charge of the SWOC in the summer of 1941.

I had to decide almost immediately whether mine would be a passive, caretaker function or vigorous leadership. Both the circumstances and my own inclinations dictated action. There were still many things that needed to be done to establish the SWOC firmly as the recognized, viable representative of the steelworkers of America. I set out to do them as quickly and as effectively as possible.

Without Murray's unspoken reservations to hold me back, I threw on picket lines where we were still unable to collect our dues. Bittner supported me in this and so did the officers of the locals who needed the money. Then I turned my attention to a major problem that had been building in the company where we thought we had our strongest position: U.S. Steel.

Grievances were piling up there at an alarming rate, even though our contract with U.S. Steel called for compulsory arbitration. When the grievances penetrated deeply enough into the bloodstream of plants about the country, they broke out in a rash of wildcat strikes. I didn't discourage the strikes because I felt they were justified by U.S. Steel's deliberate ignoring of legitimate grievance procedures.

Ben Fairless understandably didn't see it that way. He was outraged and asked for a meeting with Clint Golden and me. In Murray's absence, I entered Fairless' office for the first time as the chief representative of the steelworkers. He recognized this and directed his remarks to me. He carefully ticked off the list of wild-cat strikes, complained bitterly that they represented specific violations of our contract, accused the SWOC of doing nothing to stop them, then fixed me with his intense eyes and asked querulously: "In light of these things, I wonder whether or not we have an agreement."

The threat was implied but very much present, and I knew it was a crucial moment for me. I was being watched from both sides. My union associates and the corporation officials knew that Murray was going to be laid up for a long time. The SWOC people were wondering if I had the guts and the stature to carry on in his place; and the steel people were wondering how far they could push me in this apparent leadership vacuum. In such a situation, I was more concerned about underreacting than coming on too strong.

So I said, with as much authority as I could muster: "Ben, I don't give a good goddam whether or not we have an agreement. If you want to cancel it, go ahead and do it. But that won't solve anything, because all the trouble you're having is your own fault."

The shock effect was deeply satisfying. Golden grinned and Fairless came out of his chair, pointed a finger at me and said, "What the hell do you mean?"

I told him: "We've had a labor agreement for more than four years that provides for impartial arbitration of unsettled grievances. Yet, in all those years, there hasn't been one, single arbitration. If you want these strikes to stop, then you had better start living up to the contract and settling these grievance cases."

Lester Perry, the president of U.S. Steel's largest subsidiary, was in the room and Fairless turned to him and asked, "Is that true?"

Perry hesitated a few seconds, then nodded an affirmative.

Fairless looked at Perry, rubbed his chin and said: "Okay, if we have to have arbitration, let's have it. If we've agreed to this, then let's get on with it and get these strikes stopped right now."

I thanked Fairless, shook hands with him and told him I'd await word from Earl Moore and John Stephens, his industrial-relations specialists, on when and how the arbitration machinery would be activated. He said, a little grimly, "You'll hear from them," and Golden and I left. For me, it was the beginning of a personal relationship with Ben Fairless that was built on mutual trust and respect and would produce, over the years ahead, advances in labor-management relationships that we could only dream about then.

The immediate aftermath of that conference, however, was not very encouraging. Moore asked if I would come by to see him. He was brusque when I entered.

"About this arbitration," he said, as if he were flicking a fly off his lapel. "Supposing we arbitrate four or five cases, even if we have to manufacture them. That ought to satisfy everybody."

He looked at me expectantly, and I thought, So they're still testing me. Okay, I'll play along.

And I said, "How would you like to go to hell?"

I put on my hat, turned at the door and told him: "When you're ready to talk business, call me."

It took three days, and this time there was no nonsense. We agreed on a committee to set up the arbitration machinery and the members went to work. I passed the word to the field to knock off the wildcat strikes.

Then—with my authority established and Murray still too sick to know what we were about—I turned to the other major piece of unfinished business: organization of the remainder of Little Steel. Inland was coming around, but Youngstown, Bethlehem and Republic were still militantly antiunion. The slowly expanding ranks of union members within these companies were also militant, remembering vividly the shootings and beatings of a few years earlier. As they gained strength, they made life as miserable as possible for the Little Steel companies, pulling off repeated isolated wildcat strikes that, alone, had no chance of bringing a company to its knees but in the aggregate became a serious source of harassment. None of these companies had grievance machinery, and when a worker was badly used and could get no satisfaction from management, he and his friends would simply pull a departmental walkout. Although they were usually back in a few days, this sort of thing, multiplied hundreds of times, began to get to the Little Steel companies.

I pulled our top men in from all over the country and told them I didn't care how they went about it but I wanted Little Steel organized that summer. Then I turned them loose, and suddenly the Little Steel companies found themselves under intense pressure from both inside and out. The companies had lost their principal weapon: the threat of firing a man. The war was in full swing in Europe and employment in the United States was now high. The steel companies were making huge profits and were anxious to hold experienced workers and avoid stoppages.

The time was right, and we pulled out all the stops. We used the dues picketing technique to sign up members by posting a "committee" at the plant gate that refused to admit men who hadn't signed a union pledge card. Where that didn't work, we would sometimes pay doubtful workers a dollar—instead of extracting a dollar from them—to sign a card. As soon as we had a majority of the workers in a plant signed up, we would show the cards to management and demand an election or recognition of the union without the formality of an election. We still had the traditional union apathy of the steelworkers to counteract, even in Little Steel. Although I have no way of knowing with any precision, I would guess that about one-fifth of the workers were rabidly prounion, about 5 percent were strongly antiunion and the remaining three-fourths really didn't give much of a damn one way or the other. This is the group we prodded into signing enough cards to give us a majority.

If Murray had been healthy, he probably would have given me unbridled hell for these pseudo-strong-arm tactics. When Golden reminded me of that one day, I said: "Don't give *me* hell, give the companies hell. I'm trying to build a union for you."

We were worked over unmercifully in the newspapers. Somebody coined the name "goon squads"—after a hulking, stupid character in the Popeye cartoon strip—for our organizing pickets, and it caught on all over the country. But it didn't bother me because I was determined to complete the organization of the steel industry in this time of maximum opportunity. I believed absolutely in the fundamental theory of the CIO: that workingmen needed to be organized for their own protection. I was certain that the steelworkers who were now apathetic would be grateful one day that we had moved forcefully when we had the chance.

One by one, the recalcitrant Little Steel companies came into the union fold. Bethlehem demanded an NLRB election, it was held and we won. Van Bittner had done his work well there. Then Lee Pressman told me that Tom Patton, the general counsel of Republic Steel, wanted to see me. I went to that meeting with mixed feelings. It was hard to put out of my mind the Memorial Day Massacre, instigated by Republic, or the lies that Tom Girdler had broadcast about the CIO and those of us who believed in what it was doing. The temptation to seek vengeance, to extract an eye for an eye was very strong. I fought it out with myself, and I finally accepted the fact that time changes everything, that I was dealing with a new management at Republic and to hold these people responsible *in perpetuity* for the tragedy of 1937 would do a serious disservice to the workingmen I represented. So before I arrived, I had determined to meet with them on whatever ground they chose. If they were still militant, I would be, too. But if they were ready to be reasonable, I would let the dead past bury its dead.

Patton was ready to talk, not only—I discovered to my surprise —for Republic but for Youngstown as well. We agreed to bypass the machinery of NLRB elections. Patton told me that when and if we could show the Little Steel companies that we had signed a majority of their workers, they would enter into collective bargaining with us. That's all we needed. By the end of the summer of 1941, we had the required evidence in hand, and the final hard-core resistance to the SWOC collapsed. Youngstown signed a stipulation to reinstate strikers who had been discriminated against and pay back wages of $170,000; Republic restored five thousand strikers to their jobs with a back pay of a half-million dollars. Little Steel agreed to enter collective bargaining with us, and we now proudly represented almost 90 percent of the blue-collar workers in the American steel industry, four years after Phil Murray had pointed out a train window and said, "David, you and I are going to organize that industry."

While all this was going on, Murray was slowly recovering his health. His doctors told me flatly not to bother him with any details of the union, and I obliged gladly. What we were doing would probably have given him another heart attack. Meanwhile, some curious feelers were coming out of UMW headquarters in Washington. Lewis was healthy and back on the job, and a number of the SWOC organizers reported to me that Lewis henchmen were putting around the word that John Lewis was ready to do business with McDonald and forget about Murray. I heard it often enough that it became deeply disturbing, and it seemed that some open show of my loyalty to Murray was necessary. The opportunity arose during a speech to our statewide organization in West Virginia, many of those present doing double duty with the UMW. I devoted most of the speech to Murray's considerable contributions to the American labor movement, lauded his organization and direction of the SWOC and—in the process—denigrated Lewis, more by omission than commission. I did it deliberately, knowing what the consequences would likely be. My loyalty was to Murray and my future with the steelworkers, not the mine workers. I knew what I said would get back to Murray, and I wanted it very clear to him and everyone else that I didn't want to play footsie with Lewis and scuttle Murray.

I got precisely the action I expected. The UMW newspaper tore me apart in an editorial, and the thaw that had been developing in my relations with Lewis became, once again, a deep, deep freeze. It was destined to stay that way for many years.

Murray was released from the hospital in early fall and spent a month just prior to the CIO convention convalescing in Atlantic City. Lewis made a few perfunctory visits there, but from Murray's accounts of them, it was clear the two men were drawing farther apart daily. Murray insisted he was well enough to preside at his first CIO convention as chief executive, and John Lewis didn't even attend. The UMW delegation was headed by Denny Lewis, John's younger brother, and when the convention got to its feet to greet Murray, Lewis and his friends conspicuously remained in their seats.

The UMW delegation, accompanied wherever they went by a group of strong-arm bully boys, was truculent throughout that entire convention. Night after night, the UMW gang would show up in a bar or hotel lobby, deliberately provoke an argument then beat up the target of their wrath. They were almost totally indiscriminate in picking victims. One night they even worked over the CIO's director of research. Why? Sheer cussedness is the only explanation I can offer. For the first time in the history of the CIO, the Lewis forces were observing instead of running the show, and they didn't like it, so they took out their frustration and anger on whoever happened to be around.

There is only one language bully boys understand clearly, and when the depredations got out of hand, I spoke to them in that language. Through a friend in the UMW, I got word to Denny Lewis that if any steelworkers were beaten up, we would not bother retaliating against the attackers but would seek out Denny, personally, and see that he got the same treatment—with a few added touches. The fighting tailed off abruptly, but the UMW then transferred its hostility to the convention floor where its delegates opposed a CIO resolution offering all-out support to the Allies in their war against Germany. Passing that resolution was about the only business of any significance carried out by the 1941 convention.

When it ended, Murray came back to Pittsburgh, and I reviewed for him the results of our activities while he had been sick. Nine-tenths of the industry was organized; we were actually in negotiation with the Little Steel companies; grievance machinery had been set up at U.S. Steel and was functioning; dues, still a problem, were coming in at a better rate and negotiations were underway for a modified form of checkoff in the steel plants. We were alive, healthy and growing every day. So was the steel industry. Prospects for the future seemed unlimited.

Then, on December 7, 1941, the Japanese attacked Pearl Harbor and all these things that had seemed so desperately important the day before suddenly became almost insignificant.

As with so many crises in my life, I was in a stadium watching a ball game when the news came. This time it was Yankee Stadium, the Steelers were playing the football Giants, and my attention was distracted throughout the game by an uncommon number of military planes droning overhead in waves. I knew, instinctively, that something was wrong, and outside the ball park it was confirmed. Newsboys were hawking papers with the huge, black headline: PEARL HARBOR BOMBED. The United States was at war.

13

What happens to labor-management relations when a war starts? Usually, they're frozen, and in the case of the steel industry in the United States in December, 1941, that wasn't a very satisfactory state of affairs. We were in the midst of our first negotiations with Little Steel. Nothing had yet been resolved, and—for the moment, at least—it appeared nothing would be. Japanese bombs sank the steel negotiations just as surely as they crippled the U.S. Navy at Pearl Harbor.

President Roosevelt immediately called upon organized labor and business to forget their differences and unite to provide the material needed to prosecute the war. Murray then came forward with an idea called the Industry Council Plan that had an interesting history. Two years earlier, I had a number of long talks with some of the directors of a group called "The Catholic Radical Alliance." It had been formed to implement the rights of labor as spelled out in Pope Leo's Encyclical, which urged that labor and management learn to cooperate with one another for the common good. As we talked, a plan for making this philosophy operative began to take shape in my head. After all, both Murray and Lewis had long espoused such cooperation. Why, then, didn't it work?

The more I pondered this question, the more it seemed to me it *could* work if the proper machinery were provided. And that machinery, as I saw it, came in two models. First, each major American industry should set up a council divided equally between labor and management members. Then a National Industrial Council should be established along the same lines. In both bodies, government would have representatives sitting as observers and advisers, ready to supply any information through government sources to help council members with their work. The industry councils would meet at regular intervals to consider and seek solutions to the problems of a particular industry. The National Council would coordinate the work of the various industry councils and act as general adviser to them.

I had proposed this idea to Murray soon after he became head of the CIO, and he told me he didn't think it would work in a nation as large and industrially diverse as the United States. A few months later, I was startled to find a pamphlet in my office mail entitled *Industry Council Plan* by Philip Murray. My idea was all there, along with a few modifications added by Murray, and it brought him immediate favorable attention when it was released. I was angry at first, and I carried this anger to one of my priest friends with whom I had discussed the idea in the first place. He told me it was the spread of the idea that was important and not the credit for it, and of course he was right. It would be some years, however, before the idea was put into action. Roosevelt didn't think much of it, and ten years later, President Eisenhower brushed it aside after I'd presented it to Richard Nixon with his assurance that he would lay it before Eisenhower. It remained, finally, for John F. Kennedy to act on the Industrial Council Plan.

But in 1941, FDR urged Murray and AFL President William Green to form a Victory Committee of Labor, and for the first time in almost ten years, the AFL and CIO joined forces in a joint effort "to unleash the energies of all Americans for prosecuting the war on the most aggressive basis until final victory for the United States is achieved." So it took a global war to reactivate the dialogue between the top echelons of American labor.

Murray then convened a national conference of CIO unions to consider how best to utilize union manpower in the war effort. At Roosevelt's request, this conference urged that unions forgo demands for overtime pay during the war emergency and called on all war critical plants to operate seven days a week, three shifts a day.

While the CIO was taking this action of its own volition, Virginia's Congressman Howard W. Smith took advantage of the war fever to try to push through a vindictive piece of antilabor legislation he had long nurtured, waiting for the right moment. Smith's bill would have eliminated all collective bargaining provisions for overtime and union security. The President opposed it, pointing out that American workers didn't have to be coerced into backing the war effort. The bill never got out of committee. Meanwhile, union members of a Joint Management-Labor Conference called by Roosevelt guaranteed to eliminate all work stoppages if some sort of national forum were established to mediate inevitable disputes. The management representatives refused to accept this proposal, and in the ensuing deadlock, Roosevelt declared a national policy against strikes and lockouts and established the National War Labor Board to mediate whatever disputes might arise. Thus was the labor-management machinery constructed in the first months of World War II.

Meanwhile, I was asked by the U.S. Department of Labor to represent the United States at a Cuban Confederation of Labor meeting in Havana. My function, I was told, was to urge support for the American war effort in Cuba. This would be the first of dozens of similar assignments I would perform in the years to come.

There were some pieces of unfinished business in the steel industry—hanging fire since the Japanese attack—that had to be resolved when I returned from Cuba. U.S. Steel had requested an NLRB election to certify us as the bargaining agent for its workers. We agreed readily, sure of our ground. The result was even better than we anticipated: 94 percent favored the SWOC.

Little Steel was more complicated. Negotiations, deadlocked when the war started, were in limbo and finally had to be taken to the National War Labor Board. It was by all odds the most important problem put before that body, and arguments from both management and labor continued for several months. The main issue was union security. We demanded it; the companies resisted it. At last on July 16, 1942, the NWLB handed down its famous Little Steel Decision. It provided a 5½-cent cost-of-living increase in pay, checkoff of union dues, and a maintenance of membership provision that required every man signed up by the union to continue his membership and dues checkoff during the life of the agreement.

Nobody was satisfied. The companies didn't like the union security provisions and the union felt the pay raise was totally inadequate. Murray called a meeting of the SWOC district representatives and explained the decision to them, making no specific recommendation as to whether or not they should approve it. They were confused and undecided, and while they debated among themselves, R. J. Thomas, president of the United Automobile Workers and a member of the NWLB, cornered Murray and me. He had been listening to the proceedings as an invited guest.

He shifted a massive chew of tobacco from one side of his mouth to the other as he told us: "You fellows don't seem to understand that you got something a lot more important than wages. You got the union security you wanted and the checkoff. These things will really make your union grow. What the hell else do you want?"

On impulse, Murray introduced Thomas to the delegates and he told them what he had just told us. Murray then repeated his denouncement of the wage provisions but stressed the importance of union security. I spoke last, taking the position that the advantages of the security provisions more than offset the disappointing wage scale, and moving that the NWLB recommendations be accepted. They were, and at last we had moved permanently into the ranks of Little Steel. These same principles were applied to U.S. Steel and all other producers shortly afterwards.

The war also seemed to open a door for the unions to impress on management that a great deal of latent intelligence in the working force had never been used. In an effort to utilize the brains of labor as fully as possible, we organized some five hundred Victory Production Committees through which plant workers could submit suggestions that would expedite the war effort. The results were gratifying—for the workers, the management and the nation.

For example, the president of a steelworkers local in a small fabricating plant in McKeesport, Pennsylvania, came into the SWOC office early in the war to tell me that his plant was about to be shut down because there was no war application of its product. I knew the president of the company and I persuaded him to sit down with the union head and try to come up with a wartime product the company could make. Together they hit on hand grenades, did a minimum amount of converting and within four months were turning out 40,000 grenades a day. Similarly, one of our people in Williamsport, Pennsylvania, convinced his plant management the company could manufacture gun barrels, and labor and management worked closely and quickly to make the conversion and get into production that finally reached four hundred a day. And one big steel producer who was having all sorts of trouble operating the open-hearth process called and asked if we had anyone who could help. I sent out an SWOC expert who quickly spotted the bugs and redesigned the operation for efficient production.

I even got into the act myself. In April, 1942, Sidney Hillman— then a member of the War Production Board—told me there was a desperate need for steel plates in shipbuilding. I remembered J & L's sheet mill where I had once worked in Pittsburgh, and I began to think through the rolling process. I recalled that somewhere in the middle of the processing of automobile body sheet the steel would be just right for shipbuilding and could be removed from the line by hydraulic lift and cooled. I took my idea to the company, they looked into it and found it would work. Soon it was being adopted by other producers and the shipbuilding industry had all the steel plate it needed.

There were literally hundreds of similar examples of labor- time- and money-saving devices that originated in the minds of laboring men during World War II. The shame, of course, was that once the emergency ended, people almost instantly reverted to their old ways and old prejudices. Labor once again became labor, made up of strong backs and weak minds, and management became management, the fount of all wisdom and efficiency.

By early 1942, the time had come—regardless of the war—to change the structure of the SWOC. We were no longer an "organizing committee." That phase of our operations was almost totally behind us; we had arrived as a giant among industrial unions, representing one of the largest single blocs of workers in the world. That accomplishment now needed to be cast in organizational concrete, and it was accomplished at the SWOC convention in Cleveland in May, 1942.

First we needed a name, and Murray selected it with an ulterior motive that never quite caught on. He chose United Steelworkers of America—running "Steel" and "Workers" together in a single word—so the abbreviated designation of the union would be USA. It was a good idea (although I never favored competing with the one meaningful designation of USA), but the headline writers simply didn't cooperate, referring to us as the USWA. But we didn't know that then, so we went into the convention to seek approval of "United Steelworkers of America," and that became our legal name. (Before the convention started, we had absorbed the Amalgamated Association of Iron, Steel and Tin Workers into our union with the consent and cooperation of the Amalgamated's officers and members.)

We ran into our first problems in the adoption of our new constitution, which I had drafted and then put in the hands of a committee of directors and delegates from all over the United States and Canada. It was patterned generally on the UMW constitution with a few notable exceptions. At Lee Pressman's suggestion, it provided that any man or woman joining the union would be a member of the International and therefore able to move from plant to plant without being required to rejoin the union; he would retain his union seniority each time he moved. Although I'm not sure the delegates realized it at the time, this made the locals housekeeping bodies for the International, which would be subject only to the majority decisions of its individual members.

The constitution also provided that membership would not be subject to "race, creed, color or nationality." When this was read to the delegates, a motion was made from the floor to add "or political affiliation," opening up several hours of acrimonious debate which Murray finally cut off by speaking against the insertion.

The section was finally adopted as originally written and the Communist Party members who had suggested the change sulked visibly.

Another argument that still haunts me developed over the status of the Canadian director of the USWA. Originally, the Canadian director was to be appointed by the head of the union. But the SWOC's top man in Canada, Charles Millard, insisted the post should be made elective and the Canadian director given voting strength on the International Executive Board equal to that of the largest district in Canada. I opposed the idea, arguing that this would give the Canadians influence in the International out of all proportion to their numbers, but Murray overruled me and the provision was inserted. Twenty-three years later, that decision was to cost me my job as president of the United Steelworkers of America.

After the constitution was accepted, the delegates had to elect the officers to run their new union. Murray and I were the only nominees for president and secretary-treasurer, and we were both elected by acclamation.

In my acceptance speech, I recalled the morning Phil Murray had told me we were going to organize the steelworkers, and then said: "I never dreamed the day would come when I would be the international secretary of a union of almost 600,000 men. This is an achievement beyond anything I ever hoped for . . . Now I can see in the future buildings scattered the length and breadth of the United States, emblazoned with the name, 'United Steelworkers of America.' Inside will be fine recreational facilities, dental clinics, doctors to give advice, little theaters, all sorts of civic and social organizations . . . I have stood with Phil Murray for a long time, and I will continue to stand alongside him to build this dream and this union, helping to make it greater and stronger and helping America to realize her ultimate destiny."

There were more elective offices to fill, and Van Bittner and Clint Golden were elected assistants to the president without opposition. Then the convention was broken into regional groups for the election of district directors who would join the International officers to make up our Executive Board. I was tabulating the results on the stage, and most of them came to me rather quickly, since the directors had generally been selected in advance and chosen by acclamation. Within a few minutes all the results were in but one—from our largest district, District 31 in Chicago. They were meeting backstage, out of my view, and I dispatched one of my assistants, Howard Hague, to find out the cause of the delay.

He came hurrying back to tell us that our candidate, Joseph Germano, was in trouble. He was being challenged by a man who had consistently followed a Marxist line and whom we believed to be a Communist. The challenger had lost an eye in the Memorial Day Massacre and was looked on as a hero by a good many union members.

I said to Murray, "I don't want that man on our board. Can I do something about it?"

He said, "Go ahead."

I questioned Hague, found that one of Germano's friends was presiding and trying to delay a vote as long as possible while Germano henchmen beat the auditorium for votes. I told Hague to round up the members of our auditing staff who weren't known outside the general office and could circulate unnoticed among the Chicago delegates. Then I joined the Chicago group to offer chairman John Doherty a hand. He didn't need it. He was pretending to be confused about the vote tally and doing a magnificent job of stalling. I watched Hague's recruits drift into the room and counted them. When we had enough to swing the election, I nodded to Doherty, he dropped his act and called for a vote.

Germano won by a whisper, and in later years became a powerful voice in the union. In 1965, he expressed his gratitude by leading the undercover forces against me. In 1942, the Canadian decision was Murray's, the Germano decision was mine. In the years ahead, I would deeply regret both.

That first convention took two other far-reaching actions worthy of special note. It created an International Wage Policy Committee, made up of elected district representatives who would join the International officers in passing judgment on negotiated contracts. It also passed a resolution urging industrywide bargaining with basic steel and other industrial groupings, which was at that time a progressive and farsighted concept.

We received congratulatory messages on our new union from

every labor leader of the CIO in America except one—John L. Lewis. His indomitable spirit, his foresight and funds from his union had launched the SWOC five years earlier; now that his infant was making its own way, he sulked in Washington. Our treasury was healthy, and we had managed to pay off $645,000 of the money lent us by the UMW. We would have liked the opportunity to thank him before our delegates for that support, but he chose to ignore us.

Murray delivered an emotional closing speech in which he pleaded for unity among the 1,200 local unions of steelworkers and urged all-out support of the American war effort in the trying days ahead. Then it was over and we were a full-fledged, honest-to-God international union, well on its way—at birth—to being one of the largest and most powerful unions in the world.

Now that we had a viable existence of our own, it seemed important to me that I break all my ties with the United Mine Workers, which was still paying a portion of my salary. So immediately after the convention, I resigned from the UMW and went on the payroll of the USWA as secretary-treasurer at $12,000 per year. Murray was in much the same situation. He now held three titles: president of the CIO, president of the United Steelworkers and vice-president of the UMW. He could have saved some pain for all of us by resigning his UMW post at this point, but he chose not to do it for reasons he kept to himself.

Meanwhile, Murray's relationship with Lewis continued to deteriorate. Early in 1942, Lewis tried to reunite the AFL and CIO by proposing that he referee peace talks between Green and Murray. Green accepted, but Murray said that any such arrangements would have to be made through his office and approved by the CIO Executive Board and not just John L. Lewis. Nothing came of the move except a deepening resentment of Murray by Lewis.

Then the rift degenerated to a ridiculous level, tragic in men of such stature. Murray's niece and ward, Mercedes Daugherty, had been for many years a close friend of Lewis' daughter, Catherine. Shortly before we got into the war, the two of them took a vacation together and apparently had a violent disagreement, breaking off their trip and coming home early. There was strong enmity between them after that, and they set out deliberately to poison the minds of Murray and Lewis against each other. It sounds childish, but both men were close to the girls and these repeated diatribes had a profound effect.

An incident I witnessed in the CIO building in Washington shortly after the Japanese attack on Pearl Harbor illustrated the depth and irrationality of this disaffection. I was entering with Murray just as Lewis was emerging with a group of UMW officials. We met in the center of the lobby, and Lewis sprinted out of his entourage to plant himself in front of Murray. Scowling fiercely, Lewis accused Murray of calling him a "Jap" in private conversations.

Murray sputtered for a moment and finally said, "Whoever told you that is a goddam liar."

Lewis, angry and agitated, drew back his fist to hit Murray, and several bystanders jumped into the fray and grabbed his arm. I hurried Murray out of there and into an elevator. We rode up in silence, both shaken by this display and wondering silently where and how it might end.

We soon found out how it was going to end—formally, at least. A few days after this incident, Murray had to attend a UMW Wage Policy Committee meeting. I went along to enjoy the experience of watching it from the audience for the first time since I had met Lewis and Murray almost twenty years earlier. The auditorium smelled of trouble the instant we entered. I shot an apprehensive glance at Murray, but he squared his shoulders, looked straight ahead, mounted the stage and took his accustomed seat in the group clustered about Lewis. The people on the platform ignored Murray, but a covey of spectators clustered around Denny Lewis in the front row of the auditorium began to heckle Phil with vicious wisecracks plainly audible throughout the room. Murray continued to look straight ahead, refusing to rise to the bait.

When Lewis called the meeting to order, he ignored the reason for convening it, turned instead toward Murray, glowered at him for a moment, then launched into a bitter, personal attack on his old friend. Lewis was one of the great orators of our time when he was moved emotionally, and on this day he seemed almost para-noid in his desire to draw blood. Looking directly at Murray, he said, "This man I've raised from obscurity has turned traitor—on me and on all of us." He then excoriated Murray in the extrava-gant language he usually saved for employers who were mistreat-ing his miners. Murray sat immobile through it; the only signs that he heard were the cigarettes he lit and crushed out nervously and the crimson that started at his collar line and slowly crept up his ears.

When Lewis finished, Murray got a little unsteadily to his feet and walked to the microphone. Lewis actually cocked his fist as Murray approached, but there were shouts from the audience to "let him speak," so Lewis backed off a few paces and grudgingly permitted Murray the microphone. In a voice shaking with emo-tion, his Scotch burr temporarily forgotten, Murray denied all of the charges made against him and insisted he had always been loyal to Lewis. The front row continued to heckle him brutally throughout this talk, and all I could think was, I hope we get out of here in one piece. These were our friends, people we had worked with through the bad years, people with whom we shared a past and—we thought—a future. They were about to eat us alive, and I didn't really know why. I just wanted to get Murray out of there.

When Murray finished, he looked directly at Lewis and ex-tended his hand. Some of the miners began to shout, "Shake hands," but Lewis ignored them. Once again he drew back his fist, eyeing Murray. Then he laughed a tight little laugh and stepped back to the rostrum. Murray said he had an appointment with President Roosevelt and would have to leave the meeting. With great dignity, he walked down the steps of the stage and up the aisle of the auditorium, followed by Lewis' malevolent stare and the catcalls of his henchmen in the front row. I swung out of my seat and joined Murray, and we left that room alone. It was the end of an era and an association that had molded both of our lives.

I've never been sure why it had to happen. I've thought about it long and often, and the only possible answer—even though it be the obvious one—is that Lewis was simply incapable of sharing any public spotlight or accepting the slightest suggestion of criticism without reacting violently. The adulation of the 1920's and 1930's had apparently convinced him of his own omniscience, and when mortal men attempted to question that omniscience—as they had in turning down his demand that labor support Willkie and as Murray had in taking charge of the CIO in fact as well as theory—he reacted like the wrath of God. And most of the wrath was directed at Murray because he was the only other labor leader who had dared challenge Lewis' supremacy in this field. There simply could be no other explanation, because the policy disagreements between Lewis and Murray and the petty nagging of their daughters were certainly not sufficient cause for these two titans to be at one another's throats. And yet, there it was—a total break after a quarter-century of the closest possible association.

The UMW formalized the break with Murray that afternoon when the Wage Policy Committee—acting beyond its authority —removed Murray as UMW vice-president. Then a few months later, UMW delegates meeting in convention followed the recommendation of Lewis and withdrew the United Mine Workers from the CIO. Thus by October 7, 1942, John L. Lewis had broken with the friends closest to him and with the labor organization he had founded and led to triumphs that probably ensured the place of the labor union and the rights of the individual workingman in the United States for all time. It was a sad and tragic succession of events, and I have the feeling today that only a fundamental change in Lewis' personality could have altered their inexorable course. This was borne out by Lewis' brief flirtation with the AFL after he'd withdrawn the Mine Workers from the CIO. In a burst of public camaraderie, Lewis rejoined the AFL and presented William Green a paid-up mine workers union card, telling him he knew all along that "someday they would be together again." This idyll was shattered within six months when Lewis sent a wire reading: "Green: We disaffiliate. Lewis." Things simply had to go Lewis' way totally or he wouldn't play. The child he'd raised was now strong enough to talk back, and Lewis was never able to accept that simple fact.

14

By the end of 1942, we had finally signed contracts with all of the Little Steel companies after long and torturous negotiations. Bethlehem was relatively easy; once its management decided to go along with the union, it went all the way, a tribute to the negotiating genius of Van Bittner, who had been working with Bethlehem. Republic, which I handled personally, and Youngstown, however, were difficult.

One of the major problems was their insistence on penalty clauses for "absenteeism" among workers. This grew almost entirely out of the emotional reaction to speeches being made all over the country by Captain Eddie Rickenbacker, the World War I ace who was now president of Eastern Airlines. He was accusing American workers—absolutely unjustly from my observations—of dragging their feet in the war effort, and we refused to accept his charges as a premise for writing penalty clauses into labor contracts. The results coming off American production lines daily offered magnificent evidence of the all-out effort of American workingmen, especially in view of the strange assortment of warm bodies being added to the working force.

After Youngstown and Republic waived the penalty clause and signed, we had all of Little Steel in the fold, the checkoff system was in operation, the union treasury was robust and the Little Steel formula had been applied—despite concerted moans and groans—to the rest of the steel industry. Now we had to win the war; then we could turn our attention to the program of social reforms we hoped would follow the solid establishment of the steelworkers union.

I made several War Bond selling tours during 1943, one of them with Jack Dempsey—a big, mild tiger, affable and quiet—who became a lifelong friend after this trip. Because I could speak a sort of pidgin Spanish, I had become identified as the Latin-American expert of the labor movement, and late in 1943 the Office of Inter-American Affairs—then headed by Nelson Rockefeller—asked me to join a group of labor leaders being sent to Central and South America to encourage working people in those countries to maximum effort on behalf of the Allied cause.

The Argentine portion of our trip was canceled when we were told we wouldn't be welcome there, but we were well received in Chile, Peru (where unions, oddly enough, were outlawed), Colombia, Cuba, Panama and Mexico. We were gone six weeks and I lost twelve pounds while struggling with six different versions of South American diarrhea. But that, of course, was mild discomfort contrasted with the tribulations of our fighting men all over the world.

Most of our labor contracts were due to expire late in 1943, and we notified about five hundred companies that we wanted to open collective bargaining with the understanding that if no agreement was reached before the expiration date, we would sign an extension agreement with retroactive pay when and if a raise was negotiated. Very few of the companies accepted this proposal, so our only recourse was to take them before the NLRB. I wanted to pursue only the leading companies and use them as a pattern for the rest of the industry, but Murray insisted on citing all five hundred to the board, and the immediate result was chaotic. We finally helped the NLRB chairman pare the list to 96 companies, and the rest were permitted to go home.

We then asked for an NLRB directive for the extension agreement and retroactive pay. When it wasn't forthcoming by contract expiration time on Christmas Eve, we had the shortest shutdown on record—over Christmas Day. The NLRB issued the directive the day after Christmas and the mills all started up again. Then the hearings that were to drone on for months began. Wage levels in the steel industry were badly out of balance with steel profits, and all of us knew that when the war ended and the shutdown weapon was once again firmly in our hands, there would have to be some serious adjustments made. Meanwhile, we continued to break production records for our victorious troops who were now pushing the Japanese back in the Pacific and stockpiling material for an invasion of the continent of Europe.

On D day, 1944, I was in Hot Springs, Arkansas, concluding the amalgamation of the 30,000-member Aluminum Workers of America with the United Steelworkers. Aluminum processing was quite similar to steel, but the aluminum workers' wage level was considerably below steel, and they were eager for the security and higher rates we could offer them. During those negotiations, I had a dream one night in my hotel. I was walking down a hilly street on the left bank of the Thames River in London when I heard a frightening roar overhead and dropped to the ground as something flashed by in the sky. As I brushed myself off, I noticed two women sitting on the steps of a nearby house, and I asked them how to get to Piccadilly Circus. They gave me detailed directions, and as I walked, I saw all the landmarks vividly, even though I'd never visited London.

It was one of many times in my life when I've experienced a detailed premonition of events to come. A few days after this dream, Murray asked me to represent the CIO in a War Department tour of the European battlefields. I accepted gladly, and in July, 1944—shortly after the Normandy beachhead had been established—I was privileged to take a long, firsthand look at the state of the Allied war effort in Europe.

Our party included a half-dozen American labor leaders, among them R. J. Thomas and Sherman Dalrymple, heads of the United Automobile Workers and Rubber Workers respectively. My tetanus shot "took" in the unbearable heat of our bucket-seat DC-4 while we awaited takeoff, and I didn't care if I lived or died all the way across. Thirteen hours' sleep in London got me on my feet in time to watch a buzz bomb attack from my hotel room. The bombs fell all about us, sending up showers of brick and debris and waves of shattering noise. We had no time to get to a shelter, and we huddled in our rooms, sweating out each buzz as it grew and grew in crescendo and finally dissipated in a tremendous explosion.

From London we took a tour of the major bases in England. Then we boarded a troop carrier for a flight to Cherbourg and the fighting front. We saw the invasion beaches first, jammed with concrete gun emplacements, broken barbed wire and steel "ship traps." It was impossible for me to imagine how our troops could have fought their way through those defenses. Now, you could almost walk across the harbor on the decks of supply ships, and the beaches were one vast assembly line for war material of every description.

We had dinner with General John C. H. Lee, and over a good deal of "liberated" French wine, he explained the rest of our itinerary. Next morning, we set off through Normandy, where the Allied army had just broken through the hedgerow country. A colonel of infantry explained to me that an engineering sergeant had come up with the key to the breakthrough: he welded German ship traps to the fronts of American tanks and used them to plow a path through the hedgerows for our infantry.

We followed the German line of retreat past a series of shattered and burning French villages, snaking our way through an endless line of supply trucks and weapons and troop carriers. When we bedded down in Le Mans, I ventured out for a private look and was almost run down by a Jeep carrying an M.P. captain who shouted at me, "Get the hell back to your billet. Don't you know this city isn't secured?" His order was punctuated by a burst of machine-gun fire down the street. Back at the hotel, I learned it had been evacuated by the Germans just two days earlier. We were using their army propaganda sheet as toilet paper, a touch that somehow impressed me as symbolic.

In the fields around Le Mans, I saw literally acres of disassembled tanks and truck parts. When I asked why, I was told a significant number of vehicles were being sabotaged in the factories and would break down or explode as soon as they were fueled and driven a few yards. So the Army was disassembling the vehicles, cleaning the moving parts and putting them back together before turning the vehicle loose for field duty. We were still pondering this when we were put aboard a DC-3 piloted by an unlikely character right out of a World War I movie. Flying at altitudes that frequently seemed lower than the next hill, he took us to Allied headquarters at the famous Apple Orchard in Normandy. There I met General Dwight David Eisenhower. His warmth and simplicity impressed me instantly. So did his diplomacy. We sat down to lunch in a large tent with Eisenhower and his top generals, and when one of them began an angry attack on the British, Eisenhower stopped him and said, "Don't *ever* say that to me again." He praised the role of the British Army and Field Marshal Bernard Montgomery, then briefed us on the present situation in France, commended us on the flow of war material from the home front and said it was urgent we keep it coming.

Then he startled us by adding: "I have to take Paris tomorrow, goddammit."

I asked, "Why goddammit, General?"

And he answered: "I can't feed Paris and supply my armies, too. Here's a city as big as Chicago. If I take it, then I have to stop Patton and Hodges. The Germans will cut the wires and tear up the railroads and take vital pieces of machinery out of the power plants and waterworks and public utilities so they can't operate. And he'll mark and catalog all those pieces because he thinks he's coming back. Well, he isn't, but I don't have enough supplies to run the city and my armies both."

The next day we set out to find General Patton. He took some finding. After several hours of picking our way along roads that were axle deep in mud and hadn't yet been cleared of mines, we found Patton in a pair of trucks he used for his staff room and living quarters. He talked in a special patois of profanity that would read like outhouse gibberish but made sense to the ear. He showed us his battle maps, briefed us on his front. I asked about his right flank. He said, "Shhh, I'm holding it with two men and a boy," then sent us away with the admonition that "I know there's a bigger power than me up there, and I get down on my knees and ask for His help every morning and night."

As we left Patton's headquarters, we ran into German artillery fire and had to bail out of our Jeep and hit the ditch. When the attack ended, I tried to crawl inside my helmet for the rest of the trip back. On the way, we saw a contingent of the French Army moving forward to be the first Allied troops to enter Paris. They looked surprisingly grim and intent. Before returning to England, we looked at thousands of German prisoners, many of them frightened fifteen- and sixteen-year-olds, and visited a dozen frontline hospitals where surgeons and nurses worked over the wounded until they dropped from exhaustion.

Back in London, the buzz bombing had tapered off as our bombers punished the launch sites and our fighters learned how to knock the missiles down—or deflect them—as they crossed the channel. I made some radio tapes for transmitting behind the German lines, then we were put on board another DC-4 and shipped back to Washington, comforted by the knowledge of certain military victory but bone-weary from three of the most hectic weeks I'd ever spent. Driving home with my wife and son from the airport in Pittsburgh, I was stopped by a policeman because I didn't have an inspection tag on my car. I told him, "Officer, I just got back from France and I'm dead tired. I'll get one tomorrow." He let me go.

If the purpose of that trip was to stoke up the home-front war effort, it certainly worked with me. Once I had time to get my breath, I raced all over the country to make sure there were no wildcat strikes or anything else that might slow down the flow of war goods. Little things stuck in my mind and haunted me. The shelled-out home of a French music teacher with her piano shattered and sheet music strewn about. The vacant look of an American paraplegic in a frontline hospital. The beads of sweat on the face of a nurse about to collapse from exhaustion. For the first time in my life I hated, I *really* hated the Germans for this destruction they'd brought on the world. I felt these things deeply when I returned home, and I must have conveyed that feeling in my talks because the wildcat strikes—even though most of them were caused by management violations of contracts—disappeared and the steelworkers were breaking production records almost daily across the country. So were our armies as they swept across Europe and through the Pacific.

Shortly after I returned from Europe, my mother died quietly and suddenly. She was the last of her generation of the McDonald-Kelly family, and she had lived to see the realization of the dream she shared with my dad for a steelworkers' union.

Then, in the late summer of 1944, Franklin D. Roosevelt decided to become a candidate for a fourth term as President of the United States—and I took my first real swim in deep political waters. It grew out of my involvement with a rather widely misunderstood organization called the Political Action Committee.

For years, there had been talk of forming a Labor Party in the United States. Throughout the 1930's, the Communists and Socialists had strongly supported this movement, and several splinter Labor Parties had appeared and disappeared. When this talk picked up again in 1943, apparently with strong backing, Phil Murray and Sidney Hillman decided to fight it within the ranks of labor. Murray and Hillman—and most of the rest of the CIO leaders—believed in the two-party system and encouraged union members to work within that system for candidates holding views they could support. When a new move to create an ultraliberal political party in the name of the workingman began to gather steam, Murray and Hillman decided they should counter it with a specific, labor-oriented political action organization that could function within the two-party system. And so they came up with the idea of the Political Action Committee, sponsored and financed by organized labor to work on behalf of Democratic or Republican political candidates friendly to labor views. The idea was approved by the CIO Executive Board late in 1943; Hillman was named chairman, and I was asked to serve as treasurer. The first announced objective of the PAC was the reelection of Franklin Roosevelt in 1944.

Then began the financing nightmare of the SWOC all over again. We needed money to operate the PAC and set as our goal a voluntary contribution of one dollar from each member of the CIO; half was to be used for national activities, the other half to be divided between the local union and the state PAC. Funds trickled in—and I *mean* trickled—and Hillman and I opened an office in New York, hired some publicity people and began cranking out propaganda. As we expected, we were immediately accused in the news media of trying to take over the Democratic Party—at a time when we were having all sorts of trouble paying the rent on our office. We organized a lot of state and local groups and held dozens of meetings, but it was strictly a poverty operation. There was no duress put on CIO members to contribute, and damned few of them did.

Fortunately, we had a candidate who—at that juncture in history—probably couldn't have been beaten by any mortal man, so we concentrated most of our preconvention attention on the vice-presidency. Roosevelt had been under increasing pressure from party leaders to rid himself of Vice-President Henry Wallace, a bright and rather erratic Iowa farmer who had made an excellent Secretary of Agriculture but had been sold some pretty simple-minded ultraliberal nostrums that appealed to his strong humanitarian instincts. FDR liked Wallace and didn't want to dump him, but slowly he yielded to pressure from party leaders who were afraid the ticket would lose with Wallace on it. FDR refused to disclaim Wallace publicly, but just before the convention he passed the word that he would be willing to accept Senator Harry Truman or Justice William Douglas.

Hillman and Murray didn't see it that way, and they tried to use the rather amorphous muscle of the PAC to preserve Wallace's place on the ticket. It was my first look at power politics from the inside. I got myself elected as a Pennsylvania delegate—under the chairmanship of David Lawrence—to the Democratic Convention in Chicago in 1944. At the first caucus of the Pennsylvania delegation, Murray tried to push through a unanimous endorsement of Wallace, but Lawrence ruled him out of order and blocked the vote. Then Murray and Hillman began to buttonhole individual delegates—both in and out of Pennsylvania—to solicit support for Wallace.

The PAC was Wallace's principal base of support, and he worked directly with us during the last two days of that convention. We were in the tower of the Morrison Hotel, and I had a room one floor beneath Murray. One of my duties was to transport

Wallace back and forth from his suite at the Stevens to our suite in the Morrison. I wasn't a real Wallace fan. I thought he was pretty gullible, and I wasn't nearly as sure as Murray or Hillman that if Wallace ever became President he could slough off the people around him that worried me—and a lot of other Americans, including Roosevelt. But I was outvoted in the PAC councils, so I did my job—without a great deal of enthusiasm.

Three times during that convention, I had one of the drivers we kept on call take me to the Stevens Hotel where I met Wallace, took him down a back elevator and drove through Chicago's Loop with him to the Morrison. Although he said very little on these excursions, I had a chance to study him. He was more reserved than I had expected but showed no surface manifestations of the tensions he must have been feeling. He probably regarded me as an underling without voice or power in the PAC, and he confined himself to small talk—and little of that.

I followed his lead until our third trip together, when I thought perhaps I was well enough established in his mind to open communication. I opened and closed it in one sentence. "Mr. Vice-President," I said impulsively, "you'd better get rid of some of those left-wingers around you. They're no good for you or the country." He looked at me as if he were seeing me for the first time, chewed his lip for a second, started to answer, thought better of it and stared out the car window the rest of the way. That was the extent of my dialogue with Henry Wallace.

At the Morrison, I had bribed the elevator starter to get us an express car, and it was always waiting when we arrived. We would shoot up to my floor, then climb the fire escape to the CIO suite. I'm not quite sure why we went through this cloak-and-dagger routine. If the purpose was to keep his visits a secret, it didn't work. The word was around almost immediately each time Wallace was closeted with Phil Murray.

But these strategy sessions got nowhere. Murray wasn't even able to deliver the Pennsylvania delegation; the best he could do was divide it. He regarded Truman as a weak sister and held the labor delegates for Wallace, even after Roosevelt let it be known openly that he wanted Truman. During the late stages of the balloting, Murray left the convention floor briefly, and while he was gone, the dam broke when Dick Frankenstein—vice president of the United Automobile Workers and chairman of the Michigan delegation—got to his feet and changed the Michigan vote from Wallace to Truman. It was obvious, then, what was going to happen, and Lawrence was anxious that the Pennsylvania delegation get on the bandwagon. In Murray's absence, he asked me to release the Pennsylvania labor votes to Truman. I told him I had no authority, looked for Murray, couldn't find him and finally told Lawrence, "Go ahead and make it unanimous." I was uneasy about Murray's reaction, since he knew my personal views, but he never mentioned it to me. The Wallace cause was lost by then, and he knew it.

Roosevelt, although he didn't appear personally, was still acting from the wings like a very strong man during the convention. So it was a considerable shock to me when I saw him at a White House reception shortly after he was elected for his fourth term. It was the first time I'd seen him close up for several years, and I wasn't prepared for the degree of physical deterioration. He was sitting alone at a card table, greeting guests and picking at a buffet supper someone had brought to him. His eyes were sunken, his cheeks hollow and his complexion frighteningly pallid. He showed little of his old vigor as we filed past. His handshake was limp, and I remembered the ham hand that had gripped mine in the governor's mansion in New York twelve years earlier. Then I had a fleeting vision of Henry Wallace as President of the United States, and I shivered unconsciously just as I shook FDR's hand, and he gave me an odd look.

Early in 1945, I joined Nelson Rockefeller again for another Pan-American venture.

I returned to Washington in time to hear the directive of the NLRB in the steel cases it had been considering for so long. At least two of the conclusions were far-reaching. The board ordered a commission set up to study the matter of the guaranteed annual wage, particularly in the form of supplemental unemployment insurance to workers who had been laid off. But most important, it ordered that five cents an hour be set aside from payroll costs by each steel company to eliminate wage differentials, a problem we had been dealing with endlessly and without success in negotiations for years.

The NLRB set up the machinery to resolve the wage differential problem permanently. A committee representing both industry and labor was to spend almost three years reducing some 300,000 individual job rates to thirty-two, then establishing industrywide rates for the job rather than the man. The accumulated wage differential fund was used to standardize the rates during this period, and when the committee finished its work, we had a system that practically eliminated discrimination of all kinds— including that against workers of minority races—and was copied in a number of other basic industries.

By April, the Germans were retreating all across Europe, and I was attending a PAC meeting when we got the word of Roosevelt's death. Although I had been prepared for it after that White House confrontation, it was still difficult to realize that this man who had been so much a part of our existence for so long was actually gone. Murray and I sat for several hours in his darkened office after receiving the news, reminiscing about Roosevelt and speculating about Truman. I scarcely knew the new President, and Murray was dubious about him, even though Truman had always been a strong friend of labor and had generally followed a liberal domestic line. Truman's early speeches seemed to bear out Murray's assessment, but he was following a tough act and we really didn't have much of a reading on Harry Truman when Murray and I traveled to San Francisco in the spring of 1945 for the formation of the United Nations.

It had been decided by a representative group of labor leaders from all over the world to draw up the blueprint for a world labor federation at the same time the UN was being created. Most of us knew one another. Throughout the late 1930's, the CIO had been involved in a long series of international labor conferences with delegates from several dozen countries, including the Soviet

Union. I had attended a number of these meetings with Phil Murray, and at one of them had met a tall, rather garrulous Russian named Vasily Kuznetzov. Incredibly, Kuznetzov, as a graduate of Carnegie Tech in my same class of 1932, had worked in the mills of Jones & Laughlin and U.S. Steel as part of the curriculum for his master's degree in metallurgy, and spoke excellent English. We had much to talk about and became well acquainted, although the Russian delegates were constantly attended by dour-looking government agents and were always extremely careful about what they said. As head of the Metal Workers Union of the USSR, Kuznetzov led the Russian labor delegation to San Francisco, and I looked forward to the chance of renewing our friendship.

I was charged with finding housing for the labor delegates and finally had to enlist the aid of California Attorney General Pat Brown in order to get them all bedded down. Hotel rooms in San Francisco were harder to find than German sympathizers. That trip was especially fruitful for me, however, because I not only met Pat Brown but also A. P. Gianinni, the founder of the Bank of America, and Henry J. Kaiser, with whom I would do a great deal of business in the years ahead.

Phil Murray was a member of the U.S. delegation to the United Nations conference, and so had to divide his time between the main tent and the labor meeting, where I sat in for him when he couldn't be on hand.

One afternoon I arranged a tour for the labor delegates—which required some arm-twisting since gasoline was still tightly rationed—that took in the redwood groves north of San Francisco. We got out of our cars to inspect them and found dozens of families picnicking there. When we returned to our hotel, Kuznetzov accused me of staging the whole picnic for the benefit of the delegates. I told him he'd been around Pittsburgh long enough to know how American families lived—but apparently he'd also been back in Russia long enough to refuel on suspicion of anything American.

This suspicion poisoned all of our relationships with the Russians. One of the interpreters with the Soviet group was a delightful young girl we all admired. When the conference ended, our secretaries bought her a sweater as a going-away present. She thanked them uneasily and put it on a windowsill, unopened. A few seconds later, one of the strong-arm men who always accompanied the Russian delegates picked up the box and disappeared with it. I doubt that the girl ever saw it again. This sort of thing went on daily. The Russians had no freedom of movement or expression, and because they didn't, they found it convenient to suspect that our freedom was spurious and put on for the occasion.

While the UN was being set up, the labor delegates discussed the structure of the organization they wanted, then decided to meet later in the year in Paris to complete the formation of the World Federation of Trade Unions. We received the news of VE Day on the train from San Francisco back to a CIO meeting in Atlantic City, and the club car was a shambles by morning. We had invited the Russian labor delegation to visit us in Atlantic City, and once again I was tour director. I never found out if they thought I'd stage-managed the packed beaches, too.

President Truman was growing in strength and assurance every day. He had to grow, because late in July, 1945, he was faced with what was probably the most difficult decision ever thrust on a human being: the dropping of the atomic bomb on Japan. We were holding a USWA Executive Board meeting in Atlantic City when Truman warned the Japanese government to surrender or face obliteration from this fearsome bomb. I was driving to Washington when I heard the news that it had been dropped.

Our Russian friends from the San Francisco conference were about to depart for home, and they invited us to a farewell party at the Soviet embassy in Washington. We were standing at the door, preparing to leave when an aide hurried up to our group, shouted something in Russian and waved his arms wildly. A Russian general stood on a chair and announced to us in English that the Japanese had just capitulated and the war was over. Probably never before or since has a Russian embassy been so full of sound. For once, the Russians threw off their fear among foreigners, and we had a party.

The Russians pulled us all back into the embassy and introduced us to a drinking exercise that consisted of a shot of vodka washed down with champagne—a combination about as lethal as drinking jet fuel. A great sideboard of food was produced, and for the rest of that night, Russian-American relations reached a peak never achieved before or since. Although my memory of it is fuzzed, I know that sometime during the evening Kuznetzov and I leaned on one another in the center of the embassy ballroom and rendered "Dear Old Tech, Carnegie Tech" over and over until the rest of the celebrants learned the words and sang them with us. Kuznetzov is high in the Soviet hierarchy, now, and once invited me to visit him in Russia. I declined. I was afraid my strong views on Communism might embarrass him.

When the war ended, so did the wraps on collective bargaining, and we requested immediate negotiations throughout the steel industry. Our members had accepted inadequate wage rates throughout the war; now it was over and they wanted pay scales established that were remotely proportionate to the profits that were pouring into the steel industry. We demanded an hourly increase of twenty-five cents, and the steel companies offered half that much. After several months of hard negotiating, the spread had decreased slightly. The companies were up to fifteen cents, and we were down to twenty. At that point, both parties dug in their heels, and Harry Truman stepped reluctantly into the fray.

The President was being pulled in a number of different directions. He had always been predisposed to the labor point of view, but he was also determined to hold the postwar inflation line which meant keeping some sort of lid on both wages and prices. Late in 1945, a group of industrial leaders met with the NAM to plot ways and means of holding down the potential power of organized labor now that wartime restrictions had been lifted, and Truman—perhaps a little too impulsively—had reacted by suggesting that business open its corporate books as a means of proving its ability or inability to meet union demands. Business, of course, was outraged by such perfidy and convinced that they now had to fight both labor *and* government.

As it turned out, this wasn't an accurate assessment. Truman battled against all the forces of inflation—including labor pressures—but by the time businessmen realized this, the lines of enmity, blurred during the war, had been drawn again and we were staring down one another's throats. In the first few months of 1946, more than two million American workers walked off their jobs in an effort to establish peacetime wages commensurate with wartime profits. Two of those walkouts—the railway engineers and trainmen and the United Mine Workers—ended in government take-overs. Ours never quite got to that point.

When a fact-finding board was unable to settle the steel dispute, and a strike was imminent, Truman called Murray and Ben Fairless to his office, told them that he, personally, in the public interest, was pegging the settlement at 18½ cents an hour, and he wanted a confirmation from both parties within three days. Truman was angry and harassed and left no doubt that he meant exactly what he said.

Although our Executive Board approved the 18½ cents, I didn't feel then—nor do I feel now—that labor disputes should be settled by edict of the President of the United States or any other third party. In this instance, however, circumstances almost dictated our approval, and I was sent to the White House an hour before Truman's deadline of 3 P.M. on January 18, carrying a letter of acceptance from the union. The President's appointment secretary, Matt Connolly, asked me to wait until the industry representative arrived so we could see the President together. After an hour of waiting, no one showed up, and Connolly sent me in alone. Truman was cordial. He read our letter quickly, looked up and said, "Thanks. This is what I wanted. Now where is the steel industry representative?" I told him I didn't know, and his eyes hardened behind those rimless glasses and his mouth set in a thin line. He dismissed me, shaking hands and thanking me once again, but there was an icy edge to his voice.

Back at our Washington office, a friend reported to me from Wall Street that all sorts of rumors were floating around the Stock Exchange concerning the position of the steel industry on Truman's demand. Meanwhile, some odd things were happening with normally conservative steel stocks. U.S. Steel rose and then fell off six points and Bethlehem four points in a single day. Someone had made a considerable amount of money by keeping the steel decision quiet while floating rumors all over the Stock Exchange.

The steel emissary appeared at the White House about 4 P.M.—well after the close of the market—with a letter turning down Truman's ultimatum, and we had no alternative but to shut down the entire steel industry. So on the morning of January 21, 1946, some 750,000 steelworkers went out on strike, the largest single shutdown in the history of the United States.

There was an undercurrent to this strike I'd never sensed before. No one was really very angry, and I had the feeling from the beginning that the steel industry was conditioned to the 18½ cents and simply wanted a breather it could blame on us while its customers used up some swollen inventories. That feeling was by no means one-sided. Steelworkers who had been at it seven days a week for almost four years and had accumulated overtime savings they couldn't use during the war didn't object to a few weeks away from the mills. So the 1946 shutdown was more a vacation than a strike. Early in February, Murray got together privately with Ben Fairless, and by February 22, the steel companies had accepted the 18½ cents and we were back at work.

Meanwhile, our old friend John Lewis was in deep trouble. In January, 1946, Lewis demanded a ten-cent royalty on every ton of coal mined to build a welfare fund for his miners. The coal operators told him to go to hell, and he pulled out his miners on March 30. While American industry strangled for lack of coal, Truman caught hell from every segment of the public for not putting Lewis in his place. In May, the government seized the mines, negotiated with Lewis, gave him most of what he wanted and got the economy rolling again in spite of the outrage of the coal operators. But Lewis wasn't satisfied. He was outside the power centers of the labor movement, now, and he wanted to show the world he flexed more muscle than either Murray of the CIO or

Green of the AFL. So later in 1946, he made the mistake of throwing down the gauntlet one time too many in front of Harry Truman.

In October, Lewis insisted on reopening his contract with the government on a technicality. John Steelman, Truman's labor troubleshooter, refused, and Lewis once again pulled out his miners. This time Truman met him frontally. He had his Attorney General, Tom Clark, obtain an injunction—the weapon hated most by labor unions—to force the miners back to work. When Lewis ignored the injunction, he was brought to court and his union fined $3.5 million. As the UMW took the case to the Supreme Court and Truman prepared to go on nationwide radio to stake his prestige against that of Lewis and order the miners back to work, Lewis capitulated. Saying that "respect due the dignity of this high tribunal imperatively requires that, during its period of deliberation, the court should be free from public pressure superinduced by the hysteria of an economic crisis," Lewis ordered his miners back to work. Truman had faced him down.

Although Murray and I had no part in this affair, I recount it here because this year-long dispute seriously conditioned the feelings of the public—and of President Truman—toward organized labor. In the heat of the battle, Truman was to recommend to Congress that striking workers be drafted into the Army, a suggestion that was joyously shouted through the House but killed by cooler heads in the Senate. Truman also came very close to going on the air with a torrid speech that included these remarks: "In World War II, our young men were drafted for service and they faced bullets, bombs and disease to win the victory. At home, those of us who had the country's welfare at heart worked day and night. But some people worked neither day nor night and some tried to sabotage the war effort entirely. John L. Lewis called two strikes in wartime to satisfy his ego. He held a gun at the head of the government . . . Your President asked for legislation to cool off and consider the situation. A weak-kneed Congress didn't have the intestinal fortitude to pass the bill. Mr. Murray and his Communist friends had a conniption fit, and Congress had labor jitters . . . Every single one of the strikers and their demagogue leaders have been living in luxury, working when they pleased and drawing from four to forty times the pay of a fighting soldier. . . . I think no more of the Wall Street crowd than I do of Lewis. Let's give this country back to the people."

Although that speech was never delivered, it gives some idea of the temper of the times. This invective was coming from a man who had long been friendly to labor. Meanwhile, visceral haters of labor were using public reaction to Lewis' arrogant behavior to try and build a wall of resentment against organized labor that might set back for many years the gains we had written in the blood of our members during the 1920's and 1930's. Although labor relations in the steel industry were—comparably, at least —on a relatively solid plane of mutual respect, the danger was very real that we would be engulfed along with John L. Lewis in the tide of antiunion fervor sweeping across the country as our servicemen returned home.

Accordingly, Murray asked me to put together a publicity campaign to present our point of view to the people of America. It was rather like trying to sell ball bats in a china store, but we gave it our best effort. I hired a staff of publicity and advertising specialists, and we prepared a campaign that was directed mainly through newspapers and network radio. I arranged dozens of luncheon and dinner meetings with newspaper publishers and of luncheon and dinner meetings with newspaper publishers and radio station owners with Murray as the star attraction. He would make a brief pitch for the union point of view, then open up the meeting to questions. He handled himself well at these affairs, but the impact seemed to add up to absolute zero. The emotional climate in the United States in 1946 just wasn't conducive to listening to our message.

In such a climate, we were probably asking for trouble by reaching out to broaden the base of CIO membership. But that's what we did. In September, 1945, Murray made me chairman of a CIO committee to assess and recommend further organizing activities. We decided that the airlines offered the best immediate possibilities for organizing, with working people in the South as a secondary target. Murray turned down the airlines but told us to draft a plan for organizing industrial workers in the South. I had seen firsthand some of the organizing problems in that part of the country, and it seemed to me that a new approach was needed. Under ordinary circumstances, we wouldn't have been popular. In 1946, we were likely to be complete anathema.

The plan I presented reverted back to the concept I'd used so successfully at Jones & Laughlin a decade earlier: the concentration of organizers in a particular place at a particular time. I suggested we employ two hundred organizers in the effort and move as a team from area to area, turning over our signatories to the appropriate international affiliates of the CIO. The Executive Board bought the package, pledged us $1 million to get the campaign under way (we received an additional $200,000 from the Steelworkers Union) and turned us loose. I urged Murray to put Sherman Dalrymple in charge, but he overruled me and assigned the campaign, instead, to Van Bittner.

I knew, then, that my plan would never be implemented. Team organizing simply wasn't Bittner's style. He was strictly a hard-nosed individualist committed to the old way of doing things—and the old way simply wouldn't work in the postwar South. Employers there had no intention of giving up poverty wage scales, and they were quite ready to beat up anybody who suggested otherwise. John Riffe, Bittner's assistant in the Southern campaign, is a case in point. A hulking, gentle man, Riffe was absolutely fearless and totally dedicated. In the midst of the campaign, Riffe drove to Columbia, South Carolina, alone to offer encouragement to a group of workers who had struck a local plant in an effort to gain recognition for their union and a living pay scale.

The meeting was quiet, attended mostly by the workingmen and their families. When it was over, Riffe was warned by some anxious members of the audience to "be careful." Such warnings were not new to him; he'd lived with them for years. He drove several families home, then returned to the union hall alone to gather up his papers. Three men were hidden there, waiting for him. He was struck on the head from behind, overwhelmed by his assailants, brutally beaten with clubs, chains and blackjacks and left for dead on the floor. He never fully recovered his strength and died ten years later, in his early fifties. The assailants were never caught.

Our organizers, working individually throughout the South, didn't have a chance, and the whole campaign failed miserably. It seemed to me we were opening more offices than signing members, and the newspapers down there wrote gleeful headlines saying, OPERATION DIXIE FLOPS. They were dead right.

We came home licking our wounds to learn that the World Confederation of Trade Unions had been organized on schedule in Paris and was claiming to represent sixty-six million workers throughout the world. Although that figure included CIO members, it didn't include the AFL which refused to have any part of this organization. The Communist members that prevented the AFL from joining would prove to be a serious problem to us a few years hence. But before we worried about the Communists in a world labor federation, we had to do something about them in our own backyard—and that kept us busy during the following year.

15

In 1946, the time was approaching to bring the Communist issue inside the CIO to a head. I'm not talking about the cocktail party, bleeding-heart liberal who got worked over so brutally six years later by Senator Joe McCarthy. I'm talking about card-carrying members of the Communist Party, many of them trained in Russia and all of them dedicated to converting the United States of America into a Marxist workers' paradise. The CIO was being bloodied around the ears in the public press for harboring these people, with the result that the problem was being blown up out of all perspective and threatened to do real harm to the cause of industrial unionism for which many of us had battled so long.

Up to this time, criticism of the Communists in CIO councils had been put down because our primary thrust was to provide a union for the unorganized workingman and we didn't want dissidence within the union to diffuse that primary objective. Not all of us agreed with this line of reasoning. I'd wanted the Communists expelled much earlier, but mine was a minority view. Then in 1946, some other voices were raised alongside mine.

The opening fusillade was fired in the USWA Executive Board meeting on May 14, 1946. Communist members had been giving one of our district directors a bad time, and he made a long and passionate speech demanding that the union hierarchy do something about them. When several other directors echoed these sentiments and suggested an amendment to our constitution barring Communists from membership in the union, the argument became white hot. I kept quiet. It was good to hear someone else arguing a point of view I'd articulated alone in high councils for a long time. Finally someone asked me for my opinion, and I said, "Why? You all know how I feel. God knows, I've said it often enough."

Murray, flushed and angry, looked at me and said sharply, "Just how *do* you feel?"

So I spent a half hour explaining dialectic materialism and pointing out how the Communists had chosen the industrial-labor-union movement to try and infect the bloodstream of American life. I pointed out that, to the degree they were able to turn unions inside out and divide members, they could move in and pick up the pieces, and I suggested they were trying to do this in the Steelworkers Union by driving a wedge between Murray and Mc-Donald.

Murray pounced on that statement, interrupting me to say, "Are there any such people in this room?"

I said, "Yes, sir, there are."

He looked around the table, and three directors got to their feet and supported what I had just said. Murray seemed genuinely startled and confused, and he asked me to come to his room for lunch. When we got there, he said quickly, "Lee Pressman will be along in a minute or two, and I want you to raise all kinds of hell in front of him about this Communist thing."

This was a significant move by Murray. Pressman had long been identified with the left-wing elements of the CIO, and Murray apparently wanted to make it very clear to Pressmen where Murray stood. So over lunch I repeated loud and clear the essence of my earlier remarks, then Murray told Pressman to draft a statement of policy encompassing those points for him to deliver to the USWA convention coming up a few days later. Pressman flinched as I was talking, but he didn't give Murray an argument.

He did, however, water down considerably most of the things I had said. The statement as he produced it and Murray read it said . . . "we are run solely by our membership. This union will not tolerate efforts by outsiders—individuals, organizations or groups, be they Communist, Socialist or any other group—to infiltrate, dictate or meddle in our affairs."

There was prolonged applause when Murray read this statement, so prolonged that a hedge—written in by Pressman as an afterthought—to the effect that . . . "as a democratic institution we engage in no purges, no witch-hunts" was largely lost in the lingering applause. This was the beginning of a sequence of actions taken in successive conventions that first barred Communists from holding office in the Steelworkers Union on any level, and then denied them membership in the union entirely.

If this seems extreme, an overreaction to what was patently more a harassment than a threat, these actions must be put in the context of their time and considered against the background of the 1920's and 1930's.

From the very beginning of the CIO movement, the Communists were a constant source of irritation to many of us. They operated on every level, and it was the rare union leader who spoke out against them and their tactics in the early days. Always the word was, "Don't worry about them. Lewis will use them and then dump them."

How did they get into the unions in the first place? They were quite simply employees of the various mills and factories organized by the CIO. Some had received formal underground training, and most of them were more articulate than their fellow workers, which made it relatively easy for the Communists to seize control of important local union jobs and frequently to work their way up quite high in the district—and even the international—organization.

It was fascinating to watch them operate in meetings. They used the V technique, in which the leader would find a seat in the center of the auditorium about the second or third row. A few rows back, two of his associates would locate about ten seats apart, and this same pattern would be followed all the way to the rear of the hall. When the chief spokesman opened debate, his line would then be parroted all the way through the V behind him, giving an illusion of widespread strength. They would also wait until other union members, tired and bored, had gone home before trying to push through their own proposals. (Both of these techniques, incidentally, are being used quite effectively today in local organizations by the John Birch Society.)

In the days when our opposition couldn't be frontal, we figured out several effective methods of neutralizing these two techniques. We would put our own people alongside or immediately behind the Communists in the V, and when they spoke we would heckle them until they got angry, emotional and ineffective. And we prevented them from "sitting out" a meeting by stipulating a sensible closing time and carrying unfinished business over to the next meeting. Sometimes we would also outpromise the Communists, making their pie-in-the-sky polemics about a "workers' paradise" sound pretty ridiculous.

None of this was easy. It took a long time to persuade a workingman to take the floor at a union meeting and speak out on issues in which he believed. Most of them were shy and reluctant to pit themselves verbally against the aggressive, smooth talk of the Communists. And some were fearful of being beaten up if they did—which happened more than once.

I was vaguely aware, at the time, that some of our more vocal Communist opponents were actually double agents, recruited within the labor movement by the FBI. We'll never know how many of them there were, but it always startled me when one surfaced and identified himself—usually to pick up a fat fee for his memoirs. One I remember particularly was an aggressive Slav named Matt Cvetic who wrote a best-selling book called *I Was a Communist for the FBI* (later made into a movie) on his experiences in the Steelworkers. Matt managed to work his way fairly high in the Steel City Industrial Union Council, in Pittsburgh, and he consistently gave us a hard time. He told me later he was just "following instructions." If his instructions were to harass the union leadership, he followed them well.

For years, our conventions and our board meetings passed resolutions condemning Nazism and Fascism—but never Communism. When I was present, I would always add Communism to the list of devils and usually precipitate an argument. I lost some and won some, but I made a hell of a lot of powerful enemies in the process, and they circulated stories constantly that I was a homosexual who had never worked in the steel mills and had no interest in the well-being of the individual steelworker.

The Communists in the CIO also built a spy network designed to provide them information they could use against people who opposed them. Female secretaries were their prime source of information, and some of the techniques used on them were cruel beyond belief. A onetime Communist USWA organizer who left the party told me years later of two conquests of secretaries in the CIO Washington office. One didn't respond to his advances, and he suspected her of liking other girls, so a lesbian was imported and proved successful. The second girl believed the spy when he said he was going to marry her, turned over copies of high-level CIO documents to him, then wound up in a mental institution when he brushed her off once he had what he was seeking.

I know this all sounds pretty lurid, but it's the way the game was played in the organizing days of the CIO. There were two ways we could deal with this problem in our formative years. We could bring the whole fight out into the open, attack the Communists frontally, and go to the mat with them. Or we could play down the problem publicly while we set out privately to strengthen ourselves and win over enough of their converts to our way of thinking to render the hard-core ringleaders impotent. Murray chose the latter course, and by doing so laid himself open to attack from the press, the government, the business community and the public as being philosophically allied with the Communists in his midst. I knew Phil Murray better than any other living person, and these charges were absolutely not true. He may be open to criticism for the methods he chose in dealing with the Communist problem, but not for being sympathetic either to their point of view or their activities.

Murray believed strongly in the early days of the CIO that it would not be wise to expel the Communist-dominated unions. He reasoned that if they were summarily expelled, they would unite in a real Communist Party apparatus inside American industry. As long as they were contained in the CIO—where they were very definitely in the minority and held little power beyond the ability to harass and irritate—they were much less a danger to the nation. I didn't agree then, probably because I was too often an object of their harassment and I simply wanted to be rid of them. But I believe now that Murray's policy was wise.

Even though I questioned that it would work, I cooperated completely with Murray in his efforts to bring Communist labor leaders around to the American concept of trade unionism as an integral part of democratic capitalism. Night after night, Murray and I would take labor leaders committed to the Communist line —from the heads of locals to members of the high councils of the International—out to dinner or a prize fight or the theater and expose them to our way of thinking. We were successful in this missionary work in a surprising number of instances, usually with men who had been worked over pretty badly by employers, then sold a bill of goods by a Russian-trained Communist organizer sent over here to infiltrate the labor movement. The public statements, attitudes and actions of some of our leading industrialists of the 1930's made the job of the Communist organizers much easier. I think if one had gotten to me during the coal strike of 1925, I would have been ready to overthrow the system, too.

It was slow, plodding, dogged work, but Murray and I managed to save a lot of solid men for the labor movement within the framework of democratic capitalism, and I'm proud of that accomplishment. Dozens of our friends at the local level were carrying out similar programs—with similar success. And during this period, of course, the CIO was growing and establishing itself as a permanent, substantial spokesman for the industrial workingman in America.

Lewis' style was quite different. He wasn't addicted to friendly persuasion. Although he was just as strongly opposed to the Communists in our midst as either Murray or me, his ego and arrogance convinced him that he could simply throw them out whenever he finished using them. It might quite well have worked that way, too, except that Lewis put all his chips on Wendell Willkie in 1940, and suddenly Murray and I found ourselves facing up to the internal problems of the CIO as well as the Steelworkers Union. By that time, more forceful measures than persuasion were necessary in the CIO, even though Murray was never really totally convinced this was true.

When delegate after delegate to the CIO convention in Portland, Oregon, in November, 1946, broke ten years of silent frustration to speak out with passion against the Communists, Murray still cautioned: "Let no one create conflict within this movement. . . . I should say to you at this moment that this mighty organization is not going to be divided by anybody. It has been a united movement and will continue to be one throughout its existence . . . We have our divisions of opinion and we, I suppose, in the years to come will be susceptible to divisions of opinion. That is mighty healthy . . . If we were all united in the sense that we had one opinion on every subject, I imagine that we might become a little rusty."

The direction was clear in 1946, but Murray—still staunchly dedicated to his conviction that expulsion of the Communists from the CIO would ultimately weaken both the nation and the labor-union movement—refused to take the easy route. It would be three years before he would capitulate, convinced—at last— that he had no other alternative.

Meanwhile, there were more mundane matters that had to be settled. Our first postwar contract with the steel industry expired in March, 1947, so we were back in negotiations with U.S. Steel— where the pattern was always established—by late in 1946. As those sessions droned on, my attention was diverted to some personal problems that had gotten slowly, steadily and inexorably out of hand.

As Murray became more involved with the CIO and high-level "labor statesmanship" that kept him busy weeks on end with such matters as his service with the U.S. delegation to the United Nations, my responsibilities with the Steelworkers Union multiplied. Time and again, Murray would ask me to represent him at important public functions. Typical was the first postwar American Legion convention, where I shared the speakers' platform with General Eisenhower.

When I found I was to *follow* Eisenhower on the program, I knew I would probably be speaking to an emptying auditorium in an atmosphere of total anticlimax. Stringent measures were obviously required. It was Eisenhower's first public speech since returning to the United States, and the audience went wild when he finished and started to file off the platform with his entourage. I knew I would have to throw out Murray's prepared speech—which was something less than exciting—and I'd been making notes while Eisenhower was talking. When I was introduced I peered into the floodlights that focused on the speakers' lectern and cut loose in my best Carnegie Tech Drama School basso with what I like to call a "Bull Run" speech. I can't remember today what I said; I only know I startled the delegates of that convention back into their seats. I held my speech to fifteen minutes, pulled out all my oratorical tricks and got an ovation when I finished.

That sort of thing—perhaps at not so high a level but just as demanding of my time—was going on almost daily. Between running the business affairs of the International, I was racing all over the country, making speeches for Murray and taking care of my own speaking engagements. About the only time I was home was for dinner on a few weekday evenings. Almost every weekend I was off somewhere for a speech, and practically every evening was spent at a union meeting. All of which added up to the fact that I was an absentee husband and father.

So in June, 1946, Emmy Lou told me she couldn't take any more of the kind of life we were leading and was going to get a divorce. I couldn't really blame her, but in the weeks that followed her ultimatum—weeks in which I tried to find some way of saving our marriage—I also realized that I couldn't separate myself from my work to the degree necessary to build the sort of life Emmy Lou wanted. So I reluctantly consented not to contest the divorce after Emmy Lou agreed to let me raise our son. We were divorced in 1947, and she remarried two years later. There is no rancor between us, and I have seen her a number of times since our divorce.

In the summer of 1947, I revisited London to dedicate a convalescent home built with funds sent by the USWA during the war to our British associates. I went on to Paris for some talks with leaders of the World Federation of Trade Unions, then to Rome for my first audience with the Holy Father. In Rome, I discussed my marital problems with one of the leading lawyers of the Roman Catholic Church, hoping I might have my marriage to Emmy Lou annulled. He found no grounds for a plea, and I left Rome dejected. Our flight home was delayed by bad weather, and I missed all but the last day of the 1947 CIO convention, distinguished principally by its endorsement of the Marshall Plan over the bitter objections of left-wing members.

The 1947 settlement with U.S. Steel, signed late in April, included a substantial increase in wages. But even more important, it included the formation of a joint labor-management committee to look into the matter of health and accident plans for the steelworkers in which the corporation and the union would participate jointly. This was the harbinger of the future. The National Labor Relations Board had ruled that these were legitimate subjects for collective bargaining, and we wasted no time bringing them to the conference table. We knew we were breaking ground, and we were satisfied—that first year—with the formation of study committees. But the industry negotiators knew as well as we that more specific action in these areas would have to be taken the next time around.

But while we were making progress in our negotiations with the steel industry, we suffered a powerful setback in the halls of Congress. Ever since Harry Truman's bout with John L. Lewis and the feverish growth of antiunion sentiment throughout the country, members of Congress had been restive to take a roundhouse swing at organized labor. They finally did it in June, 1947, with the passage of the Taft-Hartley Labor Act.

We knew it was coming and did everything we could first to circumvent, then to soften it. But in 1947, we were running against the wind. The excessive behavior of a few labor leaders like Lewis and the almost psychotic fear of Communism (newspapers reported Red submarines off California, Red armies invading cities from Ankara to Detroit) that supposedly ran rife in labor unions made it easy for the forces of reaction to push through a punitive labor bill.

New York Congressman Donald O'Toole said the Taft-Hartley

Act was "written sentence by sentence and page by page by the National Association of Manufacturers," and Representative John McCormack of Massachusetts called its passage "the most vicious kind of demonstration of corporate lobbying." But the hour belonged to the NAM, they recognized it and made the most of it. And we found ourselves saddled with legislation that repealed a good deal of the letter and most of the spirit of the Wagner Labor Act under which we had won our independence fifteen years earlier.

The Taft-Hartley Act was long, complicated and written in frequently opaque language. Distilled of whereases, it basically: revived the hated injunction and empowered the courts to fine violators; established a sixty-day cooling-off period during which strikes were illegal; outlawed mass picketing; made unions legally liable for "unfair labor practices"; denied unions the right—as unions—to contribute to political candidates; abolished the closed shop; permitted an employer to interfere with the efforts of his employees to join a union; and authorized—even encouraged —the passage of "right-to-work" laws in the states.

These were the skeletal provisions of the bill. The intent of it was quite clearly to obstruct or prevent altogether the organizing of workers into labor unions and to provide employers a whole bag of legal tricks they could draw on one at a time to delay collective bargaining and strikes. We called it the "slave labor act," and that was more than a propaganda handle to those of us who had fought for so long to win the freedoms that were summarily taken away by the Taft-Hartley Act.

This punitive legislation forced organized labor into politics on a scale that never would have happened otherwise. Before Taft-Hartley, labor was politically divided and the Political Action Committee was a feeble, undernourished and underfinanced organization with about as much political clout as the Parent Teachers Association. But after Taft-Hartley was passed, we knew that our only possibility of repealing it was to elect people to Congress who agreed with us that this was a bad piece of legislation. And that meant getting into grass-roots politics in an organized way we'd never done before.

Phil Murray asked a former Clairton, Pennsylvania, mayor named John Mullen and me to recruit steelworker representatives from all over the country who were politically active and formulate a plan to use them to exert political pressure on behalf of labor candidates at every level. The men on this committee became known as "McDonald's Twelve Apostles," and they fanned out over the country to form regional and local political committees to distribute literature, encourage registration and voting, provide baby-sitters and transportation to the polls and generally work in any way they could for candidates of liberal domestic persuasion who favored a repeal of Taft-Hartley. At the same time, we passed the word to our people to get as many steelworkers as possible on the delegations to the national conventions.

While this was under way, Murray was going through a peculiar change of political heart. General Eisenhower spoke to the 1947 CIO convention, and a few days later Murray called our chief Washington lobbyist, Nordy Hoffman, and me to his office and told us he wanted as many local unions as we could get to draft a resolution in favor of Eisenhower for President on the Democratic ticket in 1948. He pulled Hoffman out of Washington to travel around the country, soliciting these resolutions. Nordy came back, beaming, with eight hundred individual resolutions. Murray told me to lock them up until the USWA convention when he would put them before the delegates, stampede them into an endorsement and hopefully start an irresistible movement for Eisenhower as the presidential candidate on the Democratic ticket. Murray never called for those resolutions. Sometime before our 1948 convention, Eisenhower either shot down the project or Murray cooled on Eisenhower. I never found out which it was because when I asked Murray what he wanted me to do with the resolutions, he insisted that he knew nothing about them and had never instructed me to get them. He had an odd look in his eye, and I let it drop. It was the first of a long series of similar incidents over the next few years that often left me bewildered and angry.

There was nothing bewildering about another action Murray took early in 1948. He ordered the *CIO News* to carry an article in deliberate violation of the Taft-Hartley ban on political activities by unions. The article, labeled "Test of Political Freedom," urged union members to vote for one candidate in a special Congressional election in Maryland. As Murray expected, the CIO was indicted and brought to trial, but Judge Moore of the Federal District Court in Baltimore ruled this section of the Taft-Hartley Act unconstitutional—and one of our freedoms was restored to us.

I was elected as a delegate to the Democratic National Convention in Philadelphia in 1948, and Murray was appointed a delegate by the Pennsylvania Democratic Committee. At the last minute, Murray decided he wouldn't go, and—as I was leaving —I asked him whom he wanted to see nominated.

"Eleanor Roosevelt for Vice-President," he told me.

"But what about the Presidency?" I asked.

"Anybody but Truman," he growled, and turned away.

That attitude may have given him a good deal of personal satisfaction, but it was totally unrealistic. A large part of the CIO leadership was still angry about the dumping of Henry Wallace four years earlier and had no affection for Harry Truman. I didn't feel that way, and when I got to the convention, I kept my views to myself while I listened to the labor caucuses desperately seeking someone to put up against Truman. The name most frequently mentioned was Senator Claude Pepper of Florida, but most of the disgruntled labor delegates knew they were just playing games because this convention wasn't about to dump an incumbent President.

It didn't. An incipient Eisenhower boom had collapsed before the convention started, so the boredom of convention rhetoric was broken only by the Southern revolt over the civil rights plank in the party platform. There was little hint of the exciting campaign Harry Truman would carry on to overcome what seemed to be insuperable odds.

Another development that made the odds so high was the formation of the Progressive Party to push the candidacy of Henry A. Wallace for President. Since this new party would siphon off ultraliberal Democratic votes (while the Dixiecrats were attracting right-wing Democrats), it was expected to ensure the election of the Republican candidate, Governor Thomas E. Dewey of New York.

Wallace told a nationwide radio audience on December 29, 1947, that "when old parties rot, the people have a right to be heard through a new party, a chance to vote for the greater good and not just for the lesser evil . . . And so I announce to you to-night that I shall run as an independent candidate for President of the United States in 1948."

The original supporters of this emotional crusade collected in an organization called the Progressive Citizens of America, and a large proportion of the movers and shakers came directly out of the CIO-PAC. Phil Murray was one of the early vice-presidents of the Progressive Citizens of America (so were Chester Bowles and Mrs. Eleanor Roosevelt), but he saw it as a liberalizing power within the Democratic Party. As Communist influence within the PAC grew during 1948, Murray and most of the other labor members withdrew their support and joined with liberals in Congress and civic leaders to form the Americans for Democratic Action, a liberal anti-Communist group committed to working within the established two-party system. As a result, by year's end about all Wallace had left were his Communist supporters and a ragtag assortment of left-wing diehards whose main function appeared to be providing victory insurance to Tom Dewey and the Republicans.

We suffered one high-level casualty to the Progressive Party. In the summer of 1948, our general counsel, Lee Pressman, announced he was resigning his duties with the Steelworkers and the CIO to become chairman of the Resolutions Committee of Wallace's party. A few days later, he showed up at my office in Pittsburgh and asked to talk with me. I always left my outside door open, and he closed it quietly, hitched a chair up close to my desk and said, "Dave, we've been good friends for a long time. Will you tell me honestly what you think of this step I've taken?"

I said, "Do you want it straight from the shoulder?"

So I told him, "Lee, I think you are nothing but a plain, stupid horse's ass. You're at the height of your career. You have great abilities that someday may put you on the Supreme Court of the United States. You have a chance to accomplish some really constructive results within the CIO and Steelworkers. To throw that away for Henry Wallace and the nut fringe around him is to be a damned fool."

Pressman stood up and walked over to a window. He stared out, his back to me, for several minutes. Then he turned around, looked at me with pain in his eyes and said, "I've got to go along with Wallace. This is the way I feel, and this is what I must do."

We shook hands silently and he left my office. That decision compromised one of the most promising legal careers in the nation. It also left an opening in our organization for a young Chicago attorney who *would* make it to the Supreme Court: Arthur Goldberg. Murray hired him while I was taking a vacation in Cuba, during which something popped in my inner ear that has seriously impaired my hearing ever since. I suffered spells of dizziness all the way home and spent ten days at Mercy Hospital in Pittsburgh where the doctors told me I had a hemorrhage in the labyrinth of my inner ear. They prescribed rest, and I spent a month in Miami; gradually the dizziness disappeared, and I was near normal by the time I got to Boston for the Steelworkers convention in October.

That convention was kept in an uproar most of the time by a handful of left-wing radicals who were angry with Murray for deserting Henry Wallace. They badgered Murray constantly from the floor until some of the Murray supporters finally took matters into their own hands. A delegate named Nick Migas made a vicious attack on the union leadership, and as his language became steadily more violent, a group of angry members formed spontaneously on the floor and began to move menacingly toward Migas. Several ushers got there first and removed Migas for his own protection. In the scuffle, a .32-caliber revolver fell to the floor. Migas was escorted to the door and turned loose on the street. The next morning I read in the newspapers that he had been beaten up a few blocks from the convention hall. Feelings were running high among the steelworkers.

Political feelings were running high, too. Henry Wallace was stumping the country with a Bible Belt road show he called "Gideon's Army," and Truman was attracting surprisingly large and enthusiastic audiences at railroad sidings as he crisscrossed the country in his private railroad car, taking the campaign "to the people." Tom Dewey played it cool. Too cool. He went to bed on election night thinking he had won a narrow victory. He woke up the next morning a loser—by two million popular votes and 115 electoral votes. Thurmond won four states, Wallace none, and Truman was given strong Democratic majorities in both houses of Congress.

I was pleased, but most of the CIO hierarchy was still disgruntled with Truman. Murray asked me to represent the CIO on the reception committee that welcomed Truman back to Washington after his spectacular victory. We boarded his train as it was backing into the Union Station. The President was flushed and elated and asked me to join the parade to the White House. Then, wringing my hand, he said, "Dave, the steelworkers did it for me"—an overstatement, certainly, but one I was to remember twelve years later when the steelworkers *did* nominate and elect a President.

16

During these years, my son, David, was in boarding school, but I saw him often throughout the school year and took him with me on my travels during the summer. He also spent a good deal of time with his mother, and there was an easy family relationship that took most of the sting out of this sort of situation. When I picked him up at school for one of our frequent outings, I usually had my new secretary with me, a strikingly beautiful brunette out of Katherine Gibbs School in New York, named Rosemary Mc-Hugh. She had spent several years as the secretary of Jim Carey, head of the Electrical Workers, before coming to our office. We were immediately attracted to one another, and she and young David liked each other, too.

The dissension in the 1948 Democratic National Convention over civil rights was a problem with which we had grappled since the beginning of the Steelworkers Union. There was no place in unionism for discrimination of *any* kind. All of the CIO and USWA officials believed this implicitly, and we had said it often and emphatically over the years. But embracing this position as an ideal and putting it into practice among men and in communities where bigotry was passionate and inborn was something else again. During the 1930's and 1940's probably no single organism of American life worked harder—or more successfully—at breaking down discrimination than the CIO and the Steelworkers.

Our Southern members were just as radically segregationist as any other Southerners, and when they moved North to seek work in the mills there, they brought their bigotry with them and infected Northern workers with it. Faced with this situation, we either had to meet it head on or accept it as a fact of American life and try to roll with it. Murray chose to attack it frontally, and he had the full support of all the rest of us at International headquarters in this effort.

Murray frequently tended to live in a sequestered world of his own, where his idealism wasn't challenged by uncomfortable facts of life with which the rest of us had to cope. To some extent, I served as his liaison with the outside world, bringing his Great Thoughts down to earth by putting practical problems before him that had to be solved. Civil rights and discrimination within the union was one of these problems. In his idealism, Murray assumed that all union members were blood brothers who loved one another regardless of race, creed or color. I didn't realize how much he believed this until he announced in 1946 that we would hold our convention in Birmingham.

I was in the South trying to help our organizers down there when I heard about this decision. I had just come from a meeting where the Negroes all sat in the rear of the hall and the white people in the front, and when I told the sponsors of the meeting I couldn't have this, they told me my whole purpose would be defeated if I raised hell about the seating arrangements. The night before I had appeared to speak at a well-publicized meeting in a suburb of Birmingham and found a turnout of twelve people in an auditorium that seated 1,500. When I asked why, our organizer there told me that the Ku Klux Klan had put out the word to boycott the meeting because I was a Catholic. These, of course, weren't isolated incidents. This was the pattern throughout the South.

So I hurried back to Pittsburgh and told Murray that we would be making a great mistake by holding a convention in Birmingham because it would have to be totally segregated. Murray seemed genuinely surprised.

"Are things *that* bad down there?" he asked me.

I assured him they were.

In the North, the situation was generally different. In the mills where I had worked during World War I, there were Negroes and Mexican-Americans, and they were simply accepted as human beings by the other workingmen. The Mexicans usually spoke highly accented English, but so did the Slavs and the Germans and the Poles. Most of the discrimination within the steel industry centered in the Southern states, and it involved not only the dignity of the men but their income as well. Negroes in the South were rather generally being paid a lower rate than white men for the same work.

Shortly after I briefed Murray on Birmingham, a delegation from the U.S. Steel plant there called on Murray and complained about wage rate discrimination against Negroes. Murray sent an investigator down, and he confirmed their complaint. It had taken us many years to wipe out the Southern wage differential in the coal industry. Now we were faced with a race differential in the steel industry. So Murray set up a national Civil Rights Committee within the USWA to look into cases of racial discrimination and recommend action to eliminate it.

At our next negotiation with U.S. Steel, I brought up the matter of the wage discrimination in Birmingham, and their director of industrial relations for that subsidiary company said he saw nothing wrong with it since the local union committee and company representatives had agreed on this policy. I told him angrily that he had a moral obligation to live up to the basic wage scale agreement and he had no right to use a bigoted union committee as a way out of that agreement. U.S. Steel's national negotiator, John Stephens, was shocked and agreed with me. He investigated, found my charges were correct, made the necessary adjustments and gave the Negroes who had been discriminated against back pay for all the hours they had worked at a reduced scale.

There were dozens of similar incidents—both North and South —during the post-World War II period. Earl Moore of U.S. Steel's Carnegie-Illinois subsidiary called me one day, said he was going to promote some Negroes from the "pit" to the "floor" of the Youngstown plant and was expecting trouble. The "floor" is where the steelworker elite operate, and no Negroes in Youngstown had ever before worked there. These men had earned their promotion, but the word was circulating that if they were sent to the "floor," the white workers would walk out. Moore wanted me to stand by with him in case there was trouble.

I hurried to Youngstown and rounded up our district director there who agreed to stand by me. When we got to the plant, our men were walking out. We rounded them up and talked to them for several hours. I needed every ounce of persuasion I could muster. I told them that if we were to discriminate against any union member because of the color of his skin or his eyes or his hair or the country he came from or the church he attended, it would cut the very heart out of the union movement. I can still remember them looking at me, brooding, suspicious, unconvinced at first but slowly—very slowly—coming around. The local officers threw in with me, and between us, we got them back to the mill the next day, working alongside their Negro associates on the "floor." And one more small step had been taken up the ladder of equal rights.

In 1948, our Civil Rights Committee sponsored a conference on racial equality at Penn State University. Speakers included a number of well-known sociologists, psychologists and anthropologists from Eastern universities, and it was attended by our Executive Board and by USWA staff representatives from all over the nation. These people then returned to their own areas to conduct conferences in which they used the material presented at Penn State to convince rank-and-file workers that there was no moral, legal, ethical or anthropological ground for racial discrimination in the United States or in the United Steelworkers of America.

Over the years, we broke down color bars in a good many hotels, restaurants and auditoriums through the South where we held conferences. There were hundreds of small triumphs like the USWA Texas district that elected a Negro Wage Policy Committeeman because he "was the best man." There were setbacks, too, but, in this area at least, our policy was always firm and unwavering and our convictions absolute.

I wish I could say the same for all of the companies with which we dealt. For every Ben Fairless—who was inflexible and courageous in his dedication to equal rights for all Americans—there were a dozen industrialists who took the attitude that their only responsibility was to make a profit for their stockholders, and if this meant practicing racial discrimination to expedite profit-making, so be it.

For example, during the school integration trouble in Little Rock, I met one of the chief executives of the Aluminum Company of America and asked him what his company—one of the largest employers in Little Rock—was doing to ease that situation. He didn't know what I was talking about and was surprised when I suggested he had some responsibility to provide enlightened leadership at such a time.

In my view, both business and labor have a primary commitment to the propagation of human happiness. Everything else is secondary—including the pursuit of the dollar. When our first objective is to build a better world and a better life for all mankind, then these other objectives will fall into their proper perspective. I always lived by that philosophy, and in later years I directed the Steelworkers Union by it.

In pursuit of that better life, we opened up the whole field of social welfare in our 1949 negotiations with the steel industry. It came in, oddly enough, by the back door. Although a study commission had been set up at our previous negotiations with U.S. Steel to look into insurance and pension plans, most of the pressure on us in the intervening year had been for an adjustment of wage scales to bring them into line with company profits—and this was the main thrust of Murray's opening statement in the 1949 negotiations.

When it was over, several local union representatives dropped into my hotel room and told me the men in their plants were more interested in pensions and insurance than in wage increases. These comments were persistent enough so that I decided to canvass all of the districts and found that this feeling was generally prevalent, so I reported my findings to Murray. He called a meeting of his top advisers, got the same intelligence from them and decided to change our strategy. We sat up all night planning a new line of attack, and we hit the U.S. Steel negotiators with it the next morning.

They reacted with satisfactory indignation through a new spokesman, a slight, diffident and rather shy lawyer with large eyeglasses and a speech impediment through which his rather torturous thinking processes were filtered with such profound deliberation that I would begin to squirm even before he started speaking. He was the general counsel of United States Steel. His name was Roger Blough, and we will hear more of him later.

Blough and John Stephens alternately rejected not only the concept but the mere discussion of company-financed pensions and health and accident benefits for union members in their employ. It could not and would not be considered, they said emphatically. Responding to this intransigent attitude, I told them, "You can't dump human beings on the scrap pile." Negotiating is frequently a battle of clichés and catch phrases, and this one caught on instantly. Murray began using it repeatedly, and it got out of the negotiating room and into the ranks where it became the rallying cry of the steelworkers. "We won't be dumped on the scrap pile," they told themselves, their employers and the world. And that became our keynote.

Blough had a rough initiation into the intricacies of high-level negotiating. Because of his apparent lack of humor and totally straitlaced attitudes on almost everything that came up, he epitomized all the unkind things labor had been saying about management since this dialogue began. Blough's surface qualities sometimes made his words seem colder and more bloodless than they really were. As Murray grew emotional over the security measures we were seeking, he became increasingly irritated with Blough's total lack of emotion and finally—in a rather unexpected burst of passion—exploded all over Blough, telling him that he didn't have the vaguest comprehension of the problems of working people because he had been born to the purple and had never known anything else.

Blough characteristically took this diatribe impassively and didn't respond immediately. But the next morning, from a carefully prepared brief, he told us about working in a factory to earn enough money for his college education. This poignant tale was delivered in the same style he might have used in arguing a tax case or a fine point of corporation law, and its impact on us was mostly incredulity. He would use the same technique fifteen years later in bumping heads with a dashing, emphatic, impatient young President of the United States. This was Roger Blough.

Another small point of rancor between Murray and me arose in these negotiations, a warning flag I didn't recognize at the time but thought about later. A negotiator learns to listen for key words in the dialectic of corporate position statements, and Blough buried a note of optimism in one of his rambling discourses that I spotted. When I asked him about it, Murray interrupted me impatiently to tell Blough, "Roger, honest to God, I don't have any idea what you're talking about."

And Blough, in an unusual moment of irritation, said, "Well, maybe you don't, but Dave does."

And Murray turned from Blough, looked at me with real rancor in his eyes, and said, "I suppose that's to be expected since you two are college men and a lot smarter than a stupid coal miner." And Murray stalked out of the room, leaving me once again chagrined and uneasy.

Childhood reminiscences don't make for labor contracts, and our talks with Blough and Stephens were stalemated from the beginning—even though the feeling persisted in me that Blough might be willing to make some small concessions if we could find ground on which to reach him. But we never did, and the negotiations collapsed. U.S. Steel, however, had painted itself into the untenable legal position of refusing even to discuss pensions and insurance. Since the NLRB had already ruled years earlier that this was a proper area of negotiation, Arthur Goldberg was able to win a favorable court decision ordering the steel companies to negotiate these matters with us.

It took weeks of interminable legal maneuverings, however, and while this was going on, Van Bittner's wife asked me to look in on Van in Daytona Beach, Florida, where he was directing a new organizing campaign. She said he wasn't well and she was worried about him. She was right. This husky, virile, intense man was suddenly and shockingly old and shrunken and sick. I hurried him off to Mt. Sinai Hospital in New York, but it was too late. He died within a few weeks.

And in the aftermath of his death, I learned another hard lesson that my ingrown optimism hadn't permitted me to accept before. I learned that gratitude and simple respect seldom survive the subject's usefulness. Mrs. Bittner asked me to handle Van's funeral, and I made arrangements for the hundreds of visitors I was certain would call to pay their respects. This man was a giant in the labor movement. He could have been either a governor or Senator simply by raising his hand, but he chose rather to devote all his energies to the movement he loved and in which he believed implicitly. Hundreds of thousands of men and women were leading better lives because of Van Bittner, and I expected at least a handful of them to appear at his funeral.

Few of them did. I stood vigil with the family in an empty funeral parlor, at first embarrassed, then hurt, then passionately angry. I went outside, phoned my office and told them to get some boys to the funeral parlor. They did—a straggling group of young staff members who knew Van as a distant organizer and infrequent visitor at the office and probably felt they were being imposed on by being asked to attend his wake. I suffered through those two days, trying to square what was happening here with my essential confidence in my fellowman, finding no way to reconcile the two, yet unable to embrace total cynicism as a way of life. Van would have smiled at this. If I had learned the last lesson that my friend, Van Bittner, had to teach, I might have been less gullible and considerably more effective in dealing with the treachery in my own staff years later.

I returned to the negotiations considerably sadder—and perhaps a little wiser. Things hadn't changed. In spite of the decision we'd won that pensions and insurance were negotiable, U.S. Steel continued to refuse steadfastly to bargain on the subject, and our pointless meetings were finally broken off on July 7, 1949. When Truman's representative at the talks, Cyrus Ching, reported his inability to make any headway with the contending parties, the

President appointed a fact-finding board of three public members and asked the union and the basic steel companies to continue operations while this board looked into the points at issue. We agreed readily, the companies agreed hesitantly. Thus began a long, hot summer in New York City, dedicated to a breakthrough of public and corporate thinking in the whole field of labor-management contributions to the economic security of working people.

In its social implications, that summer of testimony, of argument, of debate was probably as important as any labor-management conference in history. But it was also ineffably boring. The summer was hot, the days were long, the testimony repetitive, and, after the first few sessions, I was much too close to all this to be able to step back and get the broader picture that might have made the heat and ennui bearable.

I felt almost compelled to do something, anything, to lighten up those hearings, and the steel people gave me the opportunity when they brought a glib, dapper man to the witness stand one day who identified himself as the president of an insurance company and said he just happened to be passing by and felt compelled to drop in and testify against the socialistic demands of the steel-workers. Our country, he testified, was surely headed for perdition if the Pandora's box of social welfare were ever opened in company-employee relations. We called him the "Wall Street streetwalker" and let it be known that we had a surprise witness coming up, too. The musical *South Pacific* was playing in New York at that time, and I passed the rumor that we planned to bring over the lady who was playing Bloody Mary, swear her in and let her deliver her most famous line in the play: "Stingy bastards." That will offer some idea of how far we were reaching in the summer of 1949 to relieve the tedium.

The fact-finding board completed its report on September 10. It offered three principal recommendations: (1) that the union withdraw its demand for a wage increase; (2) that a noncontributory social insurance plan costing four cents per hour per worker be established and paid for by the industry; and (3) that a noncontributory pension plan costing six cents per hour per worker also be paid for by the industry. This was the breakthrough we'd been seeking, and we were elated. Murray and I took the report before our Wage Policy Committee with a strong recommendation that it be approved. It was. The steel industry, however, was outraged at the decision and turned it down summarily. Accordingly, we shut down the major steel plants on October 1, 1949.

Once the strike was under way, Murray and I had another disagreement on the direction our activities should take. My style was to visit as many picket lines and local union offices as possible, talking to the men on the lines and to their families in the union halls in small groups and using local radio to put our position before the public in the community. This meant a tremendous amount of frantic traveling, but the results in morale building seemed to me well worth the trouble. Murray, on the other hand, wanted to use the mass meeting as our sole vehicle of communication. He wanted me to go into a town, arrange for the largest public arena I could find—usually a ball park—then go all out to promote Murray's appearance there.

Murray's preference for this approach was based on two premises: (1) that he was such a powerful drawing card that people would turn out by the thousands to hear him speak; and (2) that the power of his reason and rhetoric and the mere fact of his presence would inevitably buoy up the workers and win the public to their side. Unhappily, neither premise was true. I was never able to bring myself to tell him, and I doubt that he would have believed me if I had.

The perpetuation of this illusion was as much my doing as Murray's. I couldn't bring myself to let him face up to the sort of reality that might have induced him to change his approach. Instead, I went into these towns ahead of Murray, bought gasoline for steelworkers to haul people to "mass meetings" and often handed out dollar bills to swell the attendance. Murray would give the same speech, over and over, the crowd would cheer on cue, and he would go back to Pittsburgh convinced he had whipped support for the strike to fever pitch.

In 1949, the stalemate lasted for three weeks and was broken, finally, in a rather unconventional way. I was deeply involved in United Fund work in Pittsburgh, and one of my associates on that committee—Leland Hazard, general counsel of the Pittsburgh Plate Glass Company and a legal adviser for the Mellon financial interests—invited me to lunch one day, ostensibly to discuss United Fund business. He disposed of that quickly and then began to talk about the steel strike. I knew I had a live one on the line, and I listened to him carefully. He said it was none of his business, but . . . and then launched into a series of suggestions he thought might serve as a compromise in resolving the steel dispute. His two basic points included: corporate pension benefits including social security for employees retired at sixty-five or for disability reasons; an insurance plan costing five cents an hour to be divided equally between employer and worker.

I told Hazard I would report his suggestions to Murray and call him back. Murray was getting restless at the silence and welcomed this break. He listened to me intently, said he thought Hazard's proposal might contain the seeds of compromise, and I dutifully reported this back to Hazard. Then we waited some more.

It took three days. We were attending the CIO preconvention meetings in Cleveland when Joe Larkin, a Bethlehem Steel vice-president, phoned Murray and asked if he would come to New York to discuss a new proposal for ending the strike. When he arrived, Bethlehem presented the same basic outline Hazard had put before me. Murray accepted in principle, then left Arthur Goldberg in New York to work out the details while we returned to Cleveland to put the settlement before our Wage Policy Committee. There it was quickly endorsed, and I wired the Bethlehem locals to send their men back to work, and the logjam was broken. Within the next few weeks, all of the other major steel companies accepted the same plan we had worked out with Bethlehem. The strike was over, the industry was back in full production and we had crossed a threshold of personal security for the workingman that opened whole new vistas of negotiation for labor unions.

The breaking of the 1949 deadlock illustrates a *modus operandi* I was to use over and over in later years—and one that a good many other solid union men never understood. I made it my business to be active in civic affairs and to get to know management people at many levels. This was deliberate on my part, and I had no reluctance in using these friends whenever the situation dictated. Because of this, I was often accused of being a company man, when actually I was cultivating a broad range of acquaintances in order to be a hell of a lot better union man.

But in 1949, the pension and insurance breakthrough belonged to Phil Murray, and when he mounted the podium to address the CIO convention, the ink was still wet on the new contract with Bethlehem and Murray's prestige was at its zenith. The delegates recognized that the steelworkers' achievement would soon be reflected in other CIO contracts, and they greeted Murray with the sort of wild enthusiasm that can only be generated in the personal pocketbook. Murray had the convention in his pocket, and he knew it. He also knew the time was right to take a step he'd been brooding over since the 1948 convention: the expulsion of the Communists from the CIO.

The pressures on Murray to lead this move were intense and came from every area of American society—the press, the clergy, the government, the business community. But we had bucked all of these pressures many times before. We knew that our strength lay within ourselves and nowhere else. So the pressure that finally influenced Murray to act against the Communists came from within the CIO. A good many labor leaders who had had their fill of the divisive tactics of the Communists and had spoken out, finally, in 1948, were even more vehement in 1949. And they were joined by dozens of others who attacked the Communists on the floor of the convention and in the bars and hotel lobbies outside. This pressure Murray felt, and this pressure he responded to.

He told Arthur Goldberg and me the night before the convention opened that he was going to move formally against the Communists and had selected the International Union of Electrical Workers—the CIO's third largest union with 500,000 members—

as his primary target. In 1948, the IUE had rebelled at sanctioning a CIO endorsement of the Marshall Plan, and its two leaders, Albert Fitzgerald and Julius Emspak, had resigned from the PAC in protest, insisting that "the split between IUE and the rest of the CIO insofar as it involved foreign policy resulted not from a change in IUE policy but in a change of CIO policy. . . . American corporations, including many in the electrical, radio and machine industry, have used Marshall Plan backing to set up in cheap wage areas overseas, leaving American workers without employment."

Critics of Murray's action in that convention have taken the position—whether through ignorance or malice—that he caved in to the pressures of big business, superpatriots and Red witch hunters to expel the Communists from the CIO. The simple fact is that those of us who had worked within the labor movement for many years had our bellies full of fighting the National Association of Manufacturers on the outside and the attack-and-divide tactics of the Communists on the inside. The long-gone mine worker who had wagged a finger at a Communist delegate to the AFL convention in 1923 and told him he was interested only in furthering the cause of the party and not the welfare of the American workingman was absolutely right. I had lived with it for twenty-five years because I'd been forced to accept the argument that we couldn't survive an internecine fight without seriously weakening the cause of organized labor. Now we were strong enough to throw off the participation of associates who put a foreign ideology before the cause to which the rest of us were dedicated. And so the CIO members who were fed up with the Communists and their obstructionism to our concept of democratic capitalism called on Murray to act. And this time he was ready.

After Murray's dramatic call for expulsion of the IUE, the delegates voted overwhelmingly to take this action. The convention then indicted more than a dozen other Communist-led unions and set up special panels before which the accused could defend themselves if they chose. The charges against all of the indicted unions had been prepared by Arthur Goldberg and were identical, claiming primary loyalty of the union leadership to a foreign ideology not in keeping with the purposes and ideals of the CIO. I sat on five of those panels, and they were quite honestly kangaroo courts. They had no legal standing and were not committed to legal procedures. We heard the heads of the indicted unions, but our decisions were preordained from two decades of listening to the haranguing of these same men in union councils. They were all expelled and given the opportunity of appearng before the CIO Executive Board to appeal if they chose. Most of them didn't; those who did lost their appeal, and the CIO had at last been officially purged of its Communist leadership.

Now we caught hell from *all* sides. Reactionary elements in the press and in Congress said the expulsion of the Communists from the CIO was just window dressing to make it a safe haven for the rest of the left-wingers who infested the union, and the ultraliberals accused us—with considerably more justice—of distorting democratic procedures to rid ourselves of people we claimed were destroying democracy. In the abstract, there was some merit to this argument. But the reality was quite different. The reality was a quarter-century of fomenting hatred, inciting riots and promoting chaos so the machinery of democratic capitalism would collapse and the Communists could move in and pick up the pieces.

We could tolerate this sort of attitude and behavior to a limited degree when much of management was acting almost the same way—as it did in the coalfields of the 1920's or during the Little Steel strike. But that era was behind us now. We were no longer fighting a class war with management. Labor's purpose and function had generally been accepted by the American business community, and we were ready to go on to bigger and better things for the American workingman—things that would be delayed and perhaps lost completely if we were to tolerate any longer the hate tactics of the Communists. This point couldn't have been better dramatized than the breakthrough in pensions and insurance with the steel companies just before the Communist expulsion took place.

Once the Communist unions had been expelled, there were a million workingmen and -women and many millions of dollars in union funds up for grabs, and we moved quickly to try and salvage as much of both as we could. The evening after the IUE was expelled, we met in Murray's hotel suite and formed a new union to be known as the United Electrical Workers of America. Jim Carey, the founding president of the IUE who had been pushed out by the Communist brotherhood, was designated to head the organizing effort, and I was put on the board to help the new union round up as much money as possible.

The most likely immediate source was to pick up as much as we could from IUE locals disgusted with the Communist leadership and anxious to join the new union. So I sent CIO organizers the next day to meet with the treasurers of IUE locals to suggest they convert their securities and withdraw all their funds immediately and send them to me to be held in escrow. I gathered about $500,-000 this way, even though Carey didn't seem too happy about it. Organizational priorities were divided among existing CIO unions, and disaffected members were encouraged to leave the Communist unions and affiliate with the CIO. Over the years, many thousands of them did, but most of the unions expelled by the CIO in 1949 have chosen to stay outside the machinery of organized labor.

We had no sooner disposed of the Communist-led unions than we found ourselves in another fight involving Communism—but this time from a very different direction. One of the most obnoxious sections of the Taft-Hartley Act required elected officers of labor unions to sign a non-Communist affidavit. The officers of the Steelworkers Union simply refused to comply. We considered it unjust, undemocratic and unconstitutional to single out American labor unions and compel their officers to swear loyalty to the United States of America as a condition of holding their jobs. We felt that to accept this condition would be to accept the argument that this special group of people were somehow less loyal and more suspect than other segments of American society and therefore required special treatment to protect the public against them. There was no more logic or justice in demanding loyalty oaths of union officers than in demanding them of steel company presidents or baseball players or pharmacists. And so we refused to sign the loyalty oaths.

This stand hurt us badly in our organizing efforts. As long as we refused to sign the loyalty oath, we were unable to enlist new members. For several months, we recruited members and parked them temporarily in other unions for safekeeping until the loyalty oath matter was resolved. But the housekeeping unions, we found to our sorrow, had no intention of giving up these new members without a fight, and so we finally had to yield to the pressure of our own organizers and sign the oath. I haven't changed my mind about it. I think the concept of a loyalty oath is obnoxious and outrageous and makes second-class citizens out of the Americans required to sign it.

In the midst of our trials with domestic Communism, we were dragged into a similar dispute on an international level. The World Federation of Trade Unions, organized with such high hopes in 1947, had degenerated into a platform for the Communist members to use in attacking democratic capitalism. By 1949, it was quite clear that the WFTU's usefulness as an instrument of international understanding among working people of the world had been totally subverted by the Soviet delegates. So Murray directed me to attend a meeting of the Executive Board of the WFTU in Paris in November and "smash" the organization. We felt that simply withdrawing the CIO membership wouldn't be enough; although some of the non-Communist delegations would probably follow us out, enough would remain to give the WFTU an aura of international respectability we didn't want. So Murray said "smash it"—and then, as always, left the means up to me.

Jim Carey and Elmer Cope of the CIO were already on hand in Paris when I arrived. I told them my mission, and they had no quarrel with it. The next morning as I entered the board meeting, I saw my old friend, Vasily Kuznetzov, and shook his hand.

I said, "How's my old college chum Vasily?"

And he answered, "Well, McDonald, that seems to be the one thing we have in common."

Every member of the Russian delegation had his own private

"security guard." I would have liked to talk with Kuznetzov, but there was no opportunity because his "guard" accompanied him wherever he went. And once the meeting started, he probably wouldn't have talked with me under any circumstances, because the instant it was called to order, I made a motion from the floor that the WFTU be dissolved. That threw the meeting into instant uproar. While the Soviet and Italian delegates shouted their outrage, the members of most of the Free World delegations supported the motion. I kept calling for a vote, and the motion was finally put before the delegates about noon. It passed by a large margin, and, over the screams of the Communists, the chairman declared the WFTU officially dissolved.

Following that action, I called a meeting of the non-Communist delegates to set up a new international labor federation composed of members from the free nations of the world. I urged that this new organization include the "Christian unions"—organized through the Roman Catholic Church, usually by priests who were intellectual leaders—that had been barred from the WFTU. The group moved on to London to hold a founding convention. There we were met by Walter Reuther, sent over by Murray to serve as chairman of our committee. Reuther was the new head of the United Automobile Workers, a ruddy-faced, garrulous, volatile man whom I knew only superficially through small-talk at CIO meetings.

In London, we got well acquainted—in a negative sort of way. Reuther objected strongly to inclusion of the Christian unions of Europe, and we had a real battle over this issue that ended in the division of our delegation. Reuther made the same argument I'd heard so often at the WFTU: that the Christian unions—which represented perhaps one-third of the workers of Western Europe—were controlled by the Catholic Church and therefore not free agents. The Christian union leaders, on hand in London to present their credentials and support for the new organization, finally said to hell with it and went home. So the International Confederation of Free Trade Unions came into being minus a large and influential group of member unions of great importance. And I headed home from London feeling the stirrings of a cordial dislike for Walter Reuther, an attitude which I'm afraid hasn't changed very much over the intervening years.

I returned to the United States on the *Queen Mary*, in the company of the entire AFL delegation that had journeyed to London to take part in the formation of the ICFTU. During the seven days on shipboard, I had a number of long talks with AFL President Bill Green and some of his associates about the possible reuniting of the AFL and CIO. During those conversations, the principal barrier to such an amalgamation came through to me loud and clear. Neither Green nor Phil Murray would defer to the other as head of a combined organization. I got off the ship in New York certain that until one or the other had passed from the scene, there would be no possibility of unity.

Back home, I took a personal step I'd been weighing for many months: I asked my secretary, Rosemary McHugh, to marry me. I'd been in love with her for a long time, and so had my son, who looked forward to Rosemary's visits to his school as much as he did mine. We had some serious problems with Rosemary's family. She was a devout Catholic, and since Rome had refused to annul my first marriage, Rosemary and I would have to be married outside the Church. When her family found out she was going to go through with it anyway, they consented grudgingly. Rosemary and I decided at a New Year's party to slip over to New Jersey— where there was no waiting period—and get married. The next day some of my New York friends somehow telescoped three days of tests and legal details into a single morning and State Supreme Court Justice Samuel DiFalco agreed to marry us at the Roosevelt Hotel in New York on the evening of January 3. And that's the way it was. Nordy Hoffman, dispatched to Long Island to bring my son in for the wedding, got lost on the way back and arrived just as the ceremony was ending. But young David went to dinner with Rosemary and me, and that close relationship has grown closer, if anything, over the years.

Rosemary had been working for eight years in various CIO offices, the last three years as my secretary. She knew the demands of my job and the intensity of my dedication to it. She shared that dedication and worked side by side with me when she could and released me without reservation when she couldn't. It was a relationship fortified with both love and understanding. Rosemary's faith and unflinching support made it possible for me to achieve the victories and accept the setbacks that lay ahead.

At first, there were only victories, although the most important of those victories grew out of a personal tragedy that I wasn't yet quite prepared for. Before that happened, however, the United States found itself in another shooting war in Korea, and I was asked by Secretary of Defense George Marshall to serve on a citizens' committee touring our military installations to suggest reforms that might step up efficiency or promote economy.

At that time, the Army was struggling with integration problems, and we ran into the two extremes of attitude on one post in South Carolina. When we asked the commanding general, a West Pointer, how many Negroes he had in his command, he told us: "I don't know. I can't recognize the color of the faces of my men." A Southerner who was commanding a National Guard division on the same base told us: "We know how to handle our nigras. We don't have any integration problems." We started a mild hassle at the USO in Columbia when we found Negroes weren't being admitted. Our chairman, Clarence Francis of General Foods Corporation, raised enough hell with USO officials that the doors were opened to all members of the Armed Forces before we left.

I think we made some other positive contributions. For example, we suggested the expansion of cooperative training maneuvers between ground troops and aircraft, some basic reforms in the buying and preparation of food and the more efficient handling of personnel records.

When I returned from this junket, Murray assigned me the job of drafting a program for presentation to the steel industry. Our contract expired December 31, 1951, and we entered negotiations with U.S. Steel a month earlier. We presented a 32-point program and the company turned down every proposal. The U.S. Steel negotiators then came up with a series of counterproposals that would give management the right to eliminate and combine jobs and increase work loads without any additional compensation for the employee and without permitting the employee the use of the grievance procedure long established in our contracts.

It looked like a long, cold winter ahead. And it was.

17

Nineteen fifty-two was the most fateful year of my life. It started in strife, bottomed in tragedy and ended in a personal triumph that I wish might have come about in some other way.

Our month of negotiating with U.S. Steel at the end of 1951 was fruitless. The company negotiators refused to bargain on our proposals and we obviously couldn't agree to theirs, which would have negated many of the advances we had made with such difficulty over the past decade. The result was a complete deadlock. Feelings were intense and some of the exchanges were angry. The temper of the nation in those Red-baiting years of Joe McCarthy was to kick the unions while they seemed to be down, and the steel industry, apparently intending to push this attitude as far as it could in our negotiations, was making impossible demands on us. We had no alternative to shutting down the industry. In this crisis, Cyrus Ching, director of the Federal Mediation and Conciliation Service, urged—at President Truman's request—that the union and members of the ten major steel companies meet with him to try and find some means of settling the dispute. Murray decided to accept this invitation, but for some reason he wanted to shift the responsibility for the decision elsewhere. So he called a special convention of the union to consider our position and decide whether or not to accept Ching's invitation.

This peculiar affair was an expensive waste of time, since its decision was foreordained and we had already prepared a document accepting the government's proposal. The night before the convention met, Murray held a press conference, and when a reporter he didn't like asked if he intended to accept the President's invitation, Murray answered sarcastically, "I imagine the United Steelworkers will be represented." I knew he'd blown the whole convention with that offhand remark, although he didn't seem to be aware of the implication of what he'd said.

Naturally, the morning papers carried a statement, attributed to Murray, that the Steelworkers had already decided on an action that supposedly was going to be debated that day at the convention. Murray caught up with me outside the convention hall and was furious. Brandishing a newspaper, he shouted, "How the hell did they get ahold of this story. Did you leak it to them?"

I tried to explain what had happened at the press conference, but he wasn't listening and he was still very angry with me when we opened the convention. It was, of course, a travesty. The delegates had all read the morning papers, too. During a break, one of them cornered me and said, "What the hell is this farce all about? We can read. We know what we're supposed to do. So for God's sake, let's get it over with and go home."

That pretty well reflected the attitude of most of the delegates. They didn't disapprove of our acceptance of Truman's invitation, but they were deeply resentful at being summoned to rubber-stamp a decision Murray had already made. They resisted the impulse to spit in Murray's eye, did what he wanted and went home.

Murray's behavior over the past year had grown erratic and unpredictable. He was deeply concerned about his health. In addition to a serious operation for an infected pancreas, he'd had several more mild heart attacks, and he lived in constant fear of another major seizure. This fear seldom slowed down his union activity, but it did tend to make him emotionally high-strung and excitable over things that in earlier years he would simply have ignored.

His attitude toward me had become extremely volatile. I never knew from one day to the next whether he would regard me as a loyal confidant or an ambitious rival. I knew he wasn't well, and I avoided arguing with him or giving him any cause for being upset with me. In spite of my efforts, however, he continued to regard me on and off with deep suspicion. In the aftermath of the special convention, he called me into his office, visibly agitated, and said, "David, I understand that you are planning to run against me for the presidency of the Steelworkers."

I was honestly shocked. The thought had never occurred to me.

"Whoever told you that," I said heatedly, "is a goddam liar. Bring him in here so I can tell him to his face. Who is it?"

"I'm not going to tell you," Murray said, "but it's a responsible source and I understand that's what you have in mind."

I could have wept—and almost did.

I looked Murray directly in the eye and said, "Look, boss, I've been with you since I was a kid. I've done everything that you ever wanted me to do. You've been like a second father to me. How in Christ's name could you even begin to think that I would try to upset you?" I hesitated while thirty years of loyal service ricocheted through my mind. Then I pounded his desk with my fist and said with all the emphasis I could muster, "If you don't believe me, then here is my resignation."

That got through to him. His flush receded and he said, "All right, all right, David. Take it easy, now."

But I wasn't ready to take it easy. I said, "Mr. Murray, do you think I could beat you in an election for the presidency of the Steelworkers?"

He said, very quietly, "No."

"Well then," I told him, "for God's sake give me credit for having that much sense. And please give me the chance to tell off the bastards who brought you that story."

Thoroughly mollified now, he stood up, put his arm around my shoulder and said, "Forget it, kid. Please just forget it."

The moment passed, but it would return. A perceptive columnist said of Murray at this stage in his life that he "would kick his best friends in the shins while his enemies trod on his toes." And Westbrook Pegler, the notorious union-baiter, called Murray "Saint Philip the Previous." Both assessments were painfully accurate, but in those last few months, I did my best to protect him from this sort of criticism—and from himself—with the result that he began to turn on me.

In this atmosphere of severe personal strain and strong public antipathy, the Federal Government brought us before the Wage Stabilization Board to argue out our dispute with the steel industry. And we found ourselves back in New York with the prospect of another long, dreary period of listening to the same arguments and legal briefs we could all recite almost by rote. This time, however, there was no byplay to lighten the atmosphere. This time there were anger and enmity and recrimination.

It was due in no small part to a new face on the steel team, a tall, broad-shouldered, hard-nosed former football All-American named R. Conrad Cooper, who had risen quickly through the ranks of U.S. Steel to the job of assistant to Industrial-Relations Director John Stephens. Cooper came into these negotiations with blood in his eye. Compromise wasn't part of his lexicon at that stage, and only his subordinate position on the negotiating team kept him from tearing us apart. I marked him then as a tough man to contend with; a few years later I would find out just *how* rough when we met on another battlefield as the primary antagonists.

The Wage Stabilization Board hearings continued for almost three months. When the board issued its report early in April, it granted many of the points we requested and none of the basic demands of the steel companies. The steel industry was outraged, screamed that the decision was "prolabor and inflationary" and refused to comply with it. On April 8, 1952, Harry Truman scheduled a television speech to announce his decision for dealing with the steel crisis. We settled down to watch the speech in Murray's hotel suite in New York. We had no idea what Truman was going to say, and as we waited for him to appear, Murray asked me if we were ready to order an immediate shutdown on the mills if circumstances dictated. I told him it would take only a phone call to start the machinery in motion.

Truman was angry, a state of mind not uncommon to him in these troubled days. His message was brief and to the point. He said that our involvement in Korea made it essential to keep the steel mills in operation and since the steel industry had refused to accept a settlement arrived at through duly constituted legal machinery, it would be necessary for the government to step in and operate the plants.

Once again, the steel industry was outraged. While the U.S. flag was being raised over steel plants across the country, the industry went to court to argue that Truman had acted beyond his authority. For the first time since Roosevelt's death, Murray was delighted with Harry Truman. During the President's speech, Murray kept shouting, "Attaboy, Harry," and when it was over he told me to order our workers to stay on the job. The next day we traveled to Washington to work out the mechanics of operating the plants with Secretary of Commerce Charles Sawyer. He was confused and had no desire for the job that had been thrust on him. I didn't blame him. I didn't share the enthusiasm of Murray and the rest of my associates over the seizure. The mills would be operating under the same management and the same wage rates as before. The change was technical rather than fundamental, and we would receive none of the awards granted us by the Wage Stabilization Board. I didn't say these things aloud because I didn't want to dampen the prevailing enthusiasm. But I thought them, and I had a deep distrust of the government moving this substantially into our affairs.

The government operation didn't last very long. While an angry Congress was stripping the Wage Stabilization Board of its powers, a district court ruled that the President's seizure of the steel mills was illegal. The plants reverted to the steel companies and we pulled our men out immediately. Three days later, the U.S. Court of Appeals restored Federal control and we sent our members back to work. And on June 2, the Supreme Court of the United States supported the original district court decision, declared the Federal action unconstitutional, and the entire industry was shut down by the largest strike in the nation's history.

Clarence Randall, the president of Inland Steel, who seemed to be acting as spokesman for the steel industry in this crisis, then went on the air with an intemperate and vituperative speech in which he was violently critical of the President of the United States and declared that Murray's "subversive actions" were aiding the Communists and "threatening the safety of American soldiers in Korea." It was a familiar theme that I thought had played itself out long ago. But in 1952, the steel industry was trying very hard to turn the clock backward.

Feelings were strong on both sides. The military raised hell about steel already produced lying in the plants so I set up a scheme called Operation Cleanout under which our people would release militarily crucial steel previously rolled. Several members of our Wage Policy Committee strongly opposed this plan. I remember one angry member standing and saying, very deliberately: "I have a son in Korea and I'd rather see him killed than go along with this plan." But it was overwhelmingly accepted.

The strike lasted fifty-four days and cost the nation eighteen million tons of steel. Antagonized by the adverse court decisions and the steel industry's refusal to accept the recommendations of his Wage Stabilization Board, Truman declined to invoke the Taft-Hartley cooling-off period and permitted the strike to throttle the industry. Finally, early in July when no progress had been made by his Mediation Service in getting us together, Truman convened a White House meeting of the principals in the steel strike. We met in the Cabinet Room, and the atmosphere was tense and acrimonious. When Truman entered briskly, we all stood and he made the rounds shaking hands. Each participant in turn addressed him as "Mr. President" except Randall, who called him "Mr. Truman," a distinction that wasn't lost on the President from the momentary flash of anger that reflected off his glasses.

The President told us with surprising calmness in view of the combustible ingredients of the situation that the nation's war effort and economy were both being grievously damaged by the strike and a settlement would have to be reached. He ordered us to get back to negotiations immediately and stay in them until we had some sort of accord. He was firm, sure of himself and came on very strong. He then left us in the Cabinet Room to talk.

The primary issue on which we were hung up was the matter of the union shop. The first hint of a break in the monolithic front of the steel industry's opposition to the union shop came in the Cabinet Room when Charley White, the president of Republic Steel, suggested that a union shop might be satisfactory if we would make an exception of old-line "loyal" employees who didn't want to join. Although his associates took angry issue with him then, the subsequent settlement followed these lines.

But that wasn't to come until several weeks later, when Truman, in desperation, called Murray and Ben Fairless to the White House, sent them to the Fish Room alone and told them not to come out until they had reached some sort of agreement. Then he set out on a televised tour of the newly decorated White House, while Clarence Randall and I watched on a TV set in the Presidential office and sweated out Murray and Fairless talking down the hall. They emerged three hours later with an agreement. In return for the steel industry moving off its inflexible position on the union shop, the Federal Government—through John Steelman, who was now Acting Defense Mobilizer—had overruled its own Office of Price Stabilization and granted the steel industry a price increase that soothed its feelings and enhanced its profits.

Murray and I were elated and hurried back to our hotel to summon the Wage Policy Committee. While the members were gathering, our International Executive Board endorsed the settlement, and we went before the Wage Policy Committee proud of our achievement in protecting the union shop. We got a totally unexpected reaction. Murray reported the terms of the agreement to the committee, then settled back to await its approbation. What he got instead was dead silence. This made Murray angry, and he rose and asked them what the hell they meant by giving him the silent treatment. Did this mean, he asked, that they didn't approve of the agreement? Again, silence.

I was afraid Murray was going to have another heart attack on the spot, and I stepped quickly into the breach with another Bull Run effort. I explained in highly dramatic terms the tensions and complexities of our confrontation with the steel negotiators and the highest officials of the United States. And I ended by telling the members of the committee that this was Murray's crowning effort, the greatest achievement he'd pulled off in thirty-five years of grinding conflict with the magnates of the coal and steel industries. When I finished, they were on their feet applauding. And while they were in that frame of mind, Murray topped my performance by producing Ben Fairless and introducing him to the Wage Policy Committee.

Fairless was a thick, balding, unpretentious man who came on in such low key that his easygoing manner frequently hid the brilliant mind and near-flawless judgment that lay behind it. He struck just the right tone in this meeting, ending a brief talk by saying something I believed very deeply: that there had to be another and better way of settling disputes that were injurious to everyone involved. He suggested that Murray accompany him on a nationwide tour of U.S. Steel's mills and try to build better relations from the ground up by talking with workers and management at the plant level. Fairless and Murray made a handshake agreement before the committee members to take such a tour. As I watched in silent approval, it never occurred to me that I would be making that trip instead of Phil Murray.

It was time for another Democratic National Convention, and I served once again as a delegate from Pennsylvania. This time the CIO-PAC candidate, Governor Adlai Stevenson of Illinois, was the winner of a struggle with Senator Estes Kefauver of Tennessee and a Southern coalition united behind Senator Richard Russell of Georgia. I had little enthusiasm for Stevenson. When he tried to avoid the nomination by telling his supporters before the convention that he was "not competent" to be President of the United States, I believed him. My choice was Averell Harriman, but the old-line powers of the Democratic Party—including Murray and the PAC—had agreed on Stevenson before the convention opened, and he was nominated on the third ballot. It really didn't make much difference who the Democrats nominated anyway. Eisenhower was the Republican nominee, and no man alive could have beaten him. He was swept into the White House on a plurality of 6½ million votes that also gave him a Republican Congress for the first time since Herbert Hoover. Things had been tough enough for labor the past two years under a Democratic Congress. Now with Senator Joseph McCarthy and his Red-baiting tactics scaring hell out of great segments of the population and a Republican Congress in Washington, our prospects were something less than bright.

It was in this rather sobering political and philosophical climate that we headed for San Francisco for a Steelworkers conference, then to Los Angeles for the CIO convention late in 1952. Murray had driven himself hard during the Stevenson campaign, riding trains all over the East and Midwest, trying to drum up labor support for his candidate. Murray's doctor had told him not to fly, and so long trips meant days of clattering across the country on a train. I tried to talk him out of going to San Francisco. I told him I could handle that meeting and he should go directly to Los Angeles and rest a couple of days before the CIO convention. He said he'd think about it, and we parted company. I had to make a speech near Pittsburgh, then fly to San Francisco from there.

When I arrived on the West Coast, I found that Murray was en route to San Francisco by train after all. He arrived in time to speak to a dinner meeting on the second night of the conference. I was busy with other matters and didn't see him until I got to the dinner late and found his speech under way. Murray looked tired and drawn, and someone told me that he had been speaking for almost two hours already. He went on for another half hour after I arrived. I knew he must have been rambling rather badly because the audience was restless and uneasy. When he finished, I went up on the stage to welcome him. His handshake was limp and his eyes glazed and I suggested he get to bed and rest up from his trip. He said that's where he was going, and wobbled out of the auditorium. I debated helping him across the street to his hotel, thought he would resent it and decided against it. It was the last time I saw Phil Murray alive.

I had a few drinks with some of the district directors and went to bed. The sun was streaming through my window but I was still sleeping soundly when the phone awoke me. Nordy Hoffman was in Murray's room. Mrs. Murray had been unable to rouse Phil in the morning and had called the house doctor. Nordy followed him into Murray's room and heard the verdict. Murray had suffered a massive heart attack during the night. He was dead when the doctor arrived.

I hung up the phone and sat on the edge of the bed, staring out of my hotel window into the rare San Francisco sunlight that reflected splendidly off the Golden Gate Bridge in the far distance. A thousand thoughts tumbled over one another in my consciousness. A friend was gone, a man with whom my life had been en-twined for more than thirty years. That was the first thought. The second, tumbling on top of the first was, My God, what's going to happen now? To me, to the union, to the labor movement?

For a second or two, my conscious mind refused to consider my own future, as if it were somehow irreverent so soon after the news of this tragedy. But I couldn't put it away, so finally I looked at it straight. I knew I had prepared myself well for the responsi-bility, and I knew I would have to be strong and forceful to fill this temporary power vacuum. I was certain I could handle the job. I had already handled it many times. Only the title and the author-ity had been lacking, and now these would be mine, too.

I swung out of bed, dressed quickly and hurried down to the Murray suite. Mrs. Murray was in shock, sitting in a straight chair between Phil's secretary and Nordy Hoffman, looking straight ahead, her eyes frightened and bewildered. I took her hand, ex-pressed my sympathy and asked if she would like me to take over the necessary arrangements. She accepted gratefully.

It was good to be busy at such a time. I arranged for Murray's body to be flown back to Pittsburgh and we followed the next day. There was to be a state funeral in St. Paul's Cathedral, and I was meeting with the CIO Executive Board members to explain the arrangements to them and soothe the ruffled feelings of pseudo big shots who hadn't been selected as pallbearers when the hotel manager opened the door, whispered my name and beckoned me out. In the hall, he looked away from me uneasily and said, "David has just been killed, but your wife is all right."

Rosemary had gone to school to pick up David that morning, and the enormity of what I'd just been told hit me like a bludgeon. I became light-headed, the hallway began whirling and I grabbed at a door casement. CIO vice-president Allan Heywood had fol-lowed me out of the room, and he caught me as I started down. Dimly I could hear his words in my ear, "Dave, my God, Dave. He didn't say *killed*. He said *keeled*. David keeled over at school and Rosemary took him home and that's where they are now. He's all right, Dave."

Slowly Allan got through to me, but it had been a shattering experience. I had to go home to see for myself, and I stayed there for a few hours, then, much against Rosemary's wishes, went back to the hotel.

Dozens of high-ranking government officials and every name of note in the labor field were on hand for the Murray services—with perhaps one exception. If John L. Lewis came to pay his last respects to Phil Murray, I didn't see him. When it was over, there was an aura of death over the Steelworkers Union. I knew it couldn't be permitted to linger long, and two days after the funeral, I convened a meeting of the Executive Board. The king was dead, but the kingdom had to function.

There was no question raised in the high councils of the union about my succession to Murray's job. It was accepted almost as a matter of course from the beginning. International elections were held every four years, and one was due in 1953. So the Executive Board named me as acting president until the election could make it official. We then had to resolve the problem of who would replace me as acting secretary-treasurer. At the time, it seemed less than an earthshaking decision. Later, it would turn out to be one of the most colossal mistakes I'd ever made.

Our Chicago district director, Joe Germano—whose job I had thrice saved—wanted me to name John Doherty, an International representative from Chicago, but I was afraid the board wouldn't accept him because he was associated with a group called the Western Bloc that some directors feared was gaining too much power. Some of the Eastern directors tried to pressure me into appointing Bill Hart, a Pittsburgh district director, but I knew the Germano faction would object strenuously to him. So I cast about for a compromise candidate on whom both sides could agree. I wanted to start my presidency in harmony, and it was important to me to demonstrate that I recognized no factions, had no favored group and no power center.

I listened to all suggestions, and the candidate who made the most sense to me was a rather withdrawn, quiet, deliberate district director from Canton, Ohio, named I. W. Abel. He was almost completely innocuous, seldom spoke at board meetings but always voted with the administration. His operation in Canton had been clean and efficient, and he seemed to have the requisites for a satisfactory secretary-treasurer—plus, of course, the added advantages of being noncontroversial. So I passed the word that I wanted Abel as my secretary-treasurer, and the appointment was made. A few weeks later, nomination blanks went to the individual unions, and when they were returned, McDonald and Abel were running unopposed. And in the spring of 1953, the members of the United Steelworkers confirmed by ballot the appointments made by the Executive Board.

I was officially president of one of the largest industrial unions in the history of the world. I had four years and a clear mandate to go to work on behalf of my members.

18

Before I had time to begin functioning as head of the Steel-workers, there was another void left by Phil Murray that had to be filled: the presidency of the CIO. The convention had been postponed when Murray died, but the two remaining top officers of the CIO—Jim Carey and Allan Heywood—called a meeting of the chief officers of the CIO affiliated unions to sift candidates for presentation to the delegates when the rescheduled convention met on December 1.

Although several people approached me, I had no aspirations for the job. I had a file drawer full of ideas, nurtured through fifteen years as a second banana, that I wanted to put into practice on behalf of the Steelworkers. This was my primary goal and I couldn't possibly have pursued it properly with part of my attention diverted to running the CIO. So I wasn't interested. But I *did* have a candidate—Allan Heywood—whom I felt had earned the job through many years of the most effective organizing effort on behalf of the CIO of any man alive.

When the candidate meeting got under way, I urged the selection of Heywood, and several other members present supported my nomination. Then Walter Reuther took the floor and spoke for about an hour in his best professorial style, ending up by nominating himself for the job of president of the CIO because—in his modest view—there wasn't anyone else around capable of filling Murray's shoes. Reuther had won the presidency of the UAW by a majority of six votes when Murray failed to endorse R. J. Thomas. From this position of strength, he now aspired to take over the CIO as well.

When the delegates to the fourteenth annual convention of the CIO met a few weeks later in Atlantic City, these were the two names put before them as serious candidates. And the backroom maneuverings were as complex and as heated as at any political convention. Generally, the smaller unions favored Heywood, and the larger ones—except for the Steelworkers, second only to the UAW in size and solidly behind Heywood—favored Reuther. Two men still uncommitted—Emil Rieve of the Textile Workers and Jack Potofsky of the Amalgamated Clothing Workers—held the balance of power. The night before the election, both visited my room and I broke open a bottle of cognac for them. They tried to convince me there should be no floor fight at the convention and I told them that was entirely in their hands; if they supported Heywood, there would be no fight, since Allan would have the votes he needed and Reuther would step aside rather than be embarrassed. If they supported Reuther, I intended to take the contest to the floor. We argued until 2 o'clock, and I couldn't tell whether or not I'd made any progress. When they left, we were apparently right where we started. The floor fight decision still rested in their hands.

And a floor fight was what we had. Even with Rieve and Potofsky swinging to Reuther, the lead vacillated back and forth until the position of the United Rubber Workers—the last large undeclared union to vote—became crucial. Its president, L. S. Buckmaster, was an old friend of Allan Heywood, and it looked as if we were in. But the Reuther forces had penetrated the delegation and divided it, and when the majority swung to Reuther, he was over the top. I was as disappointed as Heywood, but he continued —as I knew he would—to take care of most of the work of running the CIO. He continued, that is, until February, 1953, when he dropped dead in the middle of a speech in a union hall in Wilkes-Barre, Pennsylvania, a victim of overwork and—perhaps —of heartbreak.

In the years ahead, the newspapers were to make a great deal of my supposed feud with Reuther. Feud is much too strong a word. I didn't like Reuther, and I presume he felt the same way about me. His patronizing attitude and tendency to lecture those of us among the unwashed were difficult for me to swallow, and I considered his absentee stewardship of the CIO ineffective. But I worked with him whenever it was necessary, and he once even invited me to address a convention of his union. To profess affection for him now would be silly. But it was equally silly to assume —as some labor writers did—that our antipathy for one another was a consuming passion that colored many of our activities. It wasn't and it didn't.

I was glad when the CIO convention ended. I had a union of my own to tend, and I was eager to get at it. When I returned to my desk in Pittsburgh, a year-end surprise awaited me. Ben Fairless, newly appointed chairman of the board of U.S. Steel, phoned and asked if I would stop by his office, just a few blocks from ours. It was Christmas Eve. He was waiting for me, and he greeted me effusively. Then he introduced me to General Richard K. Mellon, head of the Mellon financial empire. Although I had the feeling I was being sized up by Mellon, Fairless insisted that his purpose in asking me over was to renew the invitation he'd made to Murray to tour the U.S. Steel plants in an effort to seek out some way of resolving our problems short of periodic strikes.

I told him: "Any agreement made by Murray is my agreement, too. Of course I'll stick by it."

Both Fairless and Mellon seemed pleased, and as I left them, I was thinking once again about that speech by John Lewis in Wilkes-Barre in 1923 and wondering if—now that I had the reins of a union in my own hands—I could make it work. I knew there was a good chance that the effort would be misunderstood by many of my own people, but I was ready to take that chance because it seemed to me that some avenue to labor peace had to be found—and I knew the exploration wouldn't be without risk. I didn't know then how great the risk would be.

A few days after President Eisenhower's Inauguration, Reuther asked me to join him in a get-acquainted session with the new President. When we were ushered into the Oval Office, Reuther did most of the talking, explaining that since Eisenhower was the first Republican President to take office since the CIO was formed, we were deeply interested in his attitudes toward the goals of the labor unions in general and the CIO in particular. Eisenhower was relaxed and affable and spoke easily. He was especially friendly to me, recalling our meeting at the Apple Orchard in Normandy and expressing pleasure that we had a close common friend in New York attorney Maxwell Rabb, the resident liberal in the Eisenhower brain trust (who, it turned out, wasn't long for Ike's second Administration). In response to Reuther's questions, Eisenhower told us that he had no intention of being reactionary and would try to follow a middle-of-the-road course. He expressed some sympathy with two of the principal CIO goals: increased Social Security and relief from some of the more oppressive portions of the Taft-Hartley Act. He said that he intended to evaluate a number of rather advanced pieces of social legislation and would try to continue, in general, the liberal domestic program of the previous Administration. Altogether, it was a satisfactory conversation, and I came away feeling reasonably confident that the Eisenhower Administration wouldn't provide a launching pad for a concerted attack on organized labor.

This high-level business out of the way, I turned my attention back to the steel industry where I was about to meet my first major test. But first, there was the formality of my election and inauguration. The uncontested election was certified in February, and the inauguration ceremony was simple, witnessed only by our field representatives and the Pittsburgh and Washington office staffs. I spent a good deal of time on my inaugural talk, though, because I wanted to spell out clearly to the Steelworkers and to myself what I believed in and what I hoped to accomplish in the years ahead. And I wanted to do it in less than an hour, because I didn't approve of long speeches.

Some of the major points made in that inaugural talk included:

—continued efforts to develop better relationships with steel and other industries on the basis of rational unionism functioning within the framework of democratic capitalism;

—seeking of improved legislation on workmen's compensation, unemployment insurance, health laws and fair employment practices;

—development of better pension plans in the steel industry and the pursuit of a guaranteed annual wage for steelworkers;

—efforts to create and place friends in political high places so the union viewpoint might be reflected in the halls of power;

—solicitation of ideas from within the union for the betterment of the organization and more effective means of attaining our goals.

A few months after my inauguration, I had my first real opportunity to begin putting some of these principles into practice. The labor agreement of a year earlier—reached only after a government take-over and a good deal of Presidential arm-twisting—was due for renegotiating on July 1. Our existing agreement with basic steel provided we could reopen on wages only, and the USWA Wage Policy Committee drafted a statement calling for a "substantial" wage increase. There were just about as many interpretations of "substantial" as there were steelworkers, but I suppose Joe Germano's view was typical when he told me, "Dave, if you can get a nickel an hour, grab it and run like a thief."

I kept my own counsel and made no public statements or commitments. I didn't want to paint myself into a corner or give the impression I was taking directions from anyone. There was a great deal of television and newspaper coverage at the opening of our meetings with U.S. Steel; the memory of the 1952 strife was still very fresh. But in spite of the new cast, it was the same old play. There was a lot of talk and no progress. Absolutely none. The extent of John Stephens negotiating mandate seemed to be the right to say, "No." He did it pleasantly, but that wasn't making my job any easier.

After a particularly frustrating session, I took Stephens aside and said, "Jack, I don't think you've been given the authority to negotiate an agreement with us. I want to talk to Fairless."

Stephens chewed his lip, apparently trying to decide whether or not to argue the premise. Then he answered, "Okay, I'll call him and tell him what you want. But I don't know if he'll see you."

He did, that same evening. He was sitting in his office alone, at dusk, when I arrived. He offered me a cigar but made no effort at small-talk, waiting for me to take the lead. I told him that a wage adjustment was very much in order, that we were getting nowhere with John Stephens who showed no inclination to compromise, and therefore it seemed that a strike was inevitable.

Then I looked directly in his eyes and said deliberately, "But,

Ben, I'm not going to call a national steel strike. I'm going to strike you alone."

He was tipping back in his chair and he stopped in midflight.

"What does *that* mean?" he asked.

"It simply means I can't get an agreement with U.S. Steel until *you* change the ground rules. I'm not getting along with Stephens because all he does is say, 'No.' So you leave me no choice except to strike U.S. Steel."

Fairless sized me up deliberately.

"I'm not going to make an agreement with you myself," he said. "That's Jack's job and I'm not going to move in on him. But I will tell you one thing: he has more money in his pocket to offer you, and you ought to keep trying to get it out of him. He also has something to straighten out the Southern differential."

That was enough for me. I knew the word would get to Stephens before our session the next day, and it did. I met with him privately and we resolved our differences in a few hours. He agreed on a general wage increase of 8½ cents an hour and the elimination of the Southern wage differential in two stages that added up to another five cents an hour. The southern differential was a problem we'd been struggling with for fifteen years, and this would wipe it out completely.

When I reported back to my Wage Policy Committee, they were elated, hugging me and cheering. Our people had no stomach for another strike, but they were prepared to go through with it to bring our wages into line. Now they wouldn't have to disrupt their lives again. For the first time in the history of the Steelworkers Union—except for the postwar contract of 1947—the industry and the union had reached a voluntary labor agreement that reflected the needs of both the working people and the industry. It *could* be done. I knew that, now, and I wondered as we signed that agreement if it could be done again—and again.

That's really what Ben Fairless and I were trying to discover when we set out early that fall on the junket of U.S. Steel plants he had first planned two years earlier with Phil Murray. Our party usually included about a dozen people, with about half the cast changing from plant to plant. We made some early mistakes. One was using chauffeur-driven limousines. Vin Sweeney, our public-ity director, told me this was leaving a bad impression among the workers, and he was right. So we made all of our group excursions after that in a bus.

It took us awhile to shake down a *modus operandi,* but as it finally evolved, we would meet first with the local union officers and grievance committee and the plant management and foremen and explain our mission. Then we would walk leisurely through the plant and office, stopping periodically to talk with individuals, sometimes at length. Then in the evening we would have a dinner with union and management leaders, and Fairless and I would both speak, drawing on our experiences in the plant that day to illustrate the framework of our remarks which were unchanged from plant to plant.

There were hundreds of individual incidents—some illuminat-ing, some hilarious, some depressing. In Duquesne, Pennsylvania, a tall, rawboned open-hearth helper looked Fairless up and down carefully, then told him, "I always thought I could beat the hell out of you, and now I know I can." They laughed and shook hands. Near Salt Lake City, a local union officer warned me to stay away from one of the rollers because he was a real hardhead; Fair-less didn't hear, accosted the roller on a handshaking tour, was rebuffed and came out shaking his head. I told him to forget it, that he had a reputation as the most miserable bastard in the mill, and Ben, exuding breath, said, "Thank God. I thought he was probably the chairman of the Grievance Committee." In Cleve-land, the president of the union told Fairless proudly that his local had settled all of its own grievances and had never taken one to arbitration. Then he showed Fairless a filthy locker room that the plant management had been dilatory about fixing up; Fairless promised on the spot that it would be done, and it was. In the South, our reception was especially good because the elimination of the Southern differential had buoyed the workers there both morally and financially, and they told us so.

What did all this accomplish? Most important of all, I suppose, it demonstrated to hundreds of thousands of union members that

Fairless didn't have horns and to management people across the nation that I could talk in complete sentences and didn't carry bombs in my suitcase. It left a strong impression among a great many working people that the most important man in the steel industry was honestly interested in their welfare. And it left an impression among management people that the union men who represented their employees were neither unreasonable nor dedicated to tearing down the company but rather were seeking many of the same goals as management. It also built a strong feeling of friendship and respect among the top-level people of management and labor who virtually lived with one another for three months.

I've been criticized on this count, for figuratively going to bed with management. There are those who still believe that labor contracts should be negotiated at arm's length, in enmity. I contend that only the results are important, and if better results can be obtained through closer relationships and increased understanding, then that's the best way to proceed. I can think of no instance where my demands on behalf of the steelworkers were watered down or I was softer in seeking those demands because I knew the people with whom I was negotiating. In my opinion, it worked the other way. Because they knew me, they respected me and the principles I represented, and for this reason I was able to negotiate better contracts than would have been possible otherwise.

The 1954 contract is a case in point. Negotiating time had arrived once again when Fairless and I returned from our trip. The country was in an economic slump, and the experts speculated that the Steelworkers would be glad to settle on the basis of the status quo. But two things continued to bother us. We felt that the previous wage boost still hadn't reflected the general condition of the industry, and—even more important—we were uncomfortable about the employee contributions to the pension plan. So we set out to obtain a further wage adjustment and the establishment of a noncontributory pension plan. We achieved both, at a time when either would have been considered a triumph for the union.

We came down to the wire, which had become more or less

standard operating procedure. The contract expired on July 1, and we had been negotiating all day and into the night. Finally Stephens and I went alone to his room to try and clear up the last hurdle. I wanted fifteen cents an hour; he finally offered fourteen, and I turned it down. He stretched out on his bed, exhausted, and promptly fell asleep. So I walked across the street to my own hotel where I was besieged by reporters waiting for me. The time was midnight, the contract had just expired and therefore the mills would be shut down.

Stephens called me when I got back to my room and wanted to know why I'd walked out on him. I told him he'd gone to sleep on me and he denied it, then said he was going home to get some rest and would meet me again at 9 o'clock in the morning. Our Wage Policy Committee had been standing by and getting slowly drunk, and I explained the situation to them and then went to bed about 5 A.M. At 9, Stephens showed up, beat and bleary-eyed. Apparently he'd read the newspapers and done some telephoning. He didn't waste any time. He told me U.S. Steel would settle for fifteen cents, we shook hands on it, and I raced back to my Wage Policy Committee and announced the agreement. They lifted me on their shoulders and carried me around the room. The mills had been down for less than twelve hours, and by afternoon steel was in production once again after the shortest shutdown in industry history.

Shortly after this agreement was announced, Walter Reuther came out publicly with what he called a "Living Document Theory." Essentially, Reuther's contention was that labor agreements, as living documents, should be subject to amendment or adjustment even before their designated expiration date. Once again, I found myself in basic disagreement with Reuther. I knew that this knife cut both ways; I could still remember vividly the misery and chaos caused by the coal companies in the 1920's when they abrogated signed contracts. I believed that these contracts should be binding on both parties for the length of the agreement.

There was a great deal of consternation among corporate officials—including many in the steel industry—after Reuther's announcement, so it seemed important to me that I make my position quite clear. The Iron and Steel Institute was holding its annual meeting in New York, and I went there on my own and called on a dozen or more steel company presidents to assure them that I disagreed with Reuther and had no intention of reopening our recently signed contract. I met a number of industry leaders under highly desirable circumstances in this way, and the trip also paid an unexpected dividend two years later when the officials of Republic Steel suggested—in the midst of a painful recession— that we reopen negotiations to discuss reducing labor costs. I reminded them of our conversations about Reuther's "Living Document Theory" and heard no more from them.

In the late summer of 1953, I was asked to help out an old foe, Clarence Randall, then chairman of the board of Inland Steel. Randall had been appointed by Eisenhower to head up a special Commission on Foreign and Economic Policy, and the President asked me to serve on it. I came up with a report advocating Federal assistance to people, companies and communities pauperized by recession conditions beyond their control. I got no support whatsoever. I did serve one function, however, for Randall. The reactionary members of the commission were about to carry the day, so I staged a two-hour left-wing tirade—with Randall's knowledge and collusion—that tilted the conclusions of the commission toward the center. Ten years later, I had the satisfaction of seeing most of my ideas that had been summarily rejected by the Randall Commission enacted into law under Presidents John F. Kennedy and Lyndon B. Johnson.

And at home I had a collective bargaining conference with my son, David, who at fourteen began to flex adolescent muscles and give Rosemary a hard time. After some serious negotiating during which I did most of the talking, we came up with a nine-point contract which he signed under penalty of losing portions of his five-dollar-a-week allowance if he failed to perform. The agreement worked admirably and never had to be renegotiated.

19

I almost blew my first convention as president of the Steelworkers. On the weekend before the convention opened, I caught a cold that turned into what must have been at least double pneumonia. But only death itself could have kept me away, and I made the opening address with a temperature of 102 and a head that kept drifting off into the kleig lights.

In addition to the tremendous satisfaction of appearing before the delegates as their president for the first time, I also had something important I wanted very badly to say. Here is a small sample of how I said it:

"We are engaged in the operation of an economy that is based on mutual trusteeship. What does this mean? It means that the days of the Andrew Carnegies are gone. The corporations of our country are no longer owned by individuals or small family groups. They are owned by hundreds of thousands of stockholders, and this is particularly true in the steel industry.

"U.S. Steel has almost as many stockholders as employees. These stockholders through a voting system employ a group of managers. The managers are simply employees of the corporation. There is another group of employees known as the working force. Together, these two groups have a mutual trusteeship to operate the steel company, and the same holds true for all steel companies.

"In the operation of this mutual trusteeship, full consideration must be given to everyone involved. The managers must give full consideration to the just claims of the workers. And the working force must see to it that the steel properties are operated successfully, because if they aren't operated successfully, they will have no jobs. And both have an obligation to the owners, the stockholders, because new money must flow in to avoid decadence. That we cannot tolerate. We have something new and vital in the world in mutual trusteeship, and we are going to develop it. This union is going to enhance its operation."

I finished in a mental haze, breathing antibiotics over the lectern and so weak I could hardly stand. They led me back to my hotel room and put me to bed, where I was told several days later that my speech had started a great deal of talk, most of it positive. I got on my feet for the last day of the convention, in time to preside over the adoption of a resolution of appreciation to Phil Murray and to urge that the Steelworkers take the lead in bringing about a united labor movement.

There was a great deal of speculation in the labor press over a ploy labeled the "Lew-Mc-Beck Organization" in which I'd been involved over the summer. It started by pure accident. I was in Washington on business and lobby sitting with one of our district directors and my friend, Chick Federoff, when the subject of John Lewis came up. His office was around the corner, and on impulse we decided to walk over and say hello to him. I had no idea what sort of reception I'd get. Lewis had been as cantankerous as ever during the Truman years, and although he was now almost eighty, he was still decidedly active in the affairs of his mine workers.

So we dropped in unannounced, he was there and apparently delighted to see us. We talked for several hours, mostly about the need to unite the labor movement. This may seem odd coming from the man who had done more than any other individual to fragment it, but Lewis felt in 1953 that labor was coming under concerted attack and it was essential to offer as monolithic a front as possible. I happened to agree, and as we parted, we made vague plans to discuss the matter further.

One of Lewis's publicity men—whether by accident or design I've never known—leaked the news of our meeting, and it scared hell out of the top echelons of both the CIO and AFL, who were still sparring with one another like a pair of dilettante boxers. The reaction in both the press and the labor movement was so satisfying that Lewis and I decided to meet again and include Dave Beck, president of the Teamsters Union, who also shared our views. Since our combined union membership was more than three million and together we controlled a major power source (coal), the basic manufactured material of our economy (steel) and the total means of over-the-road transport (teamsters), our casual combination attracted a great deal more attention than it deserved. We had one luncheon meeting, after which we gave out a statement highly critical of the foot-dragging in mounting a united labor attack on the Taft-Hartley Act and suggested we might take matters into our own hands.

That's really all there was to it. Would we have followed through on our threat? I really have no idea. Our purpose was to try and move the CIO and AFL leadership off dead center, and that we accomplished. I used the platform on the last day of the 1954 Steelworkers convention to reiterate my strong feelings about the need for labor unity and to suggest that our union take the lead in bringing this about. I scotched the rumors—started by labor columnist Victor Riesel—that we were seeking not unity, but more fragmentation. And I ended by suggesting that the so-called "Unity Committees" of the AFL and CIO get off their tails and get to work.

While Reuther and George Meany, the president of the AFL, were pondering this, I got a telephone call from General Bobby Cutler, the director of the National Security Council. He said, "Dave, I am authorized by the President to ask you to serve on a top secret committee having to do with the security of our country. If you say 'no,' then this call never happened, and if you say 'yes,' then you can't tell anybody, not even your wife, what we want you to do."

I said, "General, the answer is 'yes,'" and he told me to report to his office on the following Monday and tell no one where I was going and why. I called Rosemary, told her I had to go to Washington on business, that I might be out of touch for a while, and I would call her as soon as I could. She was puzzled, but caught the tone in my voice and didn't press me.

For the next three weeks, in the company of five highly placed associates from the fields of business and education, I got a total, detailed look at the intercontinental defense establishment of the United States. Most of the things we saw were top secret then. Some still are. Those that aren't include the Texas Towers sunk into the Atlantic Ocean, the DEW line across Northern Canada, and the picket planes (Constellations with the latest radar equipment) patrolling skies throughout the Western Hemisphere. We met with the nation's top military leaders, heard our innermost defense secrets, saw films of atomic and H-bomb tests.

When it was all over, we sat in on a meeting of the National Security Council, presided over by Eisenhower. We were there to provide this group of men charged with our national protection the benefit of outside views of our defense establishment, offered by lay citizens expert in a half-dozen different fields. This briefing had two very different and profound effects on me. First, it instilled an awe of the immense reach of our defense system and the devastating retaliatory power available to us. And, second, it damned near made a pacifist of me. When I was asked for my comments around that table, I said, "Mr. President, I can see only two answers to world problems today. The first is constant diplomatic negotiations. We've got to talk these things out, somehow, even if it takes 150 years. And I guess the second answer would have to be constant prayer." A few years earlier, when I had broken up the World Federation of Trade Unions, I had insisted that it was impossible to talk with the Soviets. Now when I saw close up the tools of destruction that were available to both of us, I knew we *must* talk with them some way. And I tried to convey that feeling to the National Security Council before the President thanked us for our time and our efforts and sent us home.

I'd been back at my desk only a few weeks when Eisenhower asked to see me again, this time on a very different matter, although I didn't know it then. The day before I was to see him, I received a copy of U.S. Steel's Annual Report. I was anxious to look it over, because it was the first report issued under the new board chairman, Roger Blough. He had succeeded Ben Fairless, who retired shortly after our cross-country junket. I was still unsure of Blough. He had shown indications of reasonableness that made me unwilling to accept at face value the generally negative attitude he displayed toward organized labor and—it seemed to me—the world in general. When I read his first Annual Report, however, I knew we were in for big trouble in the years ahead. He came through as though he were running for the presidency of the National Association of Manufacturers on a right-wing ticket. He suggested that the Steelworkers and the Eisenhower Administration were in collusion to drown the United States of America in a tidal wave of inflation. He labeled both our financial and employee security goals as irresponsible and left no doubt that he intended to resist them with every resource at his disposal.

John Stephens had the misfortune to stop by the office to discuss some technical contract details just as I finished reading Blough's blast. Stephens had no way of knowing, of course, the rage burning inside me, and when he asked for my view on the matter that brought him there, I exploded, taking out on him the anger I felt toward his boss. It was completely unfair, and I knew it, but I had to get it out of my system, and Stephens listened in an embarrassed sort of silence.

I ended by saying, "You can tell Blough that we don't like what he said a goddam bit. We never attacked Fairless, either publicly or in our own newspaper. But this sort of thing gives us no choice. We'll have to strike back, and when we hit, we'll hit hard. Just remind Blough, for us, that he started it."

Stephens tried to defend Blough, but not with very much warmth. Then he tried to talk me out of issuing a public blast on the ground that it would serve no constructive purpose. But I was much too angry even to weigh that sort of reasoning, and Stephens finally departed, shaking his head sadly at this turn of events that he feared might check and reverse a *détente* that seemed to offer the best promise for labor-management peace since the growth of industrial unions.

When I left my hotel room for the White House and my meeting with Eisenhower the following morning, I stuffed several copies of Blough's diatribe in my pocket. I met Treasury Secretary George Humphrey at the east entrance and we shared an elevator to the President's living quarters. I asked Humphrey if he had seen the Blough statement, and when he said, "No," I gave him a copy. He stuffed it in his pocket, unread.

Secretary of Labor James Mitchell was awaiting us in the Presidential living room, and Eisenhower arrived in a few minutes. He offered us all a drink, then got briskly to the business at hand. He'd asked me to come, he said, because he wanted to explain his "tight money" program and make sure I understood it. He pointed out that he regarded protecting the nation's economy and the public against inflation as one of his primary responsibilities and his "tight money" policy had been devised to that end. In order to make this policy work, it was essential to hold both the price and wage line, and he wanted to ask my cooperation in holding down wage demands in the steel industry as a good soldier in the fight against inflation.

I heard him out, although I was familiar with the essentials of his tight money program and understood it thoroughly. I also didn't agree with it, as I told him when he finished.

"We feel strongly," I said, "that higher wages are inflationary only when productivity remains constant or decreases. But in the steel industry today, the productivity per man-hour is increasing at a much higher rate than wages. When we ask for higher wages, we are simply seeking our share of the increased productivity of our own hands. We are not increasing costs, and because we aren't, there is no need for higher wages in the steel industry to necessitate higher prices."

Humphrey took me on, then, explaining that American business was solidly behind Eisenhower's program and it was important to the nation that labor cooperate as well. Suddenly I remembered Blough's statement and asked Humphrey if he'd read it. He said he hadn't, and I told him that if he believed big business was solidly supporting the Eisenhower Administration, he should read what Blough had to say. So he pulled the statement from his pocket and read it aloud. I watched the President's face and saw it flush as Blough's outspoken criticism got through to him.

That ended the meeting. I thanked the President for inviting me and said I would certainly weigh very carefully what he'd told me. On the way out, I mused over Blough's capacity to put his corporate foot in his mouth. Little did I know, then, that his exercise with Eisenhower was only a warm-up for the main event with John F. Kennedy.

Several months later, I asked for an appointment with the President to explain one of *my* programs to *him*. I had attended several of Eisenhower's famous black-tie dinners meanwhile and felt I knew him well enough to approach him with my "Invest in America Plan." The nation was in the midst of a serious recession in 1954, and it seemed to me that only by devising some means of creating jobs and putting industry back into full production could we avoid these periodic economic bellyaches.

Most of my package—which included a $1.25 minimum wage, expanded civil rights laws, Federal housing assistance, increased Social Security, National Health Insurance and Federal aid to education, among many other items—has since been enacted into law. Eisenhower read it, called it "interesting" and turned it over to George Humphrey and Jim Mitchell. Humphrey said he'd like to look it over before we discussed it. When we did, he said there were parts of it that appealed to him greatly and others he simply couldn't accept. He singled out the national road-building program as especially attractive, and several years later, construction had begun on the National System of Interstate Highways. The effectiveness of the program I suggested, however, was dependent on the results that could be produced by the entire package. Unwrapping it an item at a time destroyed much of its usefulness.

We also prepared a television film promoting the "Invest in America" idea, which was based on the concept that the more a citizen earns, the more he buys. Most of my suggestions were aimed at increasing the income of individual citizens. Most had been made before in one form or another, but never had they been packaged in a comprehensive program aimed at reducing and eventually eliminating the specter of constantly recurring recessions.

About the same time, I began to press for industrywide bargaining in steel. We had really been practicing this in spirit, but it seemed important to me that we do it by letter as well. Since Big Steel accepted the SWOC as a bargaining agent, we had been negotiating first with U.S. Steel, then using this agreement as a pattern for labor contracts with the rest of the industry. Essentially the same thing was happening with steel prices, which were set by U.S. Steel and followed by its competitors. Any suggestion of price collusion was, of course, illegal, but it seemed to me that we no longer had to be so reluctant about formalizing industrywide labor negotiations.

Under the system in operation when I took office, we would open negotiations with all the steel companies at the same time we started our talks with U.S. Steel. The other negotiators, however, would simply mark time until the varsity squad had settled matters with Big Steel. Then the others would almost always fall into line. When this process was multiplied to every plant in every company, we had a hell of a lot of people marking time until they were provided a basic economic settlement they could adjust to the smaller steel companies and the hundreds of steel fabricators with whom we had contracts. To simplify this procedure, I began talking industrywide early in my term of office.

I was also pushing hard for the amalgamation of the AFL and CIO, and late in 1954 we finally began to get some action. A joint committee, including the two presidents, was formed to explore the possibilities of a merger. When we met, we were set up like two antagonistic negotiating groups, and I suggested the long tables be discarded and we intermingle as friends. After a few days of reasonably amicable talk about the need for a united labor front, a smaller committee—of which I was a member—was named to draw up the final ground rules for a combined organization. The final stumbling block was a name. Whatever AFL-CIO lacks in imagination it compensates in exact description. Arthur Goldberg finally suggested it after a good many more exotic names had been discarded.

A merger convention was set for New York on December 5, 1955, preceded by conventions of each of the merging organizations. When Reuther turned the final CIO convention into a personal accolade without so much as a mention of either Lewis or Murray, I walked out in disgust and most of the Steelworker delegates followed me. Both the conventions approved the merger, and the marriage was consummated a few days later. The notable absentee was John L. Lewis who called the new AFL-CIO a "rope of sand" and declined to bring his miners into the fold. I was made a vice-president of the merged organization and a member of the Executive Committee.

A few days after the merger, the presidents of Jones & Laughlin, Republic and National Steel—Ben Morrell, Charley White and Tom Millsop—asked me to meet them for dinner. They said they were tired of U.S. Steel setting the labor pattern and wanted to be in on the action. Would I be willing to enter into collective bargaining with a group of steel companies instead of U.S. Steel alone? This, of course, was directly in line with union policy, and I told them we would be happy to expand the base of our primary negotiations. They said they would discuss it with the other steel companies. Twelve of them—producing about 90 percent of the steel in the United States—went along with the idea. Consequently, when it was time to negotiate our 1956 contract, we were dealing for the first time with an industry committee instead of U.S. Steel, even though the chief negotiator was still John Stephens.

We had a potent package to put before this first industrywide negotiating team. The main feature was a form of guaranteed annual wage known as the Supplemental Unemployment Benefit plan. We had worked it out the year before with the Continental and American Can Companies, and it provided that any employee laid off would have his regular state-paid unemployment compensation supplemented by the company up to two-thirds of his regular earnings for a period up to one year. I had tried to sell the same idea to U.S. Steel in 1955, but they refused to buy. In 1956, it would be the primary goal of our negotiating package that also included premium pay for weekends, a staple in most other industries that had never been written into steel contracts.

When negotiations dragged into the summer without appreciable progress, I had a study made of steel inventories, found they were unusually high and deduced—correctly as it turned out—that the steel industry would welcome a modest shutdown they could blame on the Steelworkers.

This suspicion hardened into virtual certainty one evening when I was having dinner in a New York restaurant after a trying day of negotiating. Tom Millsop, the president of National Steel, came to my table, leaned over me and said, almost conspiratorially, "Dave, no matter what happens, you and I are going to be friends. Right?"

I was puzzled, but I answered, "Right, Tom, but what's going to happen?"

He just shook his head and walked away.

A few days later, Stephens asked to see me alone and then made an offer. It was totally inadequate and made me so angry I kicked an armchair and stubbed my toe so painfully that I hobbled around for almost a week. I took the offer to my Wage Policy Committee, anyway, and they agreed it should be turned down. When I passed the word to reporters waiting outside, I told them: "The Titans have labored and brought forth a louse," and they printed it happily, a feeble parody, perhaps, but good copy.

So we had a serious shutdown on our hands for the first time since I'd taken office, although the nagging feeling persisted that as soon as steel inventories leveled out, the industry negotiators would find our demands much more palatable. The Federal Mediation Service got into the act quickly and prodded us back into meetings in Pittsburgh which continued to get nowhere as our members walked picket lines. Then, finally, I told Stephens—as I had once before—that I didn't think he had authority to modify the industry position and I wanted to talk to some of the company presidents. That night, he arranged for me to go to the apartment of U.S. Steel's president, Cliff Hood. The presidents of Republic and Bethlehem were also there, and the atmosphere was cordial. Charley White told me he didn't "think I had enough guts to call a strike," and I told him, "You don't know how much guts I've *really* got."

I explained our position in detail and told them my committee would never agree to anything less than the SUB plan and time and a quarter for weekend overtime. They listened but refused to commit themselves, insisting instead that their negotiating committee had full authority to act and I would have to deal with John Stephens.

This time it took about two weeks. Late on a Friday afternoon, when all of us were frustrated and exhausted, Stephens again asked for a private talk. He said he was determined to make an agreement and wanted to know my rock-bottom terms. I told him very quickly and started back out, but Stephens said he wanted to make it look better and would I wait with him awhile longer. We talked baseball for about an hour, then Stephens said, "Okay, let's go out. But I've got to do some checking and I want to get rid of my colleagues. You have any ideas?"

I told him, "I'll take care of it. You just go along with whatever I pull."

I stalked into the living room looking glum and angry, glared at the people who were watching me for a sign of what had happened in the bedrooom, then strode to a window air conditioner and hit it so hard I almost broke it loose from its moorings. Then I sat down and lit my pipe.

Stephens who had trailed me silently into the room said, "I'm sorry. I didn't expect to make you *that* sore."

He walked over to me, extended his hand and said, "Will you shake before we break up?"

I made a show of shaking his hand and everyone padded off quietly, sure that negotiations had reached a total impasse.

Stephens called me at home on Saturday, just before I was to leave on a trip to visit picket lines around the country. He said we should get together the next morning, so I delayed the trip and met him in a downtown hotel at 10 A.M. We got right to business. He said he had a final offer, and I listened to it in amazement. It not only included SUB and time and a quarter for overtime but also a basic wage increase and some fringe improvements we wanted. I was elated, shook hands on it and we sat down together and wrote up the agreement in longhand which we each initialed.

Our Wage Policy Committee called the contract "the greatest victory ever achieved by the United Steelworkers of America in its 20-year history." I won't quarrel with them. Its total value was $1,500,-000,000!

While we were negotiating in the summer of 1956, the national political parties were meeting to nominate a President. Eisenhower, of course, was the automatic Republican choice and almost sure of reelection. In the Democratic convention, the fight for second place was probably more significant than the nomination of the Presidential candidate, although we weren't aware of it then.

I was still an Averell Harriman man in 1956, and he asked me to make one of his seconding speeches. We all knew it was in a lost cause, for Adlai Stevenson was a certain winner. I still had little affection for Stevenson, and I stayed with Harriman to the end, then had to leave the convention before the vice-presidential fight developed. Stevenson refused to select a running mate and threw it to an open convention. Senator Estes Kefauver appeared to have the inside track, but unexpectedly and almost from nowhere came a bright, personable, young Senator named John F. Kennedy to contest for the second place on the ticket. I had known Kennedy as a rather brash young Congressman who captivated every lady he met, and later as a surprisingly perceptive Senator whom I could see grow almost daily in his grasp of the intricacies of politics and government. In 1956, he hadn't occurred to me as a presidential candidate. Before the year was out, however, he would.

Kennedy made the major nominating speech for Adlai Stevenson, and he was good, which surprised many of the delegates who had never before regarded Kennedy seriously. He coined the phrase—"one takes the high road and one takes the low"—about the campaign tactics of Eisenhower and Nixon that later became a keynote in the Stevenson campaign. It was assumed that because Stevenson had asked Kennedy to nominate him, the Senator had been dismissed as a serious vice-presidential candidate, but the support for this exciting young man was spontaneous and enthusiastic and almost took him over the top on the second ballot. He was beaten by the conviction of several key Democratic figures—

principally David Lawrence, who headed my delegation and was a Catholic, himself—that his religion would be a major political drawback. If nothing else, the 1956 convention experience proved to Jack Kennedy that he would have to meet the religion problem frontally and dispose of it if he were ever to be a serious candidate for the Presidency.

As a loyal Democrat, I worked for Stevenson, but—I'm afraid —without very much enthusiasm. Between 1952 and 1956, I had an opportunity for two leisurely looks at Stevenson, and I wasn't impressed. Rosemary and I were invited to his home in Liberty-ville, Illinois, for dinner and an evening of talk shortly after my service on Eisenhower's Intercontinental Defense Committee. Stevenson was then titular head of the Democratic Party, and I was appalled to find him totally uninformed about matters I was privy to and which he certainly should have known. Apparently the Eisenhower Administration had made it a conscious policy to keep the leader of the opposition party in ignorance on matters of national security and sensitivity, and Stevenson either didn't real-ize the degree of his ignorance in these areas or didn't want to raise hell about his exclusion from them. Otherwise he was a charming host, quieter than I expected and rather subdued in his manner and talk. He didn't come on very strong.

About a year later, Arthur Goldberg and I conferred with Stevenson in his Chicago law office. He had just returned from a trip to Asia and Africa, and he shocked me by telling us the United States was losing its markets overseas because American labor was overpaid. The premise might be debated, but the propriety of making such a statement to the head of one of America's largest labor unions struck me as downright stupid. The virtue of that sort of honesty—if that's what it was—in a candidate for high office is more than counterbalanced by its poor judgment and atrocious timing, and I'm afraid I found Stevenson guilty on both counts.

But I worked for the Democratic ticket nevertheless with the tools I had available. Murray had broken up my internal PAC or-ganization just before he died because someone convinced him I was using it as a power base to seek his job. I rebuilt it as best I

could for Stevenson, but many of the PAC workers had been involved in the effort to draft Eisenhower for the Democratic ticket
in 1948, and they had about the same degree of enthusiasm for
Stevenson as I did. A great many labor people made the right
sounds on behalf of Stevenson in 1956, but their hearts—and, I
suspect, their votes—were elsewhere.

I saw Stevenson close up only once during the campaign. I rode
his train and made some speeches for him when he campaigned in
Pennsylvania and talked with him briefly in his suite at the Penn-
Sheraton in Pittsburgh. He looked tired, beaten and discouraged,
and his campaign workers, at that stage, were reflecting the lack of
confidence Stevenson displayed and apparently felt. There was
reason for it, of course. Eisenhower was almost unbeatable, and
even a last-minute decision by Stevenson to open up the subject of
Eisenhower's questionable health was ineffective as Ike was
swept back into office by a large margin.

With the election over, I had to turn my attention to another
convention, one that I thought would be a triumph and turned,
instead, into a near catastrophe. After the Wage Policy Committee's statement that the 1956 contract represented the Steelworkers' "greatest victory," I was looking forward to a massive orgy of
gratitude and good feeling at our convention. I was also hoping to
cash in on this good feeling to put through a sorely needed recommendation of the Executive Board that I knew rank-and-file members wouldn't like: the raising of monthly dues from $3 to $5.
These dues, plus an initiation fee of $5 and the earnings on our
invested savings constituted the total sources of income for an international union that now represented 1,200,000 workers and
employed 1,200 people on its staff.

All the proper steps were taken in the evolution of this raise in
dues, which was badly needed to keep the International functioning at the level of services it was rendering. The decision was debated and passed by the Executive Board. Since a constitutional
amendment would be required to change the dues structure, the
Constitution Committee met, debated the change, then recommended it unanimously. As a part of the same package, the Execu-

tive Board had also recommended long-due salary increases for the members of the International staff—including a raise in my salary from $40,000 to $50,000 a year. I didn't seek this raise, and when I found it was going to be recommended, I wrote a letter to the Committee, asking that they drop it. They ignored my letter and recommended the raise, anyway, which was pleasing to me as a tangible token of appreciation but turned into a liability when the matter was brought before the convention.

As soon as the motion was introduced, the congenial atmosphere on the convention floor turned to acrimony. The debate became lengthy and bitter and, finally, highly emotional. (I. W. Abel, incidentally, made one of his infrequent speeches in support of higher dues.) The opponents of the raise claimed it would be spent for high living by union officials and cited my $50,000 salary as Exhibit A to prove their point. (Incidentally, I never collected the $50,000 per year because I never accepted any salary during a major shutdown.) When I finally called for a voice vote on the question, it was impossible to determine the result in the cascade of noise that poured off the convention floor. So I took a standing vote. When about 400 of the 3,600 delegates present voted against the change, I declared the constitution amended and the new dues structure adopted. There was an undercurrent of strong animosity throughout this whole affair, however, that made me certain I hadn't heard the end of it.

In the angry and rebellious spirit that persisted after the dues vote, another recommendation of the Constitution Committee was turned down. In an effort to correct that long-ago mistake by Phil Murray in providing for an elected director in Canada, the committee proposed that the national director of Canada be appointed by the International president. The Canadians organized a powerful lobby against this change, managed to sell enough delegates on the idea that I wanted to be a "dictator" and beat the proposed amendment on a floor vote. As a result, the Canadian union—which has never been able to pay its own way and is subsidized from American dues—continues to exert power in the International out of all proportion to either its size or its financial contribution. This balance of power was used against me decisively in 1965, and it will be used again to thwart majority will in the Steelworkers Union.

Arthur Goldberg summed up my feelings rather well when he told the delegates: "We have just negotiated a remarkable contract, and frankly, after watching this convention for a couple of days, I'm beginning to feel that the Steelworkers are acting like the fellow who says, 'What have you done for me yesterday?' I haven't seen very much reaction to this contract. Maybe it is *too* good."

After all the rancor, we badly needed an upbeat note, and it was supplied by the young man who came very close to winning the Democratic vice-presidential nomination, Senator John F. Kennedy of Massachusetts. He had accepted my invitation to address our convention, and he won it over almost instantly. For the second time that year, I took a long, hard look at this man. He had the remarkable facility of expressing highly sophisticated wit and decidedly earthy humor at the same time—and with almost the same degree of impact. He was charming and urbane and tough, and although he told us things we wanted to hear about the place of organized labor in American society, he did it with such conviction and high style that he captured that angry audience. Watching him from the platform, I was as much captivated as the rest of the audience, and I thought—with the same sort of surprise you feel when an adolescent you've known for years turns suddenly into a brilliant and provocative adult—there's greatness here, and we're going to hear more, much more, from this man.

I had very little time in 1956 to pursue that thought, however. As soon as our convention ended, I was in my first real internecine struggle as president of the Steelworkers. From right field, a movement appeared called the Dues Protest Committee. The front man was a millhand from McKeesport, Pennsylvania, named Donald C. Rarick. Legend has it that Rarick was so outraged over the raise in his dues that he got together with a few of his friends and organized a grass-roots movement to unseat me and put the dues back where they belonged. I made the mistake of not taking all this very seriously at first, until it slowly became clear that there was some real expertise behind Rarick. My friends told me the mover and shaker was a Pittsburgh district director (later, under a Republican governor, Secretary of Labor of the Commonwealth of Pennsylvania) William J. Hart, but I didn't believe them until Hart arrived on the last possible day for nominations with a sufficient number of nominating certificates from local unions to put Rarick on the ballot against me in the Steelworkers election of 1956.

Somebody came up with enough money to send Rarick flying all over the country, charging me with being a "silk-stocking president" and an "iron-fisted dictator." Although I didn't know it then, the attorney for the Dues Protest Committee, who sat in on the strategy meetings, told me later that Hart's plan was to run the union through a front man until he could shoulder him aside and take over, himself. My friend and personal lawyer, Ernest G. Nasser, was with me during this and subsequent meetings. I later faced Hart with this accusation and he denied it. When I offered to bring my informants for a direct confrontation, he said, "Oh, no, no, no," and departed hastily, leaving little doubt in my mind about his role in this affair.

When it became apparent that Rarick's charges were beginning to disrupt the effectiveness of the union, I asked to meet him, and a mutual friend arranged a conference in a motel near Pittsburgh. He turned out to be an earnest and determined young man totally convinced of the righteousness of his cause. I told him that many of the things he was being told to say were simply not true and were damaging the credibility and unity of the Steelworkers in the eyes of outsiders. I told him he had no chance of winning and he could best serve the cause of the union to which both of us were dedicated by withdrawing. He refused, and the campaign ran its increasingly bitter course. I won the election with about 65 percent of the votes, but it left a legacy of bad feeling and disrupted friendships that broke down the internal harmony of USWA's top echelons. I suppose that harmony couldn't have lasted indefinitely in any human situation, but I didn't expect it to founder in the aftermath of a labor contract that provided an unparalleled measure of prosperity and security to the steelworkers I represented.

While Rarick was strewing his charges all over the country, the battery of investigators and attorneys for the McClellan Committee in the U.S. Senate were industriously mining any antilabor information, rumors or fables they could dig out. The McClellan Committee was supposed to be investigating racketeering in labor and management, but they seemed to be focusing most of their attention on labor in general and Dave Beck and James Hoffa of the Teamsters in particular.

I refused steadfastly to comment on the problems of these two men beyond affirming my personal respect for them as effective labor leaders. I knew Hoffa only slightly. In the few dealings I had with him, I found him pleasant, shrewd, quick and a man of his word. I had no personal knowledge or contact with any of the racketeers who allegedly surrounded him. I was much better acquainted with Dave Beck and amazed when I heard of his conviction for mishandling union funds. Beck was a highly respected man—in his own community as well as in the labor field. His prison term certainly can't eradicate the enormous contributions he made to the labor movement and to the men he represented.

In 1957—as Beck and Hoffa, among others, discovered—the most effective way to discredit a labor leader was to drag him before the McClellan Committee and work him over there. After I survived the Dues Protest Committee struggle, some of the ringleaders of my defeated opponents made an effort to encourage the Senate investigators to subpoena me to appear before the committee. When I heard this from friends in Washington, I acted promptly to circumvent this action. I had nothing to hide and nothing to fear from the committee, but its method of operation was deadly, forcing the witness into a position of repeatedly denying charges collected from all sorts of irresponsible sources. The same thing is happening today in the investigations of the House un-American Activities Committee, and the net result of this sort of procedure is far too often a vague feeling in the public mind that where there is smoke, there must be a fire. I watched Hoffa browbeaten on television, and I wanted no part of this charade.

So I cashed some political chips and went to Washington and bought insurance with them. I had known Richard Nixon as a Senator, and Rosemary and I had been entertained numerous times by the Nixons, usually in their home but once in the old Supreme Court chamber in the Capitol to meet Queen Elizabeth and Prince Philip of Great Britain. I always made a courtesy call on Nixon when I was in Washington, and when the McClellan Committee began to breathe in my direction, I paid the Vice-President a business call. Nixon, of course, was an expert at this sort of thing, having built much of his reputation by conducting Congressional investigations.

I told him my feelings about the McClellan Committee, and asked his advice about whether or not it would be wise for me to appear.

He was emphatic in his answer. "Don't let them hit you with the black paintbrush," he said. "If you do, then you'll have to prove your own innocence. No matter how wild the lies they throw at you, you'll still be put in the position of disproving them."

This corroborated my own feelings. I called on Senator Karl Mundt, the ranking Republican on the McClellan Committee, and he told me he had been approached by some of my enemies but had no immediate intention of calling me before the committee. That left me uneasy and dissatisfied. After all, McClellan was the seat of power, and McClellan was a Democrat. I'd been talking with Republicans who could be of only limited help to me in any event.

What Democrat could be most helpful? The answer was so obvious that it had eluded me through all those calls on high-ranking Republicans. Paul Butler, of course. The chairman of the Democratic National Committee, who so gratefully received the support of the Steelworkers, both financial and political, in election years.

I called on Butler, got an immediate audience and said to him: "Paul, remember me? I was treasurer of the PAC and raised all that money for the Democratic Party. I was glad to do it, and I'd do it again, but now I want to ask a favor of *you*. I don't want to testify before the McClellan Committee. And I want you to know that if I *am* called to testify, I'm going to have to tell them that of the $23,500,000 raised through contributions to the PAC, $23 million went to the Democrats and only $500,000 to the Republicans. I'm also going to have to tell them exactly how that money was raised and how much of it went into McClellan's campaign fund. I have a feeling the Republicans might be able to make considerable political hay out of all this, and it might even dry up a pretty good source of Democratic money. So I hope you'll do whatever you can to keep me out of that hearing room. If I were a crook, I'd take the Fifth Amendment, but I'm not a crook and I have nothing to hide. I just don't want anything to do with the McClellan Committee, and I don't think you want it either."

Butler said he'd do what he could, and I took out some additional insurance by telling the same story to the Senate Majority leader, Lyndon Johnson, who also said he'd do what he could. The message apparently got through because I was never called before the committee.

One of the main reasons I wanted to avoid this exposure was because I knew it would multiply overnight the hate mail and threats I was receiving in the aftermath of the Dues Protest movement and its attendant publicity. Most of this garbage was coming to my home and it was beginning to get to Rosemary, who would open the hate mail to protect me from it and often wouldn't tell me about the obscene and threatening phone calls. We lived in a $30,000 home in a middle-class neighborhood in a Pittsburgh suburb, and our entire staff of servants consisted of old George Gunn, who did odd jobs around our neighborhood and was a close pal of our son. (Newspapers and magazines loved to refer to George as my "chauffeur" and my home as "plush.") So Rosemary and David had no protection if some nut decided—as a number of them threatened—to take out his animosity toward me on my family.

My phone at both my home and office was tapped for years. I suspected but couldn't prove it, until one of my staff found a gadget in the switchboard area of the office that phone company technicians said was a tapping device. I hired an expert to check my lines and he discovered something called a "supervisory tap." He explained that the going rate for such a tap was a $12,000 bribe to a supervisory employee at the phone company and it permitted the briber to monitor all of my telephone conversations on a tape recorder. I never found out who paid for the tap or how long it had been in existence.

Whoever it was would probably have been interested in a call I received from John Stephens about a year after my reelection. He had distressing news. "I'm retiring early," he said. "The announcement will be out tomorrow but I wanted you to know ahead of time. There's something else you have to know, too. Now don't blow your stack when you hear this, but Cooper is taking over for me. Believe me, Dave, he's a new man and I know you'll be able to do business with him."

I hung up dismayed and despairing. I had grown fond of Stephens as a courageous foe I could admire and respect and trust. I felt none of these things for Cooper. In my every contact with him up to that point, he had been cold, one-dimensional and intransigent. Negotiating with him was rather like dealing with a computer programmed to say "No." As long as he was subordinate to Stephens, I could go around him. But no longer. And the announcement the next day was even worse than I had expected. Blough made Cooper an executive vice-president with more authority than Stephens had ever owned.

I knew when I heard this that eventually I was going to have to play "chicken" with Cooper, and I was determined it wouldn't be me who would blink first. If he thought he could steamroller me, he would have the union perpetually on the run, and I couldn't permit that to happen. But I also realized that it wasn't fair to prejudge Cooper so harshly without at least attempting to put our relationship on a more positive footing. So I asked for a meeting with Cooper.

He didn't appear overjoyed to see me, but I brushed that aside and said with a sincerity I really felt: "Look, you and I and Roger are all about the same age. We have about ten years to go before retirement, and we can live those ten years in two armed camps or in some state of mutual respect and understanding. It can be a period of hell or of reasonable happiness. Now personally, I prefer the happy relationships, but you two will have to make that decision. I just wanted you to know that I'm ready to be rational and reasonable in my dealings if you are willing to offer me the same courtesy. I'm willing to understand and consider your problems if you're willing to consider and understand mine and those of the union men who work for you. So it's entirely up to you."

That sort of approach to Ben Fairless or John Stephens would have evoked a reply in kind. But not from R. Conrad Cooper—at least not in 1958. There were several seconds of silence, then Cooper said briskly: "Well, we want good labor relations, of course, but we also have to make a profit, you know . . ." And his voice trailed off and I left his office convinced we were going to have trouble. The only question in my mind was—how soon?

While I awaited the answer, I set out to protect the union's flanks by trying to build better public understanding of the labor point of view and better internal relations with the rank-and-file members of the Steelworkers. Just before Phil Murray died, he asked me to do some TV spot announcements on behalf of Adlai Stevenson's candidacy, and they turned out to be rather effective. I remembered them in 1958 and hired the same producer—Bob Post—to do a series of films for showing to new members of the Steelworkers and to college and civic groups.

About the same time, the McClellan Committee was criticizing the alleged lack of democracy in labor unions as illustrated by the relatively small number of members attending union meetings. This was a fine theoretical concept, but not very practical. We had some locals with as many as 20,000 members and trying to conduct a meeting of that size would have been chaotic. It wasn't necessary, because normal apathy kept about 90 percent of union members away from regular meetings. So why not, I asked myself, take the meeting to them? Thus was born the "Steelworkers Monthly TV Meeting."

With the Executive Board's approval of a pilot film, we produced a series of fifteen-minute shows to carry the message of the International to our membership, their families and the general public. We publicized the showing times—usually on Sunday afternoon—widely, and several surveys indicated a remarkably high percentage of viewers.

We needed all the goodwill we could store up, because we were very shortly going to have to draw on it for a long, long time. The basic steel and aluminum agreements were due to expire in mid-1959, and by the end of 1958 the steel industry made it very clear it was spoiling for a fight with the union. The steel industry went on the attack with an expensive public-relations and advertising campaign reiterating the theme of Roger Blough's polemic two years earlier: that irresponsible financial demands from organized labor in general and the Steelworkers in particular were directly responsible for the inflation that was then threatening the country. (There was no mention of skyrocketing steel prices.)

We came up with some counterpropaganda, planned and executed by singer Phil Regan who had been hired as the "voice of the steelworkers" and our public-relations consultant. Phil concocted a radio program in which I dispensed union propaganda between his songs, and for several months, we had it on 1,500 local radio stations. My constantly reiterated phrase was: "The more you earn the more you buy, and only human beings have purchasing power." The steel companies had begun something I always rejected out of hand: negotiating differences in the public entertainment and news media. But once they started it, we had no choice except to counter—even though they were doing it on prime TV time and we were on local radio.

While the battle of the tube was heating up, I had to fill a commitment in Australia, where I had been invited to address the Australian Social and Economic Council. I stopped off to see my friend, Henry J. Kaiser, in Honolulu, did a bit of sight-seeing on the Fiji Islands, then landed in Sydney, where I became a sort of good will ambassador without portfolio. The steelworkers there treated me royally, and a week of television and radio interviews and talks before Australian civic groups preceded my speech in

Canberra. From Australia, I visited Singapore, Bangkok, Hong Kong and Tokyo, and in each city I extolled the democratic capitalism of America that permitted free men to join labor unions and fight under protection of law for their own dignity, and I attacked Communist leaders at first hand.

When I returned home, Vice-President Nixon invited me to accompany him on a trip to the Soviet Union that was later to produce his famous kitchen encounter with Nikita Khrushchev. I couldn't go because the trip conflicted with the beginning of our negotiations with the basic steel industry.

That year, I would have been better off in Russia.

20

The steel industry in the winter of 1958–59 was a study in contrasts. On the surface, it was in deep trouble. The country was in a recession, steel exports were declining, and Japanese and German steel producers were trying—not very successfully—to dump their products in the American market. All of this looked very bad indeed, and the steel producers bled copiously as they told the world about their troubles in expensive advertisements and publicity campaigns. What they didn't point out was that profits—as a result of several fat price increases—were high and getting higher. Net income per ton of steel had climbed from $9.15 in 1954 to $19.31 in the last quarter of 1958, and the total value of U.S. Steel common stock had risen in value in the past ten years from $500 million to $5 *billion.*

Blough and Company had developed and honed a clever pricing gambit. Basic steel would raise its prices just before a union negotiation. Then, if the union had been granted any increases—fringe or otherwise—it would raise its prices again *after* the negotiations and blame the incipient inflation on the greed of the union. It was a clever and very nearly foolproof *modus operandi* that kept profits high and responsibility for economic ills low for the steel industry. And it was being sold to the public in spite of the fact that labor costs rose only 30 percent while steel prices were increasing 115 percent.

So thoroughly had the steel industry convinced the nation of its threadbare state in 1958 that it approached the union negotiations early in 1959 with the prospect of having the best of all possible worlds: increasing productivity, increasing profits and decreasing labor costs. In the prenegotiation skirmishes in the public press, the steel industry statements had been so militant that consumers began immediately to build up inventory against an almost certain strike.

In this strained atmosphere, R. Conrad Cooper—the new chairman of the Steel Industry Coordinating Committee—called me early in April, 1959, and asked for a private meeting. This was normal procedure. John Stephens and I used to meet privately in advance of negotiations to provide one another some idea of the procedures that would be followed in the open meetings. But Cooper introduced a new style. He handed me a letter from his committee which I tore open and read in front of him. It called, among other things, for a wage and benefit freeze and the liquidation of the cost-of-living adjustment program in the existing agreements. As I read, I could feel the heat creep up my neck, and it came to a boil when Cooper told me the letter had already been released to the newspapers.

"That's a hell of a way to start out," I told him. "Is this really the way you want to play? Do you want to argue this thing out in the newspapers or in a negotiating conference?" I waved the letter at him. "These terms are ridiculous and you know it. They're a provocation, not a serious collective bargaining proposal, and I reject them out of hand."

I stomped from his office, with the ghost of Ben Fairless mocking me all the way down the hall and the realization that we were in for one hell of a fight clutching my stomach.

I suggested we begin our negotiations two weeks early, and about 150 of us, including local union presidents, gathered in a meeting room at the Roosevelt Hotel in New York on May 5, 1959, to confront the Steel Coordinating Committee. Twelve other second-echelon groups were meeting separately at the same time, company by company, but the "economic matters"—the issues serious enough to provoke a strike—were all being negotiated by the "summit committee." Cooper and I each made an opening statement, then our district and local people presented some of their views, and I was pleased to find they were making many of the points we had discussed in our televised "Steelworker Meetings." The first session ended with a plea on my part that we "not negotiate this agreement in the press." I got my answer to *that* one when the industry negotiators held a press conference as soon as we broke up.

The union program, prepared by our Wage Policy Committee, called for wage increases, improvements in pensions and insurance, increased hospitalization benefits and a number of noneconomic items. No specific amounts were spelled out. That was to be left to the principal negotiators.

The steel companies had prepared their position on an elaborate slide screen presentation. Distilled of clever artwork, their demands added up to the right to do anything they wanted with the work force—reduce crews, change working conditions and eliminate the right of the union to appeal through the grievance and arbitration machinery. This, of course, was in addition to freezing wages and benefits.

From the beginning, there was none of the horseplay, wisecracks or inside jokes that had always lightened other negotiations and made them bearable. The steel industry members were cold, grim and aloof, and, naturally, after a day or two of this treatment, our men picked up the same attitudes. At one early session, Cooper read a statement contending that everything done in collective bargaining in the steel industry since 1941 had been wrong. I was incredulous. I asked him if he thought Ben Fairless was wrong, and he answered, "Yes." Then I ticked off the names of all the people of courage and principle who had been involved in those negotiations and asked if he thought they, too, were wrong. Although he later denied it, he responded "Yes" to each name I brought up.

It was the only time he said "Yes" to anything during the early weeks of those negotiations. Both sides were steadily becoming more angry and frustrated, and since there seemed little hope of a change inside the negotiations, I looked for one outside. I noticed in the newspapers that President Eisenhower was coming to New York for a speech, so I requested an appointment with him. I left the negotiations, knowing I would be followed by the reporters covering the meeting but saying nothing about my destination. I talked with the President for about a half hour, mostly about baseball. The steel negotiations were never mentioned. When I emerged, I told the reporters who clustered around me the God's truth, that "we didn't talk about the conference. It was just a visit of a couple of old friends."

None of them believed me, of course, which was precisely what I wanted and expected. The whole thing was a psychological ploy aimed at stirring up speculation that I had carried our case to the President to enlist his help. In light of some of the public statements of Cooper and Blough, it was a credible theory and I wanted to keep the steel people off balance. If nothing more, it at least provided a change of pace from the deadly sameness of the negotiating sessions.

By early June, we were casting about rather desperately for some means of breaking the negotiations off dead center short of simply walking out of them, which would have made it possible for the industry to blame us for whatever followed. On June 10, 1959, the steel committee thoughtfully solved our dilemma for us. Cooper handed me a "Dear Mr. McDonald" letter, couched in cold, stiff language demanding eight drastic changes in labor-management relations, including the stipulation that the union give up its right to confer with management on operating changes and waive grievance or arbitration procedures in the event of a disagreement.

It was a stupid move by the steel committee. Up to this point, our membership was apathetic and the industry negotiators should have known that. The union members were generally fat and comfortable and had little stomach for a strike; there probably would have been considerable pressure on us to capitulate on a number of points had the industry been willing to concede on others. But now we had a totally new game. The industry negotiators, through their own self-righteous intransigence, had done us a favor, handed us an issue. I couldn't have written the script better myself.

I put out an immediate public statement saying that the steel companies were apparently "determined to destroy the individual rights so carefully and painstakingly developed over the years" and that this present management group "has nothing but contempt for its employees." I answered specifically each of the points in the industry letter, then concluded: "Our answer to this proposal is that the United Steelworkers of America is not a company union."

Our sleeping members were awakening, now, and the industry compounded its mistake by launching a new and expensive advertising campaign in newspapers across the country accusing the steelworkers of featherbedding by standing in the way of improved production techniques. This was simply not true, and it made the workingmen damned angry. I remember visiting my hometown of Greenfield during this period, and some of my old millhand friends—usually rather conservative in their attitudes toward labor troubles—were fighting mad. They told me not to "let them get hold of the bull whip."

The amount of deception ladled out to the public in these industry advertisements, which stepped up steadily in frequency and tempo, was massive. Nowhere was it pointed out that the number of man-hours required to produce a ton of steel had been cut in half since 1940, and that actual labor costs per ton of steel had *decreased* steadily during that same period. And the industry bleats about the competition of foreign steel—supposedly made possible by higher labor costs in the United States—were nonsense. The steel companies knew—and had admitted to me in our previous negotiations—that steel production costs in Japan and Western Europe were higher than in the United States, and the only danger from foreign steel was "dumping," a process of selling below cost to build a foreign market. This was illegal in the United States and was a problem for Federal agents, not for the negotiating table. I suppose these sophistries brought a lot of lay citizens to the side of the steel companies, but they also solidified the ranks of the workingmen behind the union negotiators. And made them very angry.

Between mid-June and July 14, when our contract officially terminated, I had several dozen private talks with Cooper, usually after employing all sorts of devious tricks to escape the newspapermen who dogged us. But talk between contending parties of comparable strength and stature is fruitless unless there is some disposition to compromise, and Cooper showed none. Accepting his demands would have meant negating the work of all my predecessors, and he refused to modify the demands or consider the changes the union requested. And so our private conversations were no more successful than the public negotiations, and at midnight on July 14, 1959, the word went out to our members, "No contract—no work."

I was standing by the main gate of the U.S. Steel plant near Trenton, New Jersey, when the stoppage went into effect. There were thousands of workers milling about in a carnival atmosphere; and when the moment struck, a group of them lifted me on their shoulders and carried me up and down the first picket line. Then I climbed on the back of a truck, urged them to remain united and pledged an "eventual victory" that I suspected would come a great deal harder than I was prepared to tell that enthusiastic crowd in Trenton.

We were as ready as we could be for this shutdown. Since I had taken over as president, the union had brought several hundred steelworkers with special qualifications in from the field and trained them as counselors for such an emergency. They, in turn, had recruited and trained thousands of others to help them at the local level. Once the strike was called, this organization swung into action. Local union offices and halls were opened to counsel people in financial trouble and lend them money in cases of extreme need. Committees called on rental agencies and grocery stores and other merchants to explain the strike and to ask for patience with steelworkers who might be late in meeting their bills. We didn't guarantee payment to these merchants; all we could do was offer them hope. But the response from most local merchants was unbelievably good. It was, of course, in their long-range interests to maintain the friendship of their steelworker customers, but before this strike was over, thousands of merchants extended themselves far beyond the call of duty.

This was decidedly not the coalfields of the 1920's. We were prepared, financially, morally and mechanically, to deal with this strike. We had the support of other unions which lent us almost $6 million for relief of strikers—all paid back, incidentally, within two years. The atmosphere on many picket lines in the early days of the strike was congenial. One Republic plant, for example, put out wires for television sets to entertain the pickets. And the local union at a Youngstown Sheet and Tube plant near Chicago charged foremen and maintenance men $2 apiece to cross their picket line and were actually $40,000 wealthier when the strike ended.

As a matter of fact, picket line friction—once the source of beatings and bloodshed—was considerably less than the friction in the high-level negotiations still under way. During the first two months of the strike, most of the ploys on both sides were more psychological than actual. When some of the members of the AFL-CIO Executive Council were reluctant about giving us financial support, I told them in disgust: "Goddam it, I don't care nearly as much about your money as I do your public embrace. The money is tangible evidence of support, and I need a psychological show of support to demonstrate that organized labor is behind the Steel-workers. If you don't agree with that idea, then forget it." I got the money *and* the support.

We called repeatedly on the presidents of the major steel companies to meet with us because their representatives were apparently without power to move off the fixed positions they had taken before the negotiations even started. They never returned my calls. So we ran newspaper advertisements listing my home and office telephone numbers and suggesting that Blough or some other responsible principal officer of a major steel company call me. None of them did.

Once I addressed a group of Wall Street tycoons, was well received and fielded more than an hour of questions afterward that provoked some thought in that group. I was kept posted on the feelings in Wall Street by former Ambassador Joseph Kennedy, with whom I had lunch periodically during the strike. I had met him through Phil Murray, and we had become close friends. His contention, from which he never wavered during these conversations, was simple and direct: if we could hold out, the financial people would eventually bring enough pressure on the steel industry to force them to capitulate.

In between these speeches and fruitless negotiating sessions, I was flying about the country, visiting hundreds of union halls and picket lines, drinking buckets of coffee, eating hundreds of doughnuts and shaking thousands of hands. Spirits remained high on the picket lines but grew steadily more rancorous around the negotiating table. More than once, my thoughts wandered from the drone of management polemics to a better day when there was mutual respect and always a hope of compromise. I thought those years had taught us to learn to live together a bit better. Now it seemed that all this hard work had gone down the drain. The Fairlesses and Graces and Stephenses were gone, and the new heads in the steel industry had apparently decided they were going to show this union how tough they could be.

The ultimate absurdity of this sort of attitude came in chance encounters outside the meeting rooms, where industry men would go to ridiculous lengths to avoid "seeing" union representatives. I remember several times running into management men on airplanes. They would always turn their heads so they wouldn't have to speak with me. I never made it easy for them. I always sought them out and spoke, which embarrassed them. But apparently it never embarrassed them enough to change the industry policy of no fraternization with the enemy. To them, this was total war.

That's the way the nation's press played it, too, and it had no reluctance about identifying the Good Guys (the steel industry) and the Bad Guys (the union). Some of the reporters played it straight, but practically all of the publishers gave us hell. I tried to explain our position to as many of them as we could round up to listen, but it didn't help very much. Fairly typical was a session I had with the executives of the *Chicago Sun-Times,* supposedly the most liberal newspaper in Chicago. They persisted in relating our dispute to their own problems with craft unions, which made it easy for them to believe the steel industry contention that it must have absolute and unilateral controls over work rules to avoid featherbedding. Nothing I could say would change their minds.

I was also anointed during this period on the cover of *Time Magazine* and ripped apart in an article full of innuendo and half-truths in *Reader's Digest.* Both writers sought interviews when I was incredibly busy, and Rosemary gave up a chance for an infrequent private visit with me during that frenetic period by inviting the *Time* reporter to accompany her to the airport when she picked me up at the end of a swing around the country. The union had a leasing arrangement with a car rental agency in New York, and I happened to know the Teamster who was driving and spoke to him in front of the reporter. His first name was "James"—and you can fill in the rest. The *Time* article opened with me telling the driver, "Home, James."

I agreed to see the *Digest* writer—a man named Lester Velie—before a business luncheon at the 21 Club in New York on the absolute condition that he not mention the setting in which we talked. For some reason that I never quite understood, the press didn't give a damn where steel magnates ate or slept, but were intensely interested in my private habits and I didn't want to generate any publicity at that juncture that might damage our cause. Velie violated the trust, of course, because seeing me at 21 fortified the premise of his article portraying me as a "silk-stocking labor leader."

With the kind of press I got, I never stayed at just a hotel or ate at just a restaurant. When I traveled, I stayed at the "plush" Roosevelt or the "luxurious" Hampshire House. When I ate, it was at the "posh" 21 or the "expensive" Jack Dempsey's. Hell, if I had stayed at the YMCA, it would have been reported as the "luxurious" Y. This was all tied in, I suppose, with the public image that labor leaders should stay in fleabag hotels and eat at Joe's Diner; otherwise they are "squandering" the dues that are bled from the hides of the working people they represent. I had to live with this all my working life, and I suppose it will never change. But it also never failed to make me sore.

By the time President Eisenhower decided to get into the act in 1959, *everybody* was getting sore, and the lines had hardened on both sides. Eisenhower was a great believer in the Federal Government keeping hands off matters that should be resolved in the private sector, but by mid-July, the strike was beginning to hurt the economy badly and the President was under extreme pressure from the financial community to step in and try to resolve it. He called the contending parties to the White House separately. When we arrived, the industry leaders had just emerged and were holding an impromptu press conference on the White House steps. I resisted the impulse to liven it up a bit, and we went on inside. Our session with Eisenhower was brief and to the point.

He said: "Dave, this strike is hurting the whole country. It's time you meet with the heads of the steel companies and try to end it."

I told him: "Mr. President, I've been trying to do that for weeks. They won't talk with me."

And he answered: "Try again. I think they will now."

So we went back to our hotel and tried again. I called Blough's room, one floor above mine, to seek a meeting. Cooper answered the phone and said Blough wasn't there and he didn't know when he would be back. I washed up, slammed out of my room and punched the elevator button. When it opened, there before me was R. Conrad Cooper shepherding all the men I'd been trying to talk with for weeks, including Roger Blough.

It was an immensely satisfying moment, and I stood there for a few seconds with my foot in the open doorway, enjoying it. Cooper reddened and looked the other way. The rest of them stared at me blankly.

I stepped in the elevator and said cheerfully: "What a remarkable coincidence. I've been trying to reach all of you people for weeks, and now we meet in an elevator."

We rode down in silence, but I wasn't ready to let them off the hook that easily. I got out first, then stood in the elevator door so each passenger would have to shake hands with me as he stepped out. That's about all the satisfaction we got out of Eisenhower's intervention. A group of company presidents did meet with us briefly, but only to reiterate that Cooper's committee had full authority to deal with the union. Joseph Block, of Inland Steel, made an effort to get talks started but his associates wouldn't go along.

This virtually forced the President to invoke the Taft-Hartley Act. He resisted pressures to seek an injunction against us and instead set up a Board of Inquiry under Dr. George Taylor of the University of Pennsylvania to hold public hearings on the issues in dispute in the hope of finding some means of resolving them.

During a recess in the hearings, Phil Regan asked me to join him in his hotel room for lunch. When I arrived, he picked up the telephone and called Edgar Kaiser, the board chairman of Kaiser Steel and the son of my old friend, Henry J. Kaiser. Regan asked Kaiser to drop by for a chat, and Edgar was surprised to find me there when he arrived. I was uneasy, at first, that Edgar might think we were ambushing him, but he seemed unconcerned and perfectly willing to discuss the worsening steel situation. Although Kaiser Steel was one of the companies represented by the Industry Coordinating Committee, it was regarded uneasily by other members of the steel industry as something of a maverick. Henry J. Kaiser was always his own man and acted by his own lights, and his son reflected these same qualities.

I told Edgar that he was the first company president willing to talk with me since the strike began, that I was anxious to start meaningful bargaining, and that we had never opposed operating improvements arrived at by mutual agreement but I couldn't bargain away our grievance rights. He listened to me carefully, and when I finished, I caught his eyes squarely and said: "Edgar, let's break this thing open. Why doesn't Kaiser Steel cut loose from the other steel companies and make a separate agreement with us?"

He would say only that he'd think about it, and I figured he wanted to discuss it with his father before he made any final decision. So I decided to get to Henry J. first. I put in a call to him, couldn't reach him and went out to dinner. The call came through at Dinty Moore's ("plush") restaurant, and I had to strain to hear Henry Kaiser over the buzz of conversation and the clanking of dishes. I told him about my conversation with Edgar, and Henry said he was sick of the shutdown and was coming to New York in a few days to talk with Edgar about it.

He did—and things began to happen. As Henry described it to me several days later, he met with Blough and ran into the same intransigent attitude I'd been bucking since May. Then he met with his son and urged that Kaiser Steel open separate negotiations with the Steelworkers. Edgar made one last try to urge the Coordinating Committee to compromise some of their positions, got nowhere and told them he wanted his mill back in operation and planned to seek a separate labor agreement.

While the President's Board of Inquiry was taking testimony in Washington, we opened negotiations with Kaiser Steel in Washington. Within a few weeks, Kaiser had agreed to a 22½-cent wage increase package over a two-year period (less than a cent per man hour more than the last joint offer of the Industry Committee) and—much more important—to respect our traditional grievance procedure and put two joint labor-management commissions to work at investigating and suggesting solutions to future matters in contention. We also established a public-union-company committee, headed by Dr. George Taylor of the University of Pennsylvania.

When he signed the new contract, Edgar Kaiser said: "We believe if management tried to change long established work rules unilaterally, it would be making a tragic error in judgment. No man wants to be coerced. Production rises faster when men have pride in their work and company. The union's progressive attitude toward automation has been a credit to its leadership."

Shortly afterward, Kaiser received an anonymous telegram I wish I had written. It said simply: "I realized Kaiser had only 2 percent of the steel production but I didn't realize it had 98 percent of the brains."

All this, of course, caused a great deal of embarrassment to the rest of the steel companies. So did the semiannual profit-and-loss statements made public late in August. They showed total net income of the steel industry up 140 percent over the first half of 1958 and average earnings per share of common stock *up 420 percent* for the eleven basic steel companies. Some of this huge increase was admittedly due to accelerated production in the early months of 1959 in anticipation of a shutdown. But basically, the figures described graphically a fat-cat industry making fantastic profits while it tried to squeeze its workers and blame them for inflation at the same time.

Meanwhile, the Board of Inquiry was winding up hearings that often generated a good deal more heat than light. Some ludicrous things happened there. When I first appeared to testify, there was a sizable contingent of Steelworkers present, and they applauded me as I took the witness chair. Next day when Cooper was called, his claque performed as if it were competing on an applause meter. The level of some of the testimony at that hearing can be judged by Cooper's reference to me as "that ham actor," an accurate description, maybe, but somewhat out of keeping with the occasion. I landed the last blow in that exchange, however. After the "ham actor" comment, I saw a photographer shooting a picture of Cooper testifying which I knew would include me sitting alongside. So just as he shot, I pressed my nose between my thumb and forefinger, and the picture made the front page of dozens of newspapers.

This sort of nonsense only served to build up public pressures for some sort of settlement. These pressures made it difficult to resist the company's "last offer"—made through the Board of Inquiry—that would have submitted the work-rights dispute to compulsory arbitration. Enough Steelworker officials—including Arthur Goldberg—felt we should consider arbitration that I convened an Executive Board meeting to discuss it. I was opposed to arbitration for two reasons, one basic, the other ethereal. The steel companies in 1959 were challenging some of our fundamental rights, earned in blood over many years. I didn't feel these issues were proper subjects for arbitration and I didn't want to set that sort of precedent, even if they were all returned to us, as they probably would have been. The other reason grew out of the rumors I was hearing from Wall Street; I was sure that pressure on the steel industry from the financial community would eventually force them to capitulate. Although Joe Germano and several other district directors were ready to submit to arbitration, the board voted against it by a large margin.

By this time, Eisenhower was angry and the pressures on him to get the economy moving again were intolerable. So on October 21, he ordered the Justice Department to seek an injunction in the U.S. District Court in Pittsburgh, ordering the striking Steelworkers back to their jobs. Judge Austin Staley ruled in favor of the union, and the case went immediately to the Supreme Court. There, in spite of a brilliant argument by Arthur Goldberg, the lower court decision was overturned and I was told to order our members back to work on November 7 under terms of the agreement in effect on June 30 of that year. In between all these legal maneuverings, the men had been out a total of 116 days. And we were right back where we had started seven months earlier.

So once again we went back to the same old negotiating grind in Washington. The industry ignored the Kaiser settlement and remained inflexible on its work-rights position. On Christmas Eve, we broke up to go home for the holidays, and quite unexpectedly, Cooper asked me and my family to join him on the U.S. Steel plane. I started to tell him we'd made other arrangements—which we had—then hesitated. Maybe he wanted to tell me something. Maybe the spirit of the season had gotten to him. Maybe just the chance to talk in those relaxed surroundings might break through some wall of reserve. So I accepted his invitation.

My son was now playing football, and he and Cooper got into a detailed discussion of the game that lasted all the way to Pittsburgh. Although no business was discussed, I've always thought that trip marked a change in attitude that finally started us downhill.

Under the terms of the Taft-Hartley law, the "last offer" put before the Board of Inquiry had to be submitted to a vote of our members. It was scheduled for January 11, and some hurried polls indicated that the Steelworkers would support the action of our board in rejecting compulsory arbitration of our work-rule grievance rights. But I had no idea where we would go from there.

My own morale had hit bottom when I had a call from Secretary of Labor Jim Mitchell asking me to meet with him and President Eisenhower in mid-December. The President was remarkably calm, a lot calmer than I. He began to tick off all the things he would do in my situation. As I explained to him that I had already tried each one, my own anger kept rising until I finally launched into a tirade against the steel industry in the kind of soldier talk that Eisenhower understood quite well. The President was jolted, more at the strength of my feelings than my language. He explained that his options were slowly disappearing and that he might have to request Congress to act if we didn't get together soon. I told him I hoped he would tell the other side that, too, and then said good night in a bad state of depression. Eisenhower asked Mitchell to stay behind, and I returned to Pittsburgh that night. In my state of mind, I wanted to be in my own home, not a hotel room.

When I got home, there was a call waiting for me from Mitchell. He asked if I would call Blough in New York the next morning, adding that Roger would be expecting my call. Blough answered, himself, and was disarmingly affable. He asked me to meet him for breakfast at the Duquesne Club in Pittsburgh the next day.

I still remember that breakfast as an Alice-in-Wonderland exercise. I was tired, keyed up, feeling the pressure, and Blough was full of simpleminded pleasantries appropriate to a country club cocktail party. I tried to explain our position for the ten-thousandth time, and at one juncture he looked at me blandly and said, "You know, David, you are really a very attractive guy."

That was too much for me. I gritted my teeth and said, "For Christ's sake, Roger, remember me? I'm the guy who was negotiating with U.S. Steel when you were only a lawyer for the corporation. We've known each other a long time. You've heard me before and you've heard all this before. Why are we playing these games?"

I found out then that Blough was worried that if the strike weren't settled soon, Congress would pass a compulsory arbitration law. He didn't want that, but for some reason he thought I did. At last we had a point of agreement, and I jumped in with both feet. I told him I'd seen compulsory arbitration laws operating in Australia and I didn't like them one bit. "I don't want them here any more than you do," I said, "and you've got to believe me."

So he agreed to join his negotiating committee and meet with Goldberg and me in New York. At long last, I had one of the principals involved. We met several days without progress. They insisted on talking compromise in money matters; I insisted that was of secondary importance to protecting the grievance machinery on work rules. Meanwhile Congress was getting more restive.

As we wavered on the edge of compulsory arbitration legislation, Jim Mitchell called me again and asked me to come to Washington that night for a meeting with Vice-President Nixon. Eisenhower had turned the matter over to Nixon, said Mitchell, with instructions to settle it before Congress acted. When I arrived at Nixon's home, he answered the door himself. He said that Blough had visited him a few hours earlier and was convinced that I was dragging my feet in the negotiations because I wanted a compulsory arbitration law.

I rolled my eyes and said, "My God, I told him myself just a few days ago—over and over and over—that I don't want such a law. What else can I do?"

Nixon said, "Okay, now that I know that, let's get it across to Roger. Can you meet here tomorrow morning with Blough, Jim and me and talk this thing out?"

I said: "Mr. Vice-President, I would meet with anybody, anywhere, anytime to get this thing settled."

And so it was done.

We gathered the next morning at Nixon's home and he told us: "There is no question in my mind that Congress is going to enact a compulsory arbitration law in the next few weeks to get this steel matter settled if we don't settle it very quickly ourselves. Neither the President nor I want such a law. If it were enacted for steel, it might likely be extended before long to all labor negotiations and eventually free collective bargaining would end. Both of you have assured me that you don't want such a law, either. Is that correct?"

He looked at me, and I picked up the cue. Addressing myself directly to Blough, I repeated much of what I had said in the Duquesne Club. I said it with sincerity dripping off every word. When Blough looked dubious, Nixon would press me with questions—and finally we convinced him. Then Nixon asked us for our promise that we would get together alone and try to reach some sort of agreement. When he had our word on this, he put us in his car and sent us back to our hotels. On the way, we decided to meet in my suite at 10 the next morning. About 9:30 he called and asked to postpone the meeting until afternoon, and I thought, Oh, oh, there goes the old ball game again.

But he called on me at 2 P.M. and by 4 o'clock—scratching on a pair of legal pads—we reached the basis of an agreement. He consented—as he knew by then he must—not to discard the grievance protection for work-rights procedures. And I consented to the formation of a joint study group—to be called the Human Relations Committee—to look into the whole matter of work changes and alleged featherbedding. After the work-rights concession, everything else seemed almost incidental, but there were several far-reaching victories for the union in the rest of the agreement. Most important, the steel companies would pick up the entire insurance tab, thus eliminating the previous fifty-fifty arrangement. There was also a forty-cents-an-hour economic package spread over thirty months and improvements in a number of noneconomic areas.

I got quick approval from our Wage Policy Committee, and Blough did the same with the other industry leaders. The following day a memorandum of agreement was signed.

The date was January 4, 1960—eight months and two days from the opening of negotiations.

That night, Martin Agronsky interviewed me on his CBS television news show. He asked me about the people who had helped reach the settlement, and seemed surprised when I included Joe Kennedy on the list. He asked how Ambassador Kennedy had helped, and I explained about our luncheon meetings. Then I added: "We talked about other things beside the steel strike. We talked a great deal about the conviction both of us share that the Ambassador's son, Senator John F. Kennedy, should be the next President of the United States."

The contract was signed.

I was looking ahead.

21

I was as glad to be back on the payroll as any other union member when the long strike was finally settled. There's a legend I must have heard repeated a few thousand times that one reason union leaders can be so casual about pulling their members off the job is that the salaries of the top officials continue regardless. I don't know about other unions, but in the Steelworkers this simply isn't true. When the members are on strike, the salaries of the officers and staff of the International (with the exception of the clerks) stop, too. When the 1959, strike was finally settled, Rosemary and I had $234 in our cash reserve—and a lot of unpaid bills. That's why the magazine articles and the abusive letters about the plush life we were leading made us so angry. I spent a total of nineteen days in my own home in the year of 1959, and I must admit it looked plush to me on the few occasions I visited there.

But the acrimony was past, temporarily, at least, and it was time to think of celebrations and politics. Especially politics. We had a cocktail party after the final signing, and by far the greatest excitement was generated by John F. Kennedy, who bounced in to thank me for the plug on the Agronsky show. R. Conrad Cooper was a sad and neglected figure when it was all over, and I insisted that he stay for our party—although he didn't want to. One of our men, feeling the juice, asked me if he couldn't "take just one punch at the son of a bitch," but most of the Steelworkers were relaxed and glad it was over, and very slowly Cooper warmed to them. One union man pulled out a hundred-dollar bill and said, "Hey, Coop, how about autographing this. I just wanted you to see that we weren't broke yet." Cooper grinned and signed the bill and began to relax and enjoy himself.

Before he left, he took me aside and said, "Dave, I've read a lot of stories that there is a strong personal dislike between us. I just want you to know that this isn't true on my part. Not true at all."

And I shook his hand with real feeling and told him, "I have no dislike for you. You know that. We've both played enough football to know that we give the game all we have and don't carry the grudges off the field."

He left then, and our relations began to improve steadily. Cooper was put in charge of setting up the Human Relations Committee, and he seemed to believe in it. So did I. It offered the best hope of blunting issues that would force intractable positions on the negotiating parties at contract time. Although it had only study responsibilities, it could make recommendations to collective bargaining groups, and there were no wraps on the HRC when it discussed a problem, no rigid positions that had to be upheld. That was its strength and its hope.

So while the HRC was getting under way and we were working out a remarkable agreement with Kaiser Steel called a "Savings Sharing Plan"—in which individual workers and the company shared the savings in production costs from good housekeeping and careful preservation of scrap and avoidance of waste—I turned my attention to some serious politicking. In 1960, I had a candidate who had captured my heart and my imagination, and I was ready to go all out for him.

I never left any private doubt anywhere about my feelings. Early in 1960, Nixon held a stag party at his home for a number of us who had been involved in the steel shutdown. The talk turned quickly to politics, and since Goldberg and I were the only Democrats present, we were asked our views on whom the Democrats would nominate for President.

Goldberg replied instantly, "Adlai Stevenson."

I said, "I think you're wrong. I think it's going to be Jack Kennedy."

We argued a few minutes while the Republicans listened, then I nodded to our host and told Goldberg, "If your man is nominated, then we're being entertained tonight by the next President of the United States."

I set out early in the year to do what I could do to prevent that from happening. As it turned out, I was able to do quite a lot. In

October of 1959, Joe Kennedy had asked me, "Would you be willing to put your political organization to work to get the nomination for Jack?" I said that I would, and by the time the candidates were setting up shop for the first primary in Wisconsin, my Steelworker organization was in full operation. I started in February to send out the word to our district directors and regional and local Political Action Committees that Jack Kennedy was our man and we were going all out for him. This was done quietly. I made no political speeches because it would have been the end of Kennedy to put a tag on him as a labor candidate at that juncture. In spite of the fairy tales dispensed by the NAM, organized labor is decidedly a minority group in this country, and whenever we make political noises, the National Chamber of Commerce has to go to the bathroom. So our activities were low key: by word of mouth in meetings, by telephone calls, by letter—and sometimes, I suspected, by osmosis. But however it traveled, it worked.

While the message was going out to our political workers, some other candidates began cozying up to me, apparently unaware of my deep commitment to Kennedy. One of them was Senator Lyndon Johnson. An Ohio Congressman named Mike Kerwin always gave a St. Patrick's Day Party in Washington that I attended, and Johnson cornered me there in 1960 to discuss his potential run for the presidential nomination. As soon as we began talking, a group of newspapermen gathered around, and he asked if I would stop by his office the next morning.

I knew Johnson as a tough, shrewd, wheeling-and-dealing politician of the FDR, Populist school who had long ago lost all his illusions and knew where all the bodies were buried. The overwhelming support of the Steelworkers in Texas had won him his place in the Senate—by a paper-thin margin—and he knew it. Consequently, he used to call on me when he had a tough political problem and needed help, and I had no hesitation in going to him for the same purpose.

So it was natural and normal that he would expect the support of the Steelworkers in his quest for the presidential nomination, and when I told him the next morning that I was totally committed to Jack Kennedy, he was visibly distressed. He also jumped immediately to a wrong conclusion, probably because the AFL-CIO had kept him at arm's length because of his conservatism in many domestic matters. Raising his voice, Johnson told me, "Up here, Dave, I'm considered a reactionary, but in Texas I'm considered a raving Communist." I interpreted this to mean that labor shouldn't confuse his basic liberal orientation in domestic affairs just because he had to strike a conservative posture for his Texas constituents. While this was probably true, it was much too late for me to change my mind about Jack Kennedy.

Johnson refused to recognize this, however, and kept asking me why he couldn't count on my support and the support of the AFL-CIO since he had been carrying the burden of the battle for labor legislation in the Senate.

I reminded him: "You wouldn't even be here if the steelworkers in Texas hadn't worked so hard for you."

He flushed and said, "I know that, but there is one thing *you* should remember, too. If I'm not President, I'm going to be in the Senate for the next six years, and I'm probably going to be the Majority Leader."

He let the implication hang there, and it made me angry.

"If you're threatening me," I said, "that's the worst way I can think of to try and get my support. And if you're not threatening me, you should think about the implications of what you say before you say it."

He backed off, then, and calmed me down, and we parted as friends. But he must have known after that conversation that the convention was going to be an uphill fight all the way for Lyndon Johnson.

The only place I ran into resistance from my own organization on Jack Kennedy was in West Virginia, where our district director called me, said he was for Hubert Humphrey and planned to work for him. So I sent word back for our staff and the Steelworker locals to undercut the district director and go all out for Kennedy. This was the only place we were divided—and also the only place Kennedy had serious trouble in the primaries.

While he was en route from Wisconsin to West Virginia, the Pennsylvania Steelworkers PAC was meeting in Pittsburgh. I called Kennedy and suggested he make an unadvertised and un-expected appearance at the meeting and he agreed. Beyond the obvious motive of offering him as much mass exposure as possible, I had two other reasons for this play. I knew Kennedy was going to have problems in West Virginia, and I figured his exposure be-fore a labor audience just prior to launching his campaign there would be helpful. But most important of all, I wanted to bring some heavy pressure to bear on Governor David Lawrence, who was scheduled to speak to the PAC that same morning and who would head the Pennsylvania delegation to the Democratic Con-vention. Lawrence refused to accept his own political success as proof that being a Catholic would no longer bar a man from the Presidency. He had opposed Kennedy for the vice-presidential nomination in 1956 because of his religion, and he was already making the same noises in 1960. I wanted him to see, firsthand, the sort of excitement this young man generated.

Once again, the script couldn't have been better. Kennedy flew in, and I had two of my aides pick him up and escort him to the meeting. Lawrence was there and waiting to speak when Ken-nedy burst into the hall. The delegates literally went wild, stand-ing on their seats and cheering for more than a half hour. I stayed away, because I didn't want to be associated publicly with this gambit, but the lesson wasn't lost on Lawrence. I'm convinced the Pennsylvania delegation was won for Kennedy at that PAC meet-ing in Pittsburgh.

While Kennedy was demonstrating in the primaries that a Catholic *could* win Protestant support, I was traveling about the country, explaining our new Human Relations Committee pub-licly and privately urging our state political action groups to work hard at getting as many Steelworkers as possible elected to the Democratic National Convention as delegates. They heard me loud and clear, and over the summer one hundred members of the union won places on state delegations. When I arrived in Los Angeles for the convention on July 18, I controlled by far the larg-est single bloc of votes—a fact of which Bobby Kennedy and his aides were acutely aware.

We set up an operating office at the Biltmore Hotel, one floor above the Kennedy headquarters. Our sleeping rooms were at the Ambassador—although we didn't do much sleeping during the convention week. I had about a hundred people working for me on the floor—some of them delegates, some sergeants-at-arms, some laymen. They always knew they could reach me instantly, either at my aisle seat in the Pennsylvania delegation, at the club on the balcony overlooking the convention floor, or at my headquarters in the Biltmore.

During the preballot maneuverings, Bobby Kennedy beat a constant path up and down the steps to the Steelworkers' headquarters. He always came to me; I never went to him.

How about calling Pat Brown, he would say, and getting any favorite son ideas out of his head? And I called Brown and told him: "If you get into this thing yourself, we're going to have a couple of Catholics fighting each other, and the bigots will have a field day. You know you can't make it anyway, so why don't you climb on with a winner and come out for Jack?"

Do you think you could get Humphrey to make a strong Kennedy statement? Bobby would ask. I tried, and I couldn't. Humphrey was noncommittal, watching the scene.

[Robert] Meyner in New Jersey is giving us trouble, Bobby would say, and we wish you'd try to get him to commit his delegation to Jack. And I went to the floor and said: "Governor Meyner, remember how the Steelworkers helped you in New Jersey? Now we need *your* help. We need a Kennedy commitment from your delegation." And the governor rubbed his chin and replied: "Dave, you know how I feel, but I can't commit the whole delegation. They've got to caucus and make up their own minds."

Many times during that week, I was asked *why* I was going all out for Jack Kennedy, *why* someone I was pressuring should be as excited as I was about this young Senator. I had to be persuasive. To be persuasive, I had to be sincere. And to be sincere, I had to think through, myself, the reasons I felt the way I did.

I suppose basically it was the remarkable sense of integrity and dedication this man exuded constantly without ever being stuffy about it. He was an accomplished politician, but he didn't play games with politics. In my dealings with him, he was totally forth-right, always. Two examples will illustrate. During the hearings on the Landrum-Griffin Labor Act, which finally got rid of some of the more obnoxious sections of Taft-Hartley but was still a gener-ally reactionary piece of labor legislation, Kennedy served as chairman of a subcommittee holding hearings on the bill. I caught up with him privately one evening during the hearings and made him listen to my arguments against a provision that would require labor leaders to be bonded and intensely audited. This was no problem for us because we had always made our audits public, but it seemed to me to set a bad precedent of presumed dishonesty in the labor movement. It would also be expensive and difficult to administrate. He heard me out, cocking his head and squinting his eyes. Then he grinned that Kennedy grin and clapped me on the shoulder and said, "Yeah, that's all well and good. But you're an *honest* labor leader."

I was also pushing hard in 1960 for a 32-hour work week as a solution to the recession that was pinching the country and as a buffer against the encroachments of automation. Kennedy wouldn't buy it and refused to say anything kind about it, either to me privately—at a time when he badly needed my support—or to labor groups he addressed. He was a man of tremendous courage and principle, combined with a sharp, penetrating intel-ligence and a wry wit that permitted him to look and laugh at his own shortcomings. The more I saw him, the more I loved him and the harder I worked for him. And because I felt it strongly, I had no difficulty conveying this enthusiasm to others.

I suppose I saw in this man the youthful embodiment of every-thing in which I'd ever believed. And so I chivvied and bullied and pleaded and traded and threatened and maneuvered on the convention floor to get him votes. While Bobby was riding herd on the delegate strength he had painfully put together, I deliv-ered the hundred Steelworker votes, prodded the Pennsylvania delegation (headed by a Catholic who thought a Catholic couldn't win) into voting as a bloc for Kennedy, and perhaps convinced a scattering of others from the depths of my own conviction.

It was enough. Jack Kennedy was nominated on the first ballot. We were over the first hurdle.

Then the Kennedy team had to face a problem they'd refused to contemplate until the nomination was secure: the selection of a Vice-President. It was more important than usual because Kennedy was a Catholic and a New England intellectual, both qualities that provoked deep suspicion in the Middle West and the Bible Belt of the South. They had to be counterbalanced on the ticket. The race against Nixon was going to be very, very close, and the selection of a running mate might quite likely mean the difference between victory and defeat.

In such a situation, politicians find strange bedfellows. I'd heard nothing from the Lyndon Johnson camp since the start of the convention. I had apparently convinced Johnson in our meeting in Washington that there was no possibility of turning me against Kennedy. Strangely enough, the first person to mention Johnson's name to me at the 1960 convention was Bobby Kennedy. He came to my hotel room a few hours after Jack's nomination and asked, "Dave, who would you choose between Symington and Johnson for Vice-President?"

I had a good many mixed feelings. Politically, Johnson seemed the best choice to balance the ticket, but I knew many of my associates in organized labor would fight Johnson with every resource at their command. I didn't share their antipathy for him. I think I always understood Johnson better than the other AFL-CIO leaders. I never saw him as a reactionary. We worked hard for him in Texas, and I never regretted it. I wanted the Kennedy ticket to win, and Johnson seemed to me by far the best choice to bring that about.

So I told Bobby, "I'd say Johnson."

He said, "Thanks, I'll be in touch," and departed.

About an hour later, he called. "It's Lyndon," he said, "and we've talked to him."

I phoned Johnson and congratulated him immediately. He said, "Dave, now that your man has the top spot, would you do something for *me?*"

I said, "You name it, Senator."

And Johnson said, "Would you get out on the floor of that convention hall and make damn sure I get the nomination?"

Johnson's concern was legitimate. To lose the vice-presidential nomination after he had been chosen by Kennedy would have been a political embarrassment from which Johnson might never recover. And yet, in that convention, it *could* happen. Organized labor was well represented, and—except for my Steelworkers—was almost solidly opposed to Johnson.

So I said, "I'll be on the next elevator and on my way to the convention floor, Senator." And I was.

On the floor, I found Johnson trouble brewing. The first labor delegate I ran into began to complain about "that damned reactionary, Johnson," and I put my finger in his face and said, "Listen, pal, if you want to vote for Nixon, vote for Nixon. I told Kennedy I was for him all the way, and he wants Johnson. When I say all the way, I *mean* all the way."

I left him with his mouth open, watching me take dead aim on any other labor delegates I could find. I rounded up my runners and told them to pass the word that I wanted Johnson because Kennedy wanted him and we were damn sure going to give Kennedy what he wanted. I told the same thing to any TV and radio interviewers I could find on the floor. When my missionary work was done, I was called by George Meany to an AFL-CIO caucus being held in the Ambassador Hotel. It's purpose, I discovered, was to come up with some way of stopping Johnson. I had a little transistor radio to which I listened, and while they were discussing ways and means of stopping Johnson, he was nominated for the Vice-Presidency of the United States.

After the convention, the campaign and election were almost anticlimax. Nixon knew where I stood and never called me, although we were good friends. I was in close touch with Bobby throughout the campaign, and whenever he was in trouble in an industrial area, he'd call and ask me for help and I'd get an urgent message out to the Steelworker political action people there.

I had another personal illustration of the Kennedy style of in-

tegrity during the campaign. He asked me to his home in George-
town for breakfast one morning after his nomination and before
the campaign got under way. He began to probe me in that
surgical way of his about the 32-hour work week I was trying to
sell as a recession cure. When he had all my arguments arranged
in his head, he said, "I still can't see it."

It was time for Kennedy to head for the Capitol, and he drove
me downtown in his open convertible, arguing all the way about
the 32-hour week. A few weeks later, he made one of his first campaign speeches at the Steelworkers convention in Atlantic City. I
met him at the airport, and we rode into town together on the
raised back seat of an open car between massed lines of cheering
people. As he waved to them, he was still arguing the 32-hour
work week. I warned him that when he got into the convention
hall, he would see signs and posters all over the place promoting
the 32-hour week and he'd be talking to an audience that believed
in it. He just grinned and said he hadn't changed his mind and
would probably tell the delegates how he felt.

And damned if he didn't. He mentioned our friendship and
thanked the Steelworkers for their support in the convention and
said he could go along with most of labor's goals, but he couldn't
buy the 32-hour week because as President he was going to seek
an economy that could support full employment under a 40-hour
week. I watched him with new admiration for his courage and
that sharp, probing mind, and I thought, This guy is going to
make a great President.

I heard the election returns at home, went to bed as did so many
millions of other Americans thinking he was safely home, then
sweated out the returns all the next day until that tiny margin was
firm. Then I phoned my congratulations to him in Hyannis Port,
and he said, "C'mon up and see me tomorrow."

So Phil Regan and I flew up, picking our way through the thousands of people massed around the Kennedy property and feeling
pretty good about it. We found Jack on the back porch in an old
sweat shirt and blue jeans and sneakers, and we sat there and had
coffee and talked.

Every once in a while, I would catch Kennedy looking out over the ocean, his thoughts momentarily far away, and I remembered as I looked at him the prayer with which he had ended his speech at our convention.

"We know there is a God," he had said, "and we know He hates injustice, and we see the storm coming. But if He has a place and a part for us, I believe that we are ready."

22

The first year of the Kennedy Administration was a year of peace for the Steelworkers and a chance to catch our breath after a long and turbulent strike and a cliff-hanging election. We seemed to be riding high. I knew that when you ride high, you also ride for a fall, but I wasn't worried about that in 1961. Not yet.

There were some clouds. The Human Relations Committee wasn't working very well. I should have anticipated the problems, but I still carried that sunny optimism about my fellowman, and it would have taken more of a cynic than I was to predict the shoals on which the Human Relations Committee might founder.

One of the purposes of the HRC was to look into work rules and plant employment practices that were inefficient or archaic and arrive by mutual agreement at changes that needed to be made. All in all, it was a fine and progressive idea that offered considerable promise in theory. The problem was that the theory and the idealism that generated the HRC at the top simply never came to grips with the practicalities at the plant level. The plant foremen and often the plant superintendent figured the HRC was a lot of high-level hot air, and if its members were to come poking around their plant looking for practices that needed reforming, the local big shots would point down the road and say, "They went that-away. . . ." They wanted to keep the employees they had, and they simply refused to finger the people. Management knew that the only practical way to streamline the personnel of a plant was through a departmental layoff because of lack of production orders, and the rehiring of a smaller, more compact force. This had been happening all the time, and the screams of the industry leaders about the union dictating working procedures that precipitated eight months of agony in 1959 was so much hokum.

One of President Kennedy's first official acts was the appointment of the Labor-Management Economic Advisory Committee I'd suggested years earlier. We made an extended study of the impact of automation on industry, and I argued the cause of shorter work periods as a means of solving unemployment problems, supplementing the 32-hour work week concept with an extended vacation plan I had been proposing unsuccessfully in steel negotiations. During one of our meetings, the President signed into law the Area Re-Development Act, embodying the principle I had recommended to the Randall Commission in 1954. It had been turned down by every member of that commission and even ridiculed by several. And now it was the law of the land.

The President had also raided the Steelworkers for one of his Cabinet appointments. He had phoned me at my office one morning and said, "Dave, I'd like to steal Art Goldberg from you." I asked why, and he told me, "I want him for my Secretary of Labor."

There had been no prior hint of this, and I was totally unprepared. When I got my breath, I said, "Tell you what, Mr. President. I'll trade Art for Bobby."

"Can't do that. I've got some other plans for him."

When he hung up, I mused over Art Goldberg's dedication to the candidacy of Adlai Stevenson at the Democratic Convention. Goldberg had told Rosemary one evening after a party that "Dave is making a big mistake supporting Jack Kennedy. Stevenson is our man, and we should get together behind him." And now Art was Kennedy's Secretary of Labor, and I knew he would do a fine job. He was a brilliant, incisive thinker who had always been dedicated to the rights of the workingman.

Kennedy often looked our way when he needed a friend. He knew there would be a loud public howl when he appointed his brother Attorney General, so he asked Art Goldberg and the Steelworkers' Washington lobbyist, Nordy Hoffman, to stand up with him when he made the announcement. Nordy remembers that just before they emerged to meet the press, the President turned to his brother and said, "For God's sake, Bobby, comb your hair."

I needed these warm memories of 1961, because the following year the real world enveloped us again. The thirty-month duration of the contract signed in the aftermath of the 1959 strike passed with unbelievable speed. In the spring of 1962, it was contract time once again. As we made our preparations to open negotiations, I wasn't expecting a picnic. But I also wasn't expecting to find myself involved in a three-way drama with my old friend, Roger Blough, and the President of the United States that would stand the financial community on its ear and have the whole nation choosing up sides.

It all started quietly enough. In late January, 1962, the President called and said he would like to talk with Roger Blough and me about the coming steel negotiations. We were told to use the south entrance to the White House in order to avoid reporters. Both Blough and I were staying at the Carlton Hotel, and we talked briefly on the phone and decided to proceed separately to the White House.

I arrived a few minutes early for our 6 o'clock meeting and was browsing through the Presidential dinner services collected by Mrs. Kennedy when Blough arrived. He was followed by Art Goldberg who said the President was ready to see us. We took the elevator to the Kennedy living room, and after greeting us, the President sat down in his rocking chair and got right to the point. He told us he was deeply concerned about domestic inflation and our weak position in foreign balance of payments, and he pointed out that the steel industry was basic in controlling the first and improving our position in the second. Memories of 1959 were still fresh in the financial community, he said, and he felt it would be a good thing for the country if we could get our negotiations under way early and arrive at a quick agreement.

He then showed us a memorandum he had just received from Walter Heller, the chairman of his Council of Economic Advisers. Heller suggested that if a wage increase could be held between 2.5 and 3 percent, an increase in the price of steel could be avoided because these costs would be absorbed by increased efficiencies in production, which Heller called the "productivity factor." Therefore, said the President, he hoped we could see our way clear, for the good of the nation, to keep our settlement within that framework.

Then he rocked back and forth slowly and waited for a reaction.

Blough looked at me and said, "Well, Dave, I guess it's up to you to give him an answer."

I said, "That's okay with me, Mr. President. And I'm willing to start negotiations immediately."

We all waited for Blough to respond, and he was silent for several seconds, then turned to Goldberg and said, "About that 3-percent figure, Arthur. I presume you had something to do with it?"

Goldberg answered, rather grimly, I thought: "No, sir. I didn't know anything about it until this evening. I had nothing to do with its preparation and didn't know what was in Heller's report until the President handed it to me here."

Blough smiled his curious, enigmatic smile that always left the impression—true or not—that he didn't believe a word of what he was hearing. And he said nothing more.

Kennedy broke the silence by asking me directly if my answer meant that I would hold our wage increase demands within the 3-percent limit. This put me on a terrible spot, because I didn't agree with his premise. As I sat there wondering how to say it, I remembered those arguments we'd had over the 32-hour work week, and I thought, This is the same guy who debated with me over his breakfast table and had the guts to attack the 32-hour week in my own convention. So what are you waiting for? Speak your mind.

I drew a long breath and I said, "Mr. President, there are a good many other things beyond Mr. Heller's productivity factor to take into consideration in collective bargaining. Our Human Relations Committee with members from both the industry and the union have come up with thirteen factors to consider in arriving at a labor agreement. Productivity is only one of those factors. They have been put before your Labor-Management Advisory Committee, and you and Secretary Goldberg have that report. If you don't recall it, I have a copy with me."

I pulled the copy out of my pocket and read the list. Kennedy listened but said when I finished that he was quite familiar with it. Then he looked at Blough and waited. After a good deal of throat clearing, Blough said that he felt the 3-percent productivity factor had no proper relationship to the steel industry. "The productivity increase at U.S. Steel," he added, "was actually about 2 percent last year, and I think this was generally true of the industry as a whole."

I couldn't let that pass. Our economists had made detailed studies on productivity and costs per man-hour in the steel industry, using government figures. Those studies indicated that productivity increases since 1958 had averaged 3.5 percent in a period of generally low capacity and would probably be much greater in the year ahead as we pulled out of a business recession. The man-hours required to produce a ton of steel had been cut almost in half since 1940, while the selling price of steel was increasing from $53.45 per ton to $147.78 in 1958 when the industry had its last across-the-board price increase. Man-hours required per ton of steel were 19.9 in 1940; twenty years later, this figure had decreased to 12.1; and this, in turn, had gone down to 10.9 since we signed the 1960 agreement. I pointed out further that our studies showed that the payroll cost per ton of finished steel had risen from $17.01 in 1940 to $39.47 in 1962, but the margin of price over payroll costs in the same period had risen from $36.44 to $108.31.

Said Blough, "I don't know the source of your figures, but they are not acceptable to us. Our figures show an entirely different story."

The President then repeated, with great eloquence and forcefulness, his arguments about the need to compete internationally and improve our balance-of-payments situation by holding down inflationary cost and price increases. The contrast of styles— Kennedy brisk, direct, bright, earnest, intense and Blough detached, deliberate, cold, aloof, plodding—was fascinating to watch. It would have been difficult to find two men so totally unlike in their personal characteristics.

The President ended by saying, "Our major domestic economic challenge today is to build and maintain full employment of manpower and productive capacity in the United States. I'm determined to bring it about, and I need you to help me. I think that Mr. Heller's 3-percent figure is fair and just and will support those goals by preventing inflation. It would very definitely be in the public interest if you would go along with me and hold your labor agreement within that limit."

He looked at us expectantly, and I made an instant decision.

"Mr. President," I said, "as much as I disagree with your basic premise, if you'll have one of your secretaries bring us a scratch pad and pen, I'll sign an agreement here and now with Mr. Blough for a 3-percent labor cost increase each year for three years. And I'll sell it to my Wage Policy Committee."

We all looked at Blough, and he was momentarily taken aback. Then he laughed uncomfortably and said, "You know I can't do that, Dave."

I said, "Come on, Roger, if I can sell it to my people, you can surely sell it to yours."

He murmured, "No, no, no" over and over, shaking his head.

There was nothing more to be said. The President was obviously disappointed at this uncertain resolution of the talk, and we tried to salvage some satisfaction by promising to start negotiations quickly. Kennedy looked pensive as we departed. On the way back to the hotel, Blough asked me to stop by his room for a drink, and we talked aimlessly about the coming baseball season.

After that White House meeting, scarcely a day went by without some sort of reminder from the Administration urging us to get on with the steel talks. The President made a public appeal, pointing out that any delay would unsettle the economy by starting another round of inventory buildup, and on February 6, Art Goldberg sent both the union and industry a telegram urging speed. So I assembled the Wage Policy Committee and obtained its approval to start negotiations on February 14.

Somehow, the sense of urgency didn't seem to filter down to the industry troops. When we met with the old, familiar "summit committee," it appeared to be 1959 all over again. While Goldberg hovered on the fringes like a solicitous mother-in-law, we conducted business as usual—the same lengthy position papers, the same speeches for the record, the same proposals and counter-proposals, all insufficient, all rejected.

On February 23, Goldberg made a speech in Chicago in which he said that conflicts between labor and management were intolerable because of the Soviet threat and new competition from an economically united Europe. He also put in a hard sell for the 3-percent productivity factor. The speech made George Meany—meeting with the AFL-CIO Executive Committee in Miami—sore as hell. He told reporters that Goldberg was "infringing on the rights of a free people and a free society." I thought that was a little strong, but I wasn't enchanted with the productivity factor concept either.

The following day we recessed the negotiations when it became clear that the company wasn't prepared to come forward with any meaningful offer. On February 26, *U.S. News and World Report* came out with an interview with Blough in which he said, "Employment costs in the steel industry have risen 12 percent over the last three years. How long . . . can that be borne without some kind of remedy? I would give you the answer that it's not reasonable to think of it as continuing. In other words, even now there should be a remedy. If any additional cost occurs, the necessity for the remedy becomes ever greater."

At Goldberg's urging, we resumed our negotiations, but we broke them off again on March 2. We were asking for a seventeen-cents-an-hour package. The industry was trying to hold the wage line, insisting that any increase would be inflationary. We were willing to come down, but not until they showed some willingness to come up. And there we were stalled.

Goldberg jumped into the fray again, meeting with Blough and Cooper and asking if they would resume negotiations if the union modified its demands. He then met with me and said the industry would reopen talks if I would pare down the size of my package. I told him what he already knew, that it was a negotiating device and it would be pleasant for the industry to come up with a positive approach to the negotiations once in a while instead of just shooting down all of our proposals.

Meanwhile, Cooper invited me to have lunch with him and do some private exploring. Since our work together on the Human Relations Committee, we had come to know and understand one another. I considered him my friend, and I had found a medium of conversational exchange that seemed to work with him: we talked in football terms that lightened the disagreements and provided a relief from the stilted prose of the bargaining table. He expressed his unhappiness at the collapse of the talks, and I said, "Coop, you're supposed to be interested in the welfare of your employees as well as the stockholders and management, aren't you?"

He said, "That's right."

I said: "Do you realize that not once since our first agreement back in 1937 has the industry ever come up with a constructive proposal? Everything we've gotten, we had to wring out of you. You have always taken a negative position on everything. Isn't it about time for you to come up with something constructive?"

He thought a moment, then said, "The job evaluation program was constructive."

"Sure," I said, "that was great, but it was twenty years ago and it was forced on you by the National War Labor Board."

"Okay," he said, "I won't argue the point with you. Just what sort of constructive proposal do you think we should come up with now?"

"What about the Extended Vacation Plan?"

He cringed visibly.

"My God," he said, "every time my management hears you use that term in a speech, they throw a tantrum."

"Okay," I told him, "then come up with some new ideas of your own."

Three days later he called me again. Over lunch, he told me: "I've been thinking about what you said, and I might have something that will interest you."

Then he described what he called a "savings and vacation plan" that incorporated many of the elements of my extended vacation proposal. It was just the sweetener we needed to reopen the negotiations, and from that point, everything was downhill. We went back into the meetings on March 14, and two weeks later we had an agreement.

The savings and vacation plan, financed by a three-cents-per-hour contribution by the companies, was adopted. It not only provided new vacation and retirement benefits for eligible employees, but also brought new people into the industry by creating job opportunities to replace those workers enjoying the extended vacations. There were other wage and job security benefits that came to an aggregate of about eleven cents an hour, near the 3-percent "productivity factor" urged on us by the President. I took the contract before my Wage Policy Committee, told them that it not only provided another breakthrough in a better life for our members but did it within the framework of national interest outlined by the President, and the committee members endorsed it. On April 6, 1962, the agreement was signed with the eleven basic steel companies.

I called Kennedy immediately, and he was delighted. He asked to talk to the Wage Policy Committee directly, so we piped the telephone into the public-address system of the room where we had been meeting, and he praised the committee for "high industrial statesmanship" and said that the agreement was "obviously noninflationary and should provide a solid base for continued price stability."

The President told me later he made the same call to the Industry Coordinating Committee with rather curious results. Cooper received his call, answered simply, "Yes, sir," when told it was the President, and responded to Kennedy's effervescent enthusiasm with a few flat words of acknowledgment, delivered in cold and distant tones. The President was perplexed and a little irritated, but the actual significance of Cooper's discomfort at talking with the President didn't come through until several days later.

Meanwhile, the nation's press showered us in an orgy of appreciation, which was pleasant for a change. *Life* used a full-page picture of Cooper and me and said in the caption: "Never in the generally bitter and sometimes bloody history of relations between labor and steel had an agreement been so rapturously received." That was the tone of most of the comment. Even *U.S. News*, a conservative and business-oriented magazine, said that a "steel settlement—free of an increase in cash wages—is expected to have a big effect on business sentiment. The point is made that a major union in a basic industry, for the first time since World War II, has recognized broad public interest in a new contract."

I'd never felt so relaxed. I put the whole matter out of my mind and prepared to enjoy the Pittsburgh Pirates opener on April 10. It was an afternoon game, and Rosemary and I arrived early in our box seats behind the Pirate dugout. Just before we left for the game, I had a rather odd phone call from Cooper. His voice sounded strained, and he said he would like to see me at two o'clock. I told him if he wanted to see me then, it would have to be at Forbes Field, and he relaxed a little and laughed and said he was thinking of going to the game, too.

At the end of the sixth inning, the Pirates had the Phillies down 6-0, and I was thinking about beating the traffic and leaving early when Cooper showed up suddenly at my seat.

He said: "I've just had a call from my office, and I'm going to have to leave. Could I see you a little later in the afternoon?"

I told him I'd probably be back in my office by four o'clock, and he said he would call me then. I was a little irritated at this intrusion of business at the one moment of real peace in the life of a labor leader: the immediate aftermath of a contract signing. But I don't think I showed my irritation when I told him I'd await his call. Driving back downtown, Rosemary, my chief assistant Bud Flannery and I talked about the prospects of the Pirates, and I didn't turn on the car radio.

I drove Rosemary home, and the telephone was ringing as we opened the front door. She answered, handed it to me and said, "The White House is calling."

I picked up the phone with a distinct feeling of uneasiness, and Goldberg came on the line. He sounded angry. "What do you think about the steel price increase?" he rasped.

I stared at the phone. "*What* increase?" I asked.

"My God, you're kidding. You mean you really don't know?"

"Don't know *what?*"

"Wait a minute. I have a friend of yours here who wants to talk with you."

The familiar, brusque Yankee accent came on with an edge I'd never heard before. The telephone line almost smoked.

"You," he said very distinctly, "have been screwed and I've been screwed."

"What do you mean? For God's sake, will somebody tell me what's happened?"

"U.S. Steel has raised its prices $6 a ton. Blough was just here and told me, and I wanted you to know right away because it's going to put you on one hell of a spot."

I let out my breath. So *that* was why Cooper wanted to see me.

"What are you going to do?" I asked the President.

"For starters, I'm going to call some of the other steel companies and try to get them not to follow suit."

"I don't think it'll work," I told him. "Blough wouldn't have pulled this without some sort of backdoor understanding."

"Well," said Kennedy, "I'm going to put Bobby on this and we'll damn soon find out."

And he hung up. As I stared at the dead phone, wondering what all this meant, Rosemary flagged me from our other phone and formed the word "Cooper" with her lips. He was agitated. He said, "I've got to see you right away."

I told him I'd be downtown in a half hour and backed furiously out of our driveway. Cooper was waiting in front of our suite when I arrived. We went in and sat down, and Cooper said, "There's something I have to tell you." He held out his hands, palms forward, and added, "Now don't blow your stack."

"Go ahead," I told him.

"We've just announced a $6-a-ton price increase."

I pretended astonishment. "You've *what?*"

"Roger just told the President. I wanted to see you at six to tell you at the same time."

"Did you follow the usual line and blame it on the union?" I asked Cooper.

"No, no, we didn't do that at all."

"You must have issued a statement of some kind. I'd like to see a copy of it."

He didn't have one, and he literally ran out to get one from his office. I told Bud Flannery to call our lawyers and economists and get them to the office immediately. By that time, Cooper was back with the U.S. Steel statement. He handed it to me, and I read it. It was long-winded, making the point repeatedly that there had been no price increases in the steel industry since 1958 and calling this increase a "catch-up adjustment." Catch-up for what? Here came the hooker. "From 1958 through 1961," said the statement, "there have been industrywide increases in steelworker wages and benefits on four occasions amounting to about 40 cents an hour, and, also, increases in employment costs for other employees. These persistent increases have added several hundred million dollars to the employment costs of U.S. Steel, without regard to future costs resulting from the new labor agreement just negotiated."

I put the statement down and said, "You've got yourselves in a peck of trouble."

"What do you mean?" Cooper asked.

I said: "Can I talk to you as a friend, with the understanding that you won't mention what I say to *anyone* else, especially Roger." He nodded grimly. "Okay, I knew about the price raise before I talked with you. The President called me at home and told me and he is *sore as hell*. He is really going after you, and when he's sore, he's a tough man to deal with. And you know, of course, that I'm going to have to issue a statement condemning your actions."

Cooper looked miserable. He said, "I wish you wouldn't do that."

"What other choice have you given me?" I asked him. "You know it has always been our policy to stay strictly out of pricing matters. We've always regarded that as your private reservation and we've never brought up prices in collective bargaining. But this is different. You've put me on one hell of a spot. You've let me make a one-sided agreement with the President, smashed it all to hell and then blamed your actions on the greed of the union. You're goddam right I'm going to issue a statement, and I'm going to blast U.S. Steel good."

The rest of the drama was played out between the President and Roger Blough, and the details have been reported many times in many places. I followed it in the same way other American citizens did—in the newspapers and on television. But my reading and viewing was supplemented by several telephone calls from the President and from Arthur Goldberg.

While the President met with his top advisers on the morning of April 11, some major steel customers began to make noises about "exploring foreign steel if the price increase sticks." Members of Congress—including a good many Republicans—were calling Blough's action everything from "unjustified" to "arrogant" to "dumb," and Senator Albert Gore began talking about a Senate investigation of this "breach of faith with the American people." Meanwhile, Joe Block, the chief officer of Inland Steel, began to get phone calls from every friend and acquaintance associated even obliquely with the Kennedy Administration. Next to Kaiser, Inland was the maverick of the steel industry, an independent company with independent attitudes.

When the President appeared for an early-afternoon televised press conference, Bethlehem Steel had followed the lead of U.S. Steel and raised its prices, too. I watched that press conference, and it was one of the few times I saw Jack Kennedy with the glint of humor totally missing from his eyes. I knew from my talks with Goldberg that the President was almost as angry at the *way* Blough had pulled his coup as he was with the price raise, itself. Having personally sampled Blough's style under similar circumstances, my sympathies were all with the President.

He really blistered U.S. Steel, calling its action "a wholly unjustifiable and irresponsible defiance of the public interest." He continued: "The steelworkers' union can be proud that it abided by its responsibilities in this agreement . . . But at a time when restraint and sacrifice are being asked of every citizen, the American people will find it hard, as I do, to accept a situation in which a tiny handful of steel executives whose pursuit of private power and profit exceeds their sense of public responsibility can show such utter contempt for the interests of 185 million Americans."

In the question session that followed, the President said: "In all our conversations with the leaders of the steel union and the companies, it was always very obvious that they could proceed with freedom to do what they thought was best within the limitations of law. But I did very clearly emphasize on every occasion that my only interest was in trying to secure an agreement which would not provide an increase in prices because I thought that price stability in steel would have the most far-reaching consequences for industrial and economic stability and for our position abroad."

The following day, the Justice Department began to look into the possibilities of an antitrust suit and the Federal Trade Commission indicated it wanted to check up on price-fixing in the steel industry. Then Roger Blough had his day on television. He followed a tough act and he chose to keep his reply in low key, which made him even more colorless than usual. His opening remarks followed much the same lines as the statement I had read two days earlier. "Each individual company in our competitive society," he said, "has a responsibility to the public as well as to its employees and its stockholders to do the things that are necessary pricewise, however unpopular that may be at times, to keep in the competitive race." In the long question-and-answer session that followed, Blough didn't exactly cover himself with glory. Admittedly I wasn't an objective observer, but the tenor of reaction was pretty well summarized in *Business Week* which reported that other members of the steel industry "hadn't expected Blough to match Kennedy as a performer, but had expected the best possible case for the industry—and quite a few of them simply don't believe they got it."

I could have recalled our Wage Policy Committee at this point and recommended to them the retraction of our approval of the newly signed labor agreement. Several of my friends were urging me to do this, and I had gone so far as to have the legality of such a move checked. But I didn't really want to take this step. I'd never before been involved in the abrogation of a legally constituted contract, and I had no stomach for starting now, even though the circumstances were certainly unusual. So I told the Steelworker staff people who were crowding me in this direction that I wanted to await developments awhile longer.

By the following day, several other steel companies had gone along with the price raise, but several conspicuously had not. When Inland announced publicly late in the day that it would not increase its prices, the tide had been checked and turned, and by Friday, Big Steel was in retreat.

While all sorts of high-level meetings were taking place in the offices of U.S. Steel in an effort to find a face-saving device for rescinding the price raise, Rosemary and I were flying across the country to Palm Springs, California, for the vacation we'd promised ourselves when the new contract was signed. When I got off the plane in Los Angeles, I was surrounded instantly by a swarm of reporters and TV cameras, clamoring for attention to their questions.

I pushed my way off the ramp and into the terminal to an area set aside for press conferences, then asked one of the reporters I knew what the excitement was all about.

"We just got the word," he said, "that Bethlehem and U.S. Steel have backed away from their price increase, and we'd like a statement from you."

I didn't say very much. What was there to say? "If the reports I hear are true," I told them, "then I'm very happy. It seems to me that the President's position and the position of the union have been completely vindicated."

And I thanked the reporters, stepped down and headed for the plane to Palm Springs. The reporters didn't hear me say, under my breath, The winner and still champion, John F. Kennedy.

23

The days between the Kennedy-Blough confrontation and the nightmare of Dallas were, I suppose, the happiest of my life. The right man was in the White House, doing all the right things after some false starts. My Steelworkers were the highest paid, most secure industrial employees in the history of the world. Relations with the steel industry seemed on a firm and friendly footing of mutual respect. And I was surrounded by competent associates who were also loyal friends. Or so I thought at the time.

As president of the Steelworkers, I was moving in some high circles—dining and hobnobbing with Prince Bernhard of the Netherlands (who filled me in on the "royalty business"), Belgium's King Baudouin and Mexico's President Alemán, among many others. It was pretty rarefied air for a labor leader, and some of the people I rubbed shoulders with were surprised to find me there.

Right after one of our better publicized steel shutdowns, I was seated alongside a Washington society leader at a White House dinner—a buxom lady with upswept hair and a neck full of jewels. She leaned over, picked up my place card, read it, looked me over and said, "Who are you?"

"Are you kidding?" I asked. "My picture has been in the papers almost every day lately and I'm on the television news every night."

She shook her head, so I tried again.

"Don't you know about the steel strike?"

She looked blank and asked, "What steel strike?"

And I said, "Jesus Christ, you are a dumb broad."

She thought that was very funny, roared with laughter and repeated it to everyone around the table.

Then there was Prince Baudouin. Roger Blough was brought

over to meet him while Rosemary and I were chatting with him. I winked at the Prince over Blough's head and asked, "Your majesty, why is your country trying to ruin the steel industry in the United States?"

He pretended shock and said, "How could my little country with only six million tons of steel production a year ruin your great steel industry?"

"That's what I can't figure out," I told him, "but my friend, Mr. Blough, here, says that's what is happening."

I had to be careful about having my picture taken with people like Blough during chance meetings at social affairs. It looked to workingmen as if I were consorting with the enemy instead of simply projecting the image of the labor leader to a social level of equality with the leaders of other elements of our society. I had hundreds of pictures taken with political dignitaries, and I learned from my brief flirtation with show business how to dominate a picture. I always stood to the right of the central figure (picture captions read left to right), wore bow ties and exposed a broad expanse of white shirt front to the camera that caught the viewer's eye instantly.

These social encounters took place over many years, of course, and weren't by any means concentrated in the Kennedy Administration. But during those brief hundred days, we attended dozens of White House affairs as the result of a warm and sometimes almost casual relationship with the Kennedys. I remember one afternoon I was in Washington on business and stopped by the President's office to say a quick hello. He came bursting out of his office in shirt-sleeves, chatted a few minutes, then said suddenly, "What are you doing on October 12?"

When I told him I wasn't sure but I thought we were free, he said, "Why don't you come to dinner that night? We're having a party for the Duchess of Luxembourg." Then he turned to his secretary, Mrs. Lincoln, and said, "Evelyn, fix it up." As it turned out, that dinner was canceled by the Cuban crisis, but the invitation was typical of our easy relationship during the two years this vital man captured the affection and raised the hopes of the entire world.

I was moving in high-level business circles, too, in an effort to build bridges that labor and management might cross to an economy built on the mutual trusteeship concept in which I believed with growing conviction. I was aware that many of the old-line labor leaders—including some in my own union—looked on these activities with doubt and suspicion as pandering to the enemy. But I was so sure that this had to be the future direction of labor-management relations—and sure, too, that I had the strength to put down the opposition caused by these suspicions—that I took advantage of every opportunity to pursue this course.

Late in 1963, for example, I accepted an invitation to address the National Association of Manufacturers against the advice of my closest friends who pointed out that George Meany—the only other labor leader ever to speak to this group—had been booed lustily. I told them I wouldn't get that kind of treatment because "there are too many of our clients in that group we've helped in some way or other."

I was given a laudatory introduction by an industrialist whose company we had helped obtain a $50 million defense contract. I pulled no punches about the needs and aspirations of the Steelworkers, and I got a standing ovation when I finished. In the question-and-answer session, an elderly NAM member launched a vigorous attack on labor unions in the guise of a question, and *he* was booed down. I made the point emphatically—and these men listened—that an employee treated as a man of dignity will respond as a man of integrity on his job. And the better he does his work, the more company management can earn for its stockholders, the more it can pay its employees, the more the employees can buy and the more solvent is the economy. This was the thesis I repeated dozens of times during 1963 and 1964.

Then tragedy—of such magnitude that it is still difficult for me to force myself to think about it. On November 15, 1963, President Kennedy addressed the AFL-CIO convention in the Americana Hotel in New York. I was chairman of the committee to meet and escort him to the convention hall. Although on the surface he seemed as irrepressible as ever, I sensed an undercurrent of tension and nervousness foreign to him. As he was being introduced by George Meany, a young woman suddenly rocketed out of the crowd on the convention floor, raced through the circle of Secret Service men and made a grab for the President. He pulled back instinctively, then reached out to shake hands with her. And suddenly she kissed his hand as the police pulled her away.

I don't know if this incident unsettled him or if my instincts that something else was bothering him were accurate, but as he spoke, I noticed that his hands were shaking and he gripped the lectern hard to keep anyone from noticing. This was so unlike Kennedy that it made me uneasy. The uneasiness persisted through the ovation that followed his speech. As we left the stage, he spotted Rosemary, walked over, kissed her on the cheek and said, "Rosemary, take good care of Dave. I need him."

I rode down to the street with him on the freight elevator to avoid the crowds massed in the lobby. At the bottom, in a darkened hallway, we shook hands and said good-bye. His last words were, "See you soon, Dave. I have some things I want to talk to you about." And then he was gone. I would never see him again.

A week later on my birthday, I was sitting in the kitchen of our home with a group of friends. Marcia Daniell, Rosemary's pal and the wife of one of my closest friends, phoned and I answered. She said: "Do you have the radio on?" I said, "No, should I?" and she said in a tight little voice, "Turn it on. The President's been shot."

Suddenly it was the day I had been told my son had been "killed" all over again. But this time it was true. I turned on the television, my heart beating wildly, just in time to hear those dreadful words, "The President of the United States is dead."

All the life juices drained from me instantly. I don't remember what I did or said. I do recall that I wept, which gave me some relief, and that the people around me were sobbing and staring blankly at the television set.

Bobby Kennedy called me that night and asked me to come to Washington. I got there on the first plane and joined the procession in the East Room, still in a stupor of grief and disbelief. I had wits enough when I heard the funeral arrangements to call my friend Jim Rowley, the head of the Secret Service, and ask him to try to prevail on the family not to walk from the White House to St. Matthew's Cathedral. Our offices overlooked the line of march, and I knew how ridiculously easy it would be for an assassin to fire into the dignitaries who would walk with the Kennedys that day. He said he had already done everything he could to dissuade them, and they simply wouldn't listen to him.

Rosemary and I attended the services at the cathedral. We sat on the aisle and stood as the family filed out. Jackie passed by my elbow, and my eyes were drawn to her almost against my will. Her courage served a whole nation—perhaps a whole world—those three terrible days.

I knew it was necessary that life continue; Jack Kennedy would certainly have wanted it that way. When Lyndon Johnson phoned me and said, "Stand by me; I need you, Dave," I told him I was at his service, and I meant it. But I couldn't stop thinking about the promise that died with John F. Kennedy. He possessed a combination of qualities so rare in a public figure that when they come together, they are called greatness. He had a compassion for the poor people of America and a real understanding and feel for the hunger and poverty of masses of human beings throughout the world. I know he would have developed and put through an imaginative, advanced program to help them. At the same time, I never believed him to be an enemy of business, never saw any evidence that this was true. He was a warm humanitarian, blessed with an inventive mind, a thick vein of humor and wry self-deprecation, and a facility for surrounding himself with able and visionary men. He would have done much for his country and for the world. He *did* so much. He rekindled a spark of faith that things *could* be better. He would have built that spark into a consuming flame had he been given the time.

In the aftermath of tragedy, we try to immerse ourselves in work. In talking with the new President, I suggested that he make the Civil Rights Bill his first order of business as a living memorial to President Kennedy. Johnson said he thought it was an excellent idea and would push for it if he could keep Congress in Washington over the Thanksgiving holidays.

Several days later, the President called again and asked if I could help him get the Civil Rights Bill through. I told him I'd be on my way to Washington as soon as we hung up. I called Nordy Hoffman and told him to assemble the Steelworker lobbyists from all over the country. Meeting with them the next day, I instructed them to call on every Senator and Congressman in Washington and let them know the Steelworkers were backing the Civil Rights Bill. If the strong implication was left that legislators who wanted our political support had better back it, too, that was all right with me. I reported the results of this canvass to Johnson, and it was favorable enough that he decided to push for immediate enactment of the bill.

After its passage, Johnson called the leaders of the AFL-CIO to a meeting in the Cabinet Room to thank us for our help in pushing the bill. Andy Beimiller, the chief legislative representative of the AFL-CIO, stood up and said, "Mr. President, you should thank Dave McDonald because the Steelworkers did more than anyone else to put this thing over." A week later, in another meeting, President Johnson acknowledged that suggestion by stopping in the middle of a sentence, pointing a finger at me and saying, "If it weren't for the work of my good friend, David McDonald, we could never have put across this Civil Rights Bill."

As soon as the bill had been passed, the Steelworkers prepared a letter of compliance pledging full adherence to the letter and spirit of the law. We sent copies of this letter to all the companies with which we had labor agreements. When they were countersigned by the employers and returned to us, we notified the President through the Human Relations Committee that the steel industry was solidly behind his civil rights program. The HRC also voted to undertake a study of plant training for minority races and chose Youngstown, Ohio, for the pilot project because it had the most representative cross section of racial groups among all our plant cities. I have been told that this study didn't get off the ground after I left the Steelworkers.

During this same period, five years of earnest effort on behalf of my Extended Vacation Plan finally began to pay off. The presidents of the Continental and American Can Companies said they were tired of having me bring it up in negotiations, and they had an alternative plan to suggest. It turned out to be my plan under another name, and I accepted it happily. It provided that any employee with fifteen years of service would get thirteen weeks off with pay. Thus the can companies, which led the way in pensions and insurance, broke new ground once again—and I was certain the steel industry would follow.

Time had gone by mercifully fast while we worked on the Civil Rights Bill, but so many things served as reminders of our loss. Throughout the convention and political campaign of 1964, a sight, a sound, a familiar place, a remembered voice would bring me up short, time and again, and I would stare into space, recalling, then pushing it away and trying to look to the business at hand.

I became involved in the Democratic backroom maneuvering almost in spite of myself. It started in March of 1964, when Senator Hubert Humphrey phoned me and asked if I would stop by his office. I had tried hard to encourage consideration of Humphrey for the Vice-Presidency in 1952. I had also had contact with him as a result of a punitive tax burden levied by the state of Minnesota on the iron mines. The mining companies had begun to go broke as ore poured in from South America, and thousands of iron ore employees in Minnesota were thrown out of work. They appealed to our union for help.

Using the HRC and a joint union-management committee, we were able to bring enough political pressure to bear to get a bill through the Minnesota legislature to submit the "Taconite Amendment" to the electorate. This would provide tax concessions for the mining of a low-grade iron ore called taconite and thus provide incentive for a new industry offering thousands of jobs as well as a domestic source of iron ore. I toured the mining communities of northern Minnesota and found poverty and destitution almost as severe as some of the ghost towns in the coal industry. I made dozens of speeches in support of the amendment, and Duluth even held a "David J. McDonald Day" to help stir up enthusiasm. The amendment passed and the iron ore companies poured some one and one-half billion dollars into taconite development that created more than 15,000 new jobs.

We were scarcely strangers, then, when I sat down in Humphrey's office early in 1964, and he told me that he wanted the Vice-Presidency and asked me if I would work on his behalf. I told him I had to look into a previous commitment first, and I would let him know. Then I called Bobby Kennedy, who was still serving as Attorney General under Lyndon Johnson but had already been bruised by several well-publicized misunderstandings with the President.

When I got him on the phone, I said, "Bob, if you are considering a run for the Vice-Presidency, I need to know. I'm being asked to make some other commitments, and I'd like to have some idea of your intentions before I make them."

He said, "I honestly don't know, but I don't think so. If anything develops, I'll get in touch with you immediately."

He didn't call back, and when Johnson excluded Cabinet members from consideration as potential Vice-Presidents, I called Humphrey and said I'd do what I could for him. So I called Lyndon Johnson, said I had talked with Humphrey, that he wanted to be Vice-President and I wanted to put in a good word for him on behalf of the Steelworkers and organized labor.

Johnson heard me out, then said laconically, "Yeah, Hubert's been calling a lot of people lately."

I continued to nurse the hope that Bobby Kennedy might have a run at the Vice-Presidency, and I didn't want to be caught in a fight between Humphrey and Kennedy, because my sympathies would all be with Bobby. When I was convinced he wouldn't go after it, I let Johnson know several times that Humphrey was satisfactory to us. The Massachusetts crowd wanted badly to push RFK right to the end and talked to me several times about it. (They even suggested once that I run, and I told them I couldn't think of a less likely winner than a divorced Catholic labor leader.) Bobby could have been nominated by acclamation after his convention speech: it would have taken only a single spark to ignite that convention for Kennedy in spite of all the elaborate preparations Johnson had made to prevent it. But Bobby didn't want it, and the spark was never struck.

I was one of the first to know about Johnson's choice of Hubert Humphrey as his Vice-President. I was idling backstage at the convention when the chief of the New Jersey state police told me Johnson was arriving, and I went to the door with him. Johnson saw me when he got out of the elevator and said, "Dave, I want you to meet my new Vice-President." And Hubert emerged grinning, threw his arms around me and said, "Thanks, Dave, for all you've done." I remember that incident with special vividness today because two years later Hubert Humphrey had a chance to return the favor and never called back.

During the 1964 Johnson landslide, the Steelworkers Union got far too much publicity mileage out of a flirtation of two rank-and-file Texas members with the candidacy of Governor George Wallace of Alabama. He enlisted them in his racist cause, and the public-relations firm handling Wallace promoted them as union leaders, which they definitely were not. When the Wallace circus arrived in Baltimore, Senator Joseph Tydings called and asked me to come down to help discredit the Wallace candidacy, particularly since he was citing support from official quarters in the USWA. I went gratefully, since I was as anxious as Tydings to stop this nonsense. I shared the platform with Senator Ted Kennedy and made a tough anti-Wallace speech, pointing out that the "officials" cited by Wallace were not officers of the union at all and that the top USWA officials in Alabama were violently opposed to Wallace, to the Ku Klux Klan and to racial discrimination of every nature. One of the proud chapters in the USWA operation in the South is the fact that, during the racial violence in Birmingham in 1964, not a single incident took place in any of the long integrated Alabama steel plants.

Even before Johnson was swept back into the White House on a tidal wave of votes that swamped Barry Goldwater's supposedly resurgent conservatism, I began to sniff out some election problems of my own. My trouble was that I didn't recognize the odor as lethal. At first—hell, until the very end—it just smelled rank to me.

Toward the end of the Johnson-Goldwater campaign, my secretary brought me a copy of the newspaper published by the Steelworkers local at the Timken Roller Bearing works in Canton, Ohio. This, of course, was I. W. Abel's home base; he had been our district director in Canton when I selected him as my secretary-treasurer in 1952. The paper was folded open to an editorial that said in very strong language that McDonald had lost sight of the rank-and-file steelworker, it was time to return to the philosophy of Phil Murray, and I. W. Abel was just the guy who could bring that about. Therefore, said the Canton paper, the Steelworkers should vote out McDonald in the upcoming election and replace him with Abel.

It was quite honestly the first time that the thought of formal opposition to my reelection had occurred to me. I was aware that some of the old liners didn't like my style, but I figured I would be judged on results, not personal antipathies. And the results were spectacular. Maybe they were too spectacular.

The ideas advanced when Lewis sent Murray and me off to organize the Steelworkers in 1936, the program of the founding convention in 1942, the goals I had set in my inaugural speech had all been realized—and, in many instances, surpassed. High wages, industry-supported pensions and insurance, a form of guaranteed annual wage and the Extended Vacation Plan were all in operation early in 1964. The Steelworkers were the best paid, most secure industrial workers in history. Under such circumstances, it scarcely seemed credible to me that the people enjoying these benefits could get too excited about voting out of office the men who obtained them.

So I wasn't worried when I saw that story. But I was curious, and I called Abe into my office and asked him if he'd seen it. He said he had, was incensed about it, had absolutely nothing to do with it and "wouldn't have my goddam job for all the money in the world."

So I left for Palm Springs, California, on a brief vacation, certain the Canton editorial was merely an isolated straw in the wind. It was driven completely out of my mind shortly after I got to Palm Springs when Secretary of Labor Willard Wirtz phoned me there, said President Johnson was going to spend two days looking into the Appalachian Poverty Program and campaigning around the Pittsburgh area and could I possibly come home to make sure that he had spectacular turnouts. I had to charter a plane to get to the Los Angeles airport, then took a jet back to Pittsburgh in time to convene my political action leaders on the afternoon before the President was expected to arrive.

By working all night, we painted hundreds of welcoming signs and produced a crowd of 25,000 people at the Pittsburgh airport to greet the President when he stepped off his plane. The chief of the county police escorted me to the door of the plane, and the President and I walked down the steps into the shouting crowd together, with Johnson beaming. We drove downtown in an open car to the Hilton Hotel, where we had another huge crowd assembled. I couldn't help thinking of Dallas as we shouldered our way through the mob at the hotel entrance. Any one of the thousands of people surging around Johnson could have been an assassin, but he was enjoying himself tremendously, touching hands, waving response to shouted words of encouragement.

He made a brief speech at the hotel in which he said some laudatory things about me, then we hit the streets again for an automobile tour through the southside mill district of Pittsburgh. This was my country, and the steelworkers and their families—urged by local Political Action Committees—turned out by the thousands along the parade route.

The President and I were seated on the tonneau of an open convertible, and every few minutes he would shout "Whoa" to the driver, pick up a bullhorn and make a speech to the crowd, then climb out of the car and shake hands. I often recognized faces when we stopped, so I would get out with him and introduce him to friends from the mills. He liked that so well that we might have been at it all afternoon if the head of the Secret Service detail, a perspiring and harassed man that day, hadn't told me finally, "For

God's sake, would you please stay in the car the next time he stops. We've got enough trouble without you complicating it."

The tour ended at the David J. McDonald Hall of USWA Local 1272, where the Steelworkers' officials (except I. W. Abel, who declined to attend) were congregated, waiting for the President. He made a short speech, thanked me profusely again, dove into the crowd and shook every hand in sight, then raced for his car to catch a plane for West Virginia, where I'd alerted our people to make sure he was properly and enthusiastically received.

I walked to the car with him to say good night, and he grabbed my arm and pulled me inside. There where we couldn't be overheard, he asked me to do anything I could to defeat Senator Williams of Delaware, who was giving him a bad time. I told him we couldn't be much help in Delaware because our numbers were small, but I'd look into it. Then he asked for Rosemary, bounded out, put his long arms around her and bussed her, climbing back in the car and sped away to the airport. The police told me later there had been 750,000 people on the streets of Pittsburgh that day, and the President had no illusions about how most of them had been produced. He wrote me a "Dear Dave" letter a few days later thanking me.

Again the Abel matter arose and he emphatically denied any idea of running against me. I believed him. I had no reason not to believe him. I could recall vividly Murray's completely unfounded suspicions about my opposition to him, and I didn't want to be sucked into the same neurotic frame of mind. Abe and I had always been able to work together. All of the International's basic decisions were talked out thoroughly between Abe, vice-president Howard Hague and me before they were made. Generally Abe was quiet and rather reserved in these meetings. If he had any strong objections to our policies, he certainly didn't express them.

But during the past few years, Abel had been making speeches at all of the district conferences while I was involved with broader affairs. Hague read some of these speeches and had others reported to him, and several times Howard dropped into my office after hours, when the staff had gone home, to tell me, "Abel is building a machine out in the districts. You'd better keep your eye on him." I laughed it off. I couldn't see Abel as a serious competitor, and I also knew there was a growing personal antipathy between Hague and Abel that quite likely made Howard read into Abel's words and actions things that simply weren't there.

So I accepted Abe's denial to me, and his denial at Gary, Indiana, in a public statement, at face value. I wanted to keep peace in the family, so I assigned Hague to jobs that took him away from Pittsburgh a great deal and kept him and Abel apart. I felt that after the election period had passed and Hague saw that Abe had no ulterior motives, the breach could be healed.

Then there was a letter. It went out postmarked both Canton and Washington, and was signed by the president of the Timken local. It repeated most of the things said in the earlier editorial, and ended by urging the Steelworkers to throw me out in favor of Abel. The thing that disturbed me particularly about this letter was that apparently—according to dozens of reports I received from the field—it was sent to the names on an old union mailing list we kept in International headquarters.

So again I talked with Abe, and he denied any knowledge. "What I said in Gary still goes," he told me. And again, I believed him. And again Hague warned me I was in the middle of a power play and I'd better start doing something about it.

The charade couldn't last much longer. Under the Steelworkers constitution, nomination blanks for International officers are distributed to the various locals in November, the balloting takes place in February, and the four-year administration begins in June. Locals may make nominations as they please, but in order to appear on the February ballot, a candidate must have been selected by at least forty local unions. Thus spontaneous nominations are hard to come by; they have to be cultivated by long and careful political spadework.

Two days before the nomination blanks were sent out, Abel's chief assistant told me, "Abe wouldn't think of running against you. Forget it."

Once they went out, however, friends from all over the country began to call to tell me that Abe was getting nominations in their locals and some sort of movement was obviously afoot. Several people reported that Abel had sent out auditors from the International to check the books of locals just before the nominations, and these people from Abel's office were urging his nomination. The rumors were too persistent to ignore, and I called my old friend, Joe Germano, and asked him if he was hearing them in Chicago. He said he was, and I said, "It sounds like Ohio politics"—a term we used to describe rump political movements that always seemed to be turning up in union elections in Ohio. "No," said Germano, "I think it's more than that. I think if Abe's a serious candidate, you're in trouble."

I hung up concerned and perplexed. I didn't know, then, that Joe Germano was a cornerstone of the Abel undercover campaign and had been hard at work undermining me for almost a year.

Before I could confront Abe directly with this new intelligence, he surfaced publicly. With nominations pouring in from the field for Abel, he could no longer preserve the hypocrisy. And so he called a press conference and announced himself formally as a candidate. It gives some indication of the degree of my gullibility that even then I wasn't sure that Abel hadn't been virtually drafted into this position. Only when the nominations were tallied and showed Abel with more than McDonald and I began hearing how long and subtly he had been electioneering in the boondocks did I have to believe that Abel had been working assiduously for several years at taking over the union in 1965.

So now it was in the open. And the timing couldn't have been worse. Contract negotiations were due to open with the steel industry in December. Abel and I would be sharing the negotiating table—as we had for thirteen years—at the same time he and his friends were attacking me from union hall rostrums all across the country. It was an uncomfortable and untenable situation and Abel compounded it by insisting that we enlarge the union negotiating team to include the men running with him on his slate, a condition I refused to accept. It was also clear that I was going to have to go out on the hustings to protect myself against the attacks being made on my record and my character. Consequently, when Cooper came to me and suggested that we suspend the negotiations until after the union election, I readily agreed. So the time wouldn't be lost completely, we made arrangements for the union district directors to carry on preliminary negotiations with representatives of the Steel Coordinating Committee in the interim.

And so I found myself flying around the country, talking to the same union locals I had wet-nursed for fifteen years as Phil Murray's front man, telling them all the things the International had done for them since I took over as president. Every once in a while I had to stop and shake my head to make sure this was really happening. My attitude changed very, very slowly from total incredulity to nagging doubt to consternation and finally to anger. Seeing people you've considered close and loyal friends turn suddenly against you without the slightest warning is a shattering experience, and it happened to me in those two months before our election with a frequency that left me often despairing and heartsick.

There appeared to be two matters primarily at issue. The first was my philosophy of mutual trusteeship, my strong conviction that as management and labor explored and learned to use new avenues of cooperation, workers, management and the whole nation would benefit. Abel, by contrast, was quoted as saying he wanted to return to "hard-nosed, arms-length bargaining." The other issue was my personal style. Abel and his cohorts accused me of "tuxedo unionism"—whatever that is—and apparently traveled a good deal of emotional mileage by portraying me before audiences of tough steelworkers as a dilettante who had lost all touch with the workingmen he represented. Where this kind of talk wasn't effective, they used other means. When I appeared at Aliquippa for a speech, one of the men who remained loyal to me told me that an erstwhile friend had been passing out hundred-dollar bills to recruit campaign leaders for Abel in the aftermath of his campaigning there.

All sorts of vignettes of that period dance through my memory when I recall it—which I try to avoid. There was the roller from a Bethlehem mill who told me he was off the next week on a thirteen-week vacation trip I'd made possible and he was sorry he wouldn't be at home to vote for me but I "wouldn't need his vote anyway." In Birmingham, a Steelworker stood in the audience, held up his paycheck and shouted, "I'm making four times as much now as I did when McDonald came on the job. Hell, yes, I'm going to vote for him." And in Pittsburgh when I cast my vote, a crane worker grabbed me and kissed me on the cheek and said, "God bless you."

I never attacked Abel or the people who had turned on me in any of my speeches during that campaign. I stood on my record and on the philosophy of labor-management relations that had produced that record. And as I had done so often in contract negotiations, I called on friends for whom I had done favors to give me a hand. Some of them responded, some didn't. One who didn't was Hubert Humphrey, whom I had helped make Vice-President of the United States and whose fences I had mended in Minnesota through my work for the taconite amendment. I phoned several times to ask him for help in his home country. He was never in and somehow never got around to returning my calls. I found out why after our election. A conversation with me would have been quite embarrassing to Humphrey since he put his entire organization in Minnesota and Wisconsin and the prestige of the Americans for Democratic Action to work for my opponent.

In spite of these disappointments, it never occurred to me that I would lose. It just didn't make sense to me that the members of an organization would throw out a leadership that had delivered on every promise it ever made. Consequently, where Abel's campaign approach was negative—all the things that were wrong with McDonald, personally—mine was positive. I dealt with issues, with goals, with results, with hopes for the future and how they might be attained. And except for one minor incident in Buffalo where the union hall was picketed by Abel supporters, my audiences were enthusiastic and encouraging. Consequently, when election day arrived, I was still very sure of myself, confident that my administration would be given a strong vote of confidence—in spite of the vast amounts of money behind the Abel candidacy, the high-powered public-relations firm that had directed his campaign and the rather disconcerting fact that all three International Vote Tellers were avowed Abel men.

I was anxious that there be no opportunity for either side to shout "Foul" afterward, so I suggested that the storing, certification and counting of the ballots—which came in over a period of several weeks from locals all over the United States and Canada—be supervised by the American Arbitration Association. I was shocked to hear this proposal turned down by our Executive Board. Although a majority of the directors were loyal to me in all the controversies that grew out of the campaign, the decisions of the board always went against me because the balance of power was held by the Canadian national director. For years, the Canadians had resented my earlier efforts to trim their voting strength. They also resented my refusal to lend them union funds for the formation of a Labor Party in Canada. Now they had an opportunity for revenge, and they used it to vote against a proposal for third party auditing of the election returns. During this same period, the board also turned down a contract I had signed with a group of our own staff workers who had organized a union to bargain with the International.

The returns straggled in but no clear trend was visible. Then I began to pull away slightly, and when I went to bed one night about ten days after the balloting, it looked as if I were home free. It was that morning I was shaken awake by Howard Hague and Nordy Hoffman and told that the Canadian returns had just come in overwhelmingly for Abel and that he had apparently won the election by a few thousand votes.

For days I vacillated over whether or not to contest the election. Jim Carey had been in a similar situation a year earlier with the United Electrical Workers, had fought a suspect election through the courts and a recount and had finally lost his case after almost six months of conflict and bitterness that tore the

union apart at the seams. I didn't want that to happen to the union
I'd helped create; I didn't want to damage the structure of an organization with an almost limitless potential for service to its
hundreds of thousands of members. And so I told an Executive
Board meeting that I wouldn't contest the election, they cheered
me, I announced the decision to the press—and then it was all
over.

I found some solace in the conviction that the impact of almost
forty-two years of a philosophy learned at the knee of John Lewis
and administered first with Phil Murray and then on my own
could never be lost on the workingmen of the steel industry. That
was my satisfaction—that and the knowledge that there was little
left to seek for my steelworkers except periodic wage adjustments. We'd done it all. Throughout 1964, I'd been wondering
what new directions we could explore, and the only thing that
came to mind was a concept of total job security, patterned, perhaps, on the Japanese plan that guarantees a job for life. That
wouldn't work here, but some variation of it might, and I was
thinking along these lines when our election problems came up. I
knew I was reaching, and therefore I knew also that the Steelworkers had achieved just about everything a union could provide them under Murray and me.

When negotiations resumed after the election, an Abel
spokesman suggested I resign early, and I told him I intended to
serve out my term of office to its expiration date of June 1. And so I
did. I was determined to leave one last agreement with the steel
industry behind me, and I met with Cooper and signed for a retroactive 2.7-percent increase over a two-year period and the
Wage Policy Committee accepted it as an interim agreement.
When I departed, my successors tried to negotiate the increase up
to 3.2 percent—the government's current production increase
formula—didn't know how, and finally forced President Johnson
to step in and impose an agreement. This, I presume, is "hard-
nosed, arm's-length bargaining."

But that, too, is past now. I said my good-byes to the union I
helped create and to the people of that union I knew and loved at

the inauguration of my successor. My last speech as president of the Steelworkers was brief and, I suppose, emotional, because that's the way I felt. I reminisced a little, as old soldiers scuffing off a battlefield tend to do, and then I quoted a passage from the writings of Theodore Roosevelt that hung on a plaque in the kitchen of my home.

"It is not the critic who counts, not the man who points out how the strong man stumbled, or where the doer of the deeds could have done better. The credit belongs to the man who is actually in the arena; whose face is marred by dust and sweat and blood; who strives valiantly; who errs and comes short again and again; who knows the great enthusiasms, the great devotions, and spends himself in a cause worthy to himself alone; who, at best, knows in the end the triumphs of high achievement and who, at worst, if he fails, at least fails while daring greatly, so that his place shall never be with those cold and timid souls who never know either victory or defeat."

Then I turned the keys of my desk and office over to I. W. Abel, handed him the gavel and told him to "dare greatly" and wield it well. And I turned to the audience, opened my arms and said, "Now, my beloved Steelworkers—good-bye and God bless you."

I could have walked off the stage then and dramatized the disruption in the Steelworkers Union. But the union was more important to me than a dramatic gesture. I wanted it solidified, not divided further, and I wanted the memory of that solidity ingrained in this audience. So I stayed and watched my successor sworn in. I even went to the reception afterward, and had one drink, and then Rosemary was tugging at my sleeve and her eyes were saying, "Let's go."

So we went. I wept a little on the way out.

And she looked at me and said, "Cut it out. We're starting a new life. Let's do it the way we ended this one—with our heads high."

And we did.

24

On Saturday, November 28, 1953, the City of Pittsburgh sponsored a "David J. McDonald Day." There were speeches and parades and banners and dinners and more speeches, all of which was warming to the ego of a fifty-year-old Irishman who had just taken over leadership of one of the world's great labor unions. But years later, what I remember best about that day were two talks, one by Mayor Robert Wagner of New York City, the other by Ben Fairless of U.S. Steel.

Said Fairless: "Americans are a patient people, but they will not go on forever allowing us to settle our private quarrels at the expense of the public welfare. I know that both labor and management want to find a better way, but we shall never do so in an atmosphere of recrimination, suspicion and distrust of each other's motives. We can only do so in an atmosphere of mutual respect, understanding and confidence in one another."

Said Bob Wagner: "The very proof that labor achieved a partnership with industry that it had never had before is in this room. There are some who can remember the days when a corporation executive would not have spoken to a union member. And as far as eating at a union dinner is concerned, he would have preferred to eat the union, or otherwise dispose of it. But those days are gone. Now, Mr. Fairless and Mr. McDonald are doing everything they can to see that the United States Steel Company and the United Steelworkers of America are partners in the task of building a greater and stronger and more prosperous nation. If they succeed, they will also be building a greater and more peaceful world, and for that they will have earned the thanks of every responsible citizen in this nation."

Never was it said better. Ben Fairless caught precisely the goals

I sought as a labor leader. And Bob Wagner summarized perfectly the results I hoped attainment of those goals might achieve.

I've had a few years to think since leaving the frantic day-by-day hurly-burly of running a huge labor union. I've used some of that time to reexamine the dream that Ben Fairless and I pursued. I still think it's a dream worth capturing. We almost had it, Ben Fairless and I. And then Ben retired and his successors decided to show the union who was boss, and when they learned *their* lesson, some hard liners in the union decided to shoulder me aside to show the company who is boss. And so it will continue until management and labor are willing—as Ben Fairless said—to put aside an "atmosphere of recrimination, suspicion and distrust of each other's motives."

Once that has been done, there are many ways—most of them unexplored—that labor and management can work together toward common ends with an immense potential for good in the society as a whole.

For example, the major labor unions now have millions of dollars parked away in banks and securities. This money came out of a social need of the workingman and it should be put to work for social enterprises that will help him. Union pension funds can be used very easily to insure loans for doctors who want to build badly needed clinics, to cite but one specific. They can be used as effectively for building social institutions as they can for building steel plants. The job I left undone was convincing those companies that serve as guardians of the Steelworker pension fund money that the funds should and could be used for social good without dissipating any of it. The Kaiser Foundation does this sort of thing, and does it well. Other industrial and labor leaders need to study some of the imaginative and far-reaching devices adopted by the Kaiser companies for the benefit of their employees and of society without harming—indeed, while increasing—the commercial success of the company.

At the same time, labor and management are going to have to learn to find some cooperative means of coping with the technological revolution that has produced automation. I've been told that America can produce all the goods it needs with 10 percent of its present work force. An electronics executive told me recently it could actually be done by one-tenth of 1 percent. These are the sort of revolutionary changes that should be governing the thinking and gripping the imagination of today's labor leaders.

Automation is not going to go away. Nor can it be ignored. Productivity can't be permitted to decrease because of competition in world markets. So labor unions are going to have to adjust their thinking to the reality of automation. But business is also going to have to accept the fact that the worker must be permitted to share in the increased profits permitted by automation. This, of course, will intensify the wage-price argument. There is no end to the argument of which came first. We firmly believe that prices pull wages up, that when increasing prices make it impossible for a man to subsist at his present level of earnings, he seeks more money for his labor so he can feed and clothe his family. Business claims just the opposite—that increased wages must push prices up. This argument will probably never be resolved. So the problem becomes learning to function within it.

Shorter work periods to provide job continuity and security is the only solution I know to the growing problem of automation. We can't turn our backs on improved mechanical and electronic methods of doing a job that once required only a man's muscle. But we also can't turn away from the needs of the workingman to keep busy at productive activity and to provide for his family. So the best answer I've been able to come up with is the shorter work period that keeps everyone employed at the old earnings or better but for briefer lengths of time.

The important thing, however, is that the answers to these problems are going to be found more quickly and more effectively if management and labor tackle them jointly. I believed this throughout forty-two years in the labor movement, and I put it into practice wherever and whenever I could—with some frequently spectacular results.

One example that comes quickly to mind is the Jesop Steel Company, a small specialty steel producer in western Pennsylvania. During World War II, Jesop had fallen into the hands of some sharp operators who sold its products on the black market for grossly inflated prices. The workers, who knew what was going on, demanded their slice, and some of the top production people were earning as much as $64 an hour. When a man named Frank Rackley took over the company and got its feet on the ground, he was faced with a wildly impossible wage scale. He wanted to keep the company in business but he couldn't pay black-market wages. So he came to me for help.

I toured the plant with him and found his equipment antiquated and often inefficient. I sent down one of our industrial engineers to help him redesign the plant and went over his books with him to figure out an equitable pay scale. Then I met with the local union officers and the USWA district director and told them that the company was now out of orbit, would be making normal earnings and the union members would have to accept normal pay. They told me to go to hell. Rackley told them the same story, then notified them of an adjustment in rates. They promptly went on strike. I told him to sit tight, then explained once again to the striking workers that the mill had to become competitive or it would be shut down and sold for scrap.

This time I got through. The strike was called off, and the union and the company began to cooperate to reduce production costs. A few months later, Rackley called to tell me that he and the president of the local union were painting his office on their own time, and the company was growing and prospering. Six hundred jobs and the livelihood of several thousand people in the small town where Jesop was located had been saved through patient steps toward cooperation. When last I heard, the company had 1,800 employees and strong lines of communication between labor and management. This was not paternalism; there was a strike at the plant a few years later because of sloppy grievance procedures. But they have an example of cooperation before them, and if they look to it, they'll find their way out of whatever troubles may arise.

There are literally hundreds of similar instances that took place during my years with the Steelworkers. We had a department that helped companies obtain government contracts. We had specialists in pensions and insurance who were available to consult with local unions and plant officials who couldn't afford specialists on the intricacies of International contracts.

When we started the SWOC in 1936, employment costs in the steel industry averaged 62½ cents an hour, and the common labor rate ran about thirty cents, just about what it was when I worked in the mills in 1917. There were no fringe benefits and damned few holidays. When I became president of the USWA, the hourly employment cost—including fringe benefits—was $2.31. When I left office, the figure had risen to $4.81 and steelworkers were the highest paid workingmen in America, with security provisions and fringe benefits ranging from unemployment insurance up to two-thirds their previous wages to thirteen-week vacations every five years.

Yet, it is vitally important that the leaders of organized labor today understand that the methods and techniques that brought all this about are no longer applicable today because the whole structure of the American work force is changing rapidly and drastically. The collars are turning from blue to white, and the labor leaders in America are color-blind. The AFL-CIO unions are still following the philosophy of the men who founded it, and that philosophy is as outdated now as the Pinkerton strikebreaker. The men who are high in the hierarchy of organized labor today got there through seniority; most of them couldn't organize their own families in the Jet Age. They have proved this by consistently turning away from the crucial—if disturbing—fact that the percentage of organized workers to the total work force in America is constantly decreasing—now only about 20 percent.

What can be done about it? The only possible answer is to organize the white-collar worker. Only in this way can labor unions begin to grow again and exert social and political power in the United States. And the possibility it will be done successfully by the present crop of American labor leaders is very slim indeed. White-collar workers cannot be seduced into a union by the same blandishments that attracted industrial workers two decades ago.

Until today's labor leaders understand this, they will make no progress with the white-collar worker, and unions will continue to wither in strength and power and usefulness to society.

Statistics from the U.S. Department of Labor indicated that in 1968 there were about 34 million white-collar as compared with 24 million blue-collar workers, and the trend is toward a steady widening of this gap. About two-thirds of the blue collars are organized, but only about 10 percent of salaried workers belong to a union.

Labor leadership has become much too conservative in seeking an effective approach to unionizing this army of white-collar workers. Its attitudes resemble quite closely those of the AFL when the CIO came into being in 1935. They are conservative in the basic sense of resisting change and insisting on doing things the "good old way." The tough, antimanagement campaigns so successful in attracting industrial workers to the unions thirty years ago will simply drive salaried people away. Reaching them can be accomplished only by a new concept of organizing activity. The white-collar workers are there for the asking—many of them badly needing the services a union might offer—but, so far, management has generally shown itself to be more flexible and responsive to the needs and hopes of white-collar workers than have the unions.

Some of the factors favorable to unionization of salaried employees include: wholesale layoffs without protection or recourse; the growth of automated office equipment that is undermining the security of many office workers; discontent over low level of earnings as contrasted with blue-collar workers; loss of fringe benefits, historically the province of salaried people, to the blue-collar workers; unjust handling of day-to-day grievances and resultant loss in individual dignity; lack of an effective means of communication with top management; lack of recognition from the top.

Most of the salaried people coping with these problems have been brought up in the business world to believe that unions are dirty and corrupt. But slowly, as labor leaders have joined the mainstream of American life, the unions have become more socially acceptable to the white-collar worker. This fact plus the very specific needs of the white-collar worker for help the unions could offer add up to the fact that now is the time to try to organize them.

What stands in the way? The deterrents—in addition to the clubfooted approach of today's labor leaders—fall into two basic categories: the negative attitude of many salaried employees toward unions and the counteroffensive being carried on by management against white-collar unions. These two are closely related because management has become quite adept at playing on antiunion sentiment that may be latent among white-collar workers, who have no tradition of unionism. The salaried employee generally feels that he is more socially acceptable than the blue-collar worker and therefore it would be demeaning for him to consort with union people. White-collar workers might not admit these attitudes, but they are demonstrably true, and until labor leaders understand they are true and come up with a means of counteracting them, very little progress will be made toward organizing the white-collar worker.

There is also an image of violence associated with unionism that generally repels white-collar workers. They oppose the concept of strikes as a means of achieving their ends, possibly because many of them still remember the bloody resistance to the organizing efforts of the CIO in the 1930's. Those who didn't see it have been told about it, probably from a management point of view in which the union people were made out as thugs or crooks. This view of union leaders persists among many white-collar workers and remains a strong deterrent to their affiliation with a union. They feel that union leaders are often dishonest dictators who control the votes of members in political elections. The fact that this isn't true shouldn't prevent it from being recognized and met frontally by labor organizers seeking to move into the white-collar ranks.

This feeling of political repugnance has grown to large extent because organized labor has permitted itself to become a political shirttail to the Democratic Party in the United States. Union members have made the point, time and again, that they no more feel committed to this political position than they felt committed to vote for Wendell Wilkie in 1940 because John L. Lewis told them to. If organized labor is to be effective in the field of political action, it must become truly bipartisan—by maintaining a friendly relationship with the leaders of both major parties, supporting the candidates rather than the parties and contributing funds to candidates who merit it on a bipartisan basis.

Finally, and probably most important of all, many white-collar workers feel they will lose any chance of promotion if they join a union. Inducing this feeling is one element of management's strong counteroffensive against white-collar unions. Management has also played loyalty to a union off against loyalty to the company, insisting a worker can't function effectively with divided loyalties. On the positive side, more and more companies are now providing employees:

—a statement of personnel policies that eliminates many of the uncertainties in employee-management relationships;

—a well-defined compensation system, including job evalua-tion and salary classification similar to that provided the blue-collar worker through insistence of the unions. Union negotiated wage increases are thus often passed along to salaried office workers;

—salary and benefit programs different—but not necessarily better—than those provided union employees;

—statements of seniority policy that protect white-collar work-ers from arbitrary layoffs.

Throughout all these countermeasures, the idea is stressed that if the employee joins a union, he will find himself on the other side of the fence from his bosses and will therefore no longer be in a position of confidence with the company. Although few white-collar workers understand it and few managements would con-cede it, most of the progressive policies adopted on behalf of white-collar workers have come about through fear that the unions will move into the salaried ranks. These benefits, therefore, are almost directly attributable to the building of a blue-collar union strong enough to stand up to management and defend the rights of company employees to dignity, fair treatment and just compensation.

Today's labor leaders, however, cannot trade on this fact in seeking to organize white-collar workers because it won't be believed. Rather they must take into account fully the problems indicated above and then develop an organizing plan that will overcome them.

Is that possible? I think so, although it is also going to be extremely difficult. Most white-collar unionization programs have failed because the organizers have attempted to convince salaried employees that they should join a division of an already established union. Trying to persuade a file clerk to join the Plumbers or a draftsman the Longshoremen is to lose the battle before it begins, because most salaried workers have a psychological block against blue-collar unions. Yet this sort of myopia has consistently governed the efforts of labor unions to reach salaried workers.

Unions must approach the problem from a modern standpoint; they must find out what today's salaried worker wants and needs and then show him how the unions can obtain it for him in a form he will accept. Salaried employees today are deeply concerned about job security, equal opportunity for promotion and more equitable salaries—among many other things—and some are almost as badly abused in these areas as were blue-collar workers during the rise of the unions. Yet salaried employees today have no means of involving themselves in the collective action necessary to demand these reforms. Any union leader who can develop the proper approach to this huge cadre of white-collar workers and win general public acceptance of his organization has an almost unlimited opportunity for national membership.

I proposed a plan to my last Steelworkers' convention in 1965 aimed at mining this lode. It was received enthusiastically, but I had no chance to put it into operation and I doubt that it can or would be implemented by the present leaders of the USWA who are dedicated to "hard-nosed, arms'-length bargaining."

The first—and possibly the most important—step is to eliminate the word "union" from an organization approaching salaried workers. Doctors, for example, call their union the American Medical Association; movie stars belong to the Screen Actors Guild, writers to the Author's League. Drives to organize salaried workers almost always get off on the wrong foot when the original solicitation comes on the letterhead or under the sponsorship of an established "union." So for starters, a white-collar union should be a guild or association or institution.

Next, a whole new type of organizer must be recruited and trained. The man who can influence a factory worker would probably be useless with salaried people; he might be intimidated by them, and they repelled by him. These new organizers must be young, college-trained men and women, and they must be paid a salary reflecting their education and training. Only this type of organizer can meet the salaried worker on an equal level. These organizers should be trained by a professional educator who is favorable toward unionization but isn't brainwashed with current union methods.

A massive program of education and public relations should then be undertaken to change some of the misconceptions among salaried workers about unions and to let them know about employment rights that often can be secured only through collective bargaining. Most salaried workers have long accepted employer propaganda as Gospel; they should be told it is something less than that. This campaign would be expensive and would have to be well and tastefully done. The results quite possibly wouldn't be apparent for several years, perhaps longer. The unions have the money to underwrite such a program. What is needed principally is proper direction. Each organizing drive would have to be planned as a separate project, designed to meet the needs of the particular group involved after a careful analysis has been made of management attitudes, previous union history in the area, worker morale, current wage rates and benefits and other relevant data. When this has been done, then the trained organizers should live with the local situation and develop a tailor-made organizing program, encouraged and broadly supervised by the national organization.

These same comments apply to all future organizing efforts by the existing blue-collar unions. Those of us who launched the American labor movement have had our day. We've fought the Pinkertons and venal industrialists and myopic government, and our victories have done much to raise America by her industrial bootstraps. Now that day is past. The educational level of factory workers is growing every year; often even common laborers must have a high-school education. The good-natured, tough-minded, hard-working illiterates who made an X on our pledge cards are almost gone; their children are high-school and college trained, and they must be appealed to on a different level. It isn't happening, and that's why the unions are hurting so badly.

Hundreds of thousands of educated men and women are now working in the mills and factories of America. Most of them have the ability to think for themselves. They aren't interested in the Great Depression or the Homestead Massacre, except perhaps as historical curiosities. They must be appealed to through the things that *do* interest them. Then they can be reached.

Why don't I do it? If I were thirty years younger, I'd be out on the firing line right now building unions among clerical and technical workers where they are badly needed. Some of our present labor leaders are actually afraid to bring these people into the unions because they fear their intelligence. But I regard that as an asset, not a liability. I would start at the factory offices where the blue-collar workers are organized and the white-collar staff can see the benefit of the unions to the membership. Then I'd move into banks and insurance companies, where the people are generally very poorly paid. From there, the sky is the limit.

If I had remained as president of the United Steelworkers of America, I might have tried it. It would have taken money, and we had the money to do it. Since leaving the USWA, I've been approached several times to have a try at organizing various white-collar groups. I've turned all these proposals down for a variety of reasons, but mostly, I suppose, because I could never give my heart to another union.

Epilogue

And so it ends.

When I left office as president of the United Steelworkers of America, a columnist who didn't like my style wrote: "His days of power and glory are over."

Maybe so. Power is a relative thing. I never thought of myself as wielding power, but if I did, I hope I used it well. And glory? I'm sure what glory means, but there is very little glory in spending nine-tenths of your life in hotel rooms, airplanes or trains when you would rather be home, in making the same arguments to the same people year after year and meeting the same opposition, in seeing a vision of what *could* be and having that vision shredded by people who question your motives, then lack either the imagination or the courage to examine the vision with you. If this is glory, then I find special comfort in the way the Romans dismissed it: *Memento mori, sic transit gloria mundi.* "Remember death," they said. "The glory of the world is only transient."

In the end, "glory" and "power" are merely words, value judgments put on us by other mortals with *their* special axes to grind. What stays behind, what lives on, what provides other generations a positive yardstick by which to measure us are our deeds and the legacy that derives from them.

Often, years later, the legacy isn't even associated with the man who left it. When I admired a piece of comedy recently and identified it as the outgrowth of a school introduced by Will Rogers, a thirtyish friend who is a producer of entertainment asked me, "Who's Will Rogers?"

Throughout the empire of United States Steel, all that remains of the man who founded it—Andrew Carnegie—is a modest bronze head in the lobby of the headquarters building. Even his name has disappeared from view. The Carnegie-Illinois Steel Company has been renamed by a bloodless corporation "Central Operations Division, U.S. Steel." But Andy Carnegie's legacy of corporate arrogance and consuming hatred toward organized labor has never been washed completely away, even by the ministrations of a fine and thoughtful human being like Ben Fairless.

What did *I* leave behind?

I have time to think on that question, now, and when I do, I'm proud of the things that come to mind. But always there is doubt, too. Do the men I represented understand what they have? Is it substantial enough to them that they will fight, if necessary, to protect it? And do they have a clear view of the concept of mutual trusteeship that brought it about and can offer almost limitless possibilities to the workingman in the future?

Only to the degree that these things are recognized and understood has my life's work been truly productive. The material gains are very real and very much present—and very important. But they are transient. The idea, the concept is *truly* important. Here lies the future and the hope.

That's why the following letter was worth a lifetime of effort to me. When I read it, I knew the idea was alive and would stay alive, and I was deeply grateful.

The letter came from James Huntermark, president of the Steel City Local in Pittsburgh, and it said:

Enclosed herewith is your Honorary Life Membership card in the United Steelworkers of America, which is a very small token, indeed, of our esteem for you and the loyal services you have rendered to your Union.

History will record that it was you who introduced an entirely new concept in the manner of negotiating with the steel industry which has brought us benefits and blessings that would have been beyond our wildest hopes and dreams some thirty years ago. Not only has our Union been the beneficiary of your courage and foresight, but many millions of Americans have also reaped the benefits of prosperity through the patterns formulated by your Union and by your efforts.

We wish you and Mrs. McDonald a most happy and wonderful retirement and may God bless you both.

Rosemary and I have found warmth and peace in our new life in these words of St. Peter: "Do not return evil for evil or insult for insult, but on the contrary return a blessing."

Index